DATE DUE

MY 2 5 03			

DEMCO 38-296

Reopening
the
American
West

Reopening the American West

Edited by
Hal K. Rothman

The University of Arizona Press
Tucson

The University of Arizona Press
© 1998
The Arizona Board of Regents
All Rights Reserved

♾ This book is printed on acid-free, archival-quality paper.
Manufactured in the United States of America
First printing

Library of Congress Cataloging-in-Publication Data
Reopening the American West / edited by Hal K. Rothman.
p. cm.
Based on papers presented at, and having their origin in followup
to, a symposium held in Prescott, Arizona in November 1993,
sponsored by the Arizona Humanities Council.
Includes bibliographical references and index.
ISBN 0-8165-1600-6 (alk. paper). —ISBN 0-8165-1625-1 (pbk. :
alk. paper)
1. Environmentalism—West (U.S.)—History. 2. West (U.S.)—
Environmental conditions—History. I. Rothman, Hal, 1958–
GE198.W47R46   1998
333.7'2'0978—dc21   97-21138
CIP

British Cataloguing-in-Publication Data
A catalogue record for this book is available from
the British Library.

Publication of this book is made possible in part by the
proceeds of a permanent endowment created with the
assistance of a Challenge Grant from the National Endowment
for the Humanities, a federal agency.

Developed in Partnership with the
Arizona Humanities Council

Contents

Part 3. Understanding

Introduction

In November 1993, the Arizona Humanities Council sponsored an outstanding meeting in the mining-turned-resort town of Prescott, Arizona. Supported by a grant from the National Endowment for the Humanities, the "Second Opening of the West" project, as the twenty-two-month-long endeavor was called, utilized the ideas of people such as John Wesley Powell, John Muir, Gifford Pinchot, Mary Austin, and Aldo Leopold to articulate and assess the changing relationships between people and environment in the American West. The Prescott symposium highlighted the endeavor, as more than three hundred people from all over Arizona and the West attended.

The weekend in Prescott proved enlightening; snow fell and threatened the activities, reminding the attendees of the presence of powerful nature as they trudged through the landscape. In the clear, cold, high-elevation air, a range of talks, meals, and discussions took place, offering new thinking and covering existing ground. From the ideas expressed during this conference comes the core of this book, an effort to reach a wide public with the ideas of the environmental history of the American West.

The idea of a "second opening of the American West" is in itself ironic, and perhaps the collection of essays here is more of a reopening of the American West to new and different realms of intellectual inquiry. A second opening requires a first opening, a concept that seems to belie the thrust of many of the articles contained in this volume; a reopening suggests another look at issues that seem decided, that have been widely accepted and made part of the historical canon. Here we have a genuine reopening, a post–new western history approach to the environmental history of the American West, a series of articles that delve into the premises that underpin not only an older generation of scholars and thinkers, but also those who have redefined the field in the past two decades.

As the authors in this collection demonstrate, the idea of an "opening," at least in physical terms, may be specious. An ongoing series of collisions, as the famed Swiss historian of colonialism Urs Bitterli might call them, and even catalytic moments, permeated both the pre- and the post-European contact West, but these interactions represented an ongoing process that continues today. Native peoples of the region appeared in waves; the most clearly defined was the Athapaskan invasion of the fifteenth, sixteenth, and seventeenth centuries. After arriving in the Southwest, these invaders from the north became an overlay upon the existing Mesoamerican cultures, labeling their predecessors the Anasazi, or the "old enemies." The Lakota people of the Great Lakes region also entered the West, pushed first by the westward migration of refugees from the Iroquois-Algonquin wars. When the Lakota reached the plains and acquired the horse, they began a 150-year expansion that dominated the region from the Minnesota border to the Yellowstone. Crows, Pawnees, Otoes, Iowas, Omahas, and others were swept aside in their wake; Hidatsas and Mandans became vassals. The Lakota entered a turf that was already contested.

Euro-Afro-Asian peoples arrived in the West in small numbers over an extended period of time. As a generation of environmental historians have pointed out, in the initial contact the impact of these newcomers was far greater than their numbers. Disease—especially smallpox, unnamed strains of pneumonia, influenza, related respiratory ailments, and venereal disease—as well as other forms of engagement such as the alcohol trade created an enormous impact on Indian populations. So did the arrival of the horse, which transformed the lives of people who had seen neither the Spanish nor other Europeans, and the trade in weapons that made warfare far more deadly among competing native groups.

The so-called physical opening, which is part of American mythology and is still recapitulated in the public memory of the nation, occurred much later, after the American Civil War, when the military focused its energy on the region and as transportation technology brought thousands of people, from hunters to farmers, to clear the West of native groups and settle it in the manner of the humid climes to the east. With the advantage of the railroad, that great pipeline to the machined miracles of industrialization, the people who came west soon outnumbered the existing Indian populations. These latest of newcomers limited the access of native groups to the resources on which they depended for survival, and through political, military, and economic strategy drove Indian peoples in the West onto reserved areas for which the dominant culture could see no apparent economic use at the time.

The conventional approach to an opening, the Turnerian idea of successive frontiers of dominant culture bringing the power of "civilization" to bear, has been seriously challenged in recent years, for its triumphalism as well as for its ethnocentrism, its limited ways of seeing the world, its discounting of the role of native peoples and nonwhite migrants in this history of the region, and its lack of concern for the environmental cost of the transformation of the West. Despite my attempts to couch it in modern analytical language, this definition of "opening" falls within the triumphalist tradition that has dominated the study of the history of the American West for most of the past century. In many circles, the idea of an "opening" of the West would seem as archaic as the use of the term "frontier." The West was always there, such thinkers might argue. The idea of opening ignores the prior populations of the region along with earlier patterns of trade, internecine conflict, and every other aspect of their lives. "Opening" the region to European trade and settlement, such scholars would say, is hardly an opening at all, but rather a continuation of patterns of replacement of population that began in the dim mists of prehistory, when people crossed the land bridge that has become the Bering Straits and likely decimated the animal populations of the Americas.

If "opening" is construed as an intellectual or ideational exercise rather than a physical presence, then it may have greater and more wide-ranging utility in analyzing the western past. In this context, the "reopening" of the title refers to the penetration of ideas about nature and its utility in the region and the application of the values encoded within these ideas to the West. Then we have a different picture, one shaped by ideas rather than the expansion of newcomers into occupied territory. In this construction, the changes in thinking about western land—from precontact ideas that revere the physical world to the concept of the "Great American Desert" (a humid-clime description of the semiarid plains) to the protocapitalist systems of organization and their revisions, and finally to a modern, and eventually postmodern construction of the meaning of western land, resources, and land-scapes—come clear. These changes suggest both continuity and discord, both similarity and difference, in way that older definitions could not.

This reopening itself is malleable, borrowing from existing traditions in an effort to go beyond them and forge a new understanding. The reopening of the West describes not an event or series of events but an ongoing process without beginning or end, one that involves all of the people of the region no matter what their ethnic, racial, cultural, or religious heritage. Frederick Jackson Turner would recognize that concept, although the process these writers describe would be foreign to his late nineteenth-century sensibility. Building from the insights of the new western history, the authors here accept the continuity of regional history, seeing no clear demarcation in the Census of 1890. The problems they relate typically stem from the twentieth century, but none of the issues discussed here would be foreign to the people of the nineteenth century. In the view of the authors here, the West never "closed." "Reopening" in physical terms would be silly. Reopening the discussion of the issues in a post–new western history manner might have more merit.

In this collection, the essays focus on the changes wrought in the environment of the American West. They reflect a wide range of issues and styles, including literary pieces that address the passage of peoples through the region, social scientific analyses of the regulatory system of the West, stabs at providing ways to solve current dilemmas, efforts to explain the diversity of human experience in the region, analyses of the relationship between humans and the physical world, and examples of the consequences of what noted historian Richard White has called "the weirdness of late capitalism." Some were initially given as talks, both at the symposium in Prescott that gives this book its name and in other places. Others are part of larger works, and a few stand independently, written specifically for this collection. The authors include journalists, historians, social scientists, and others, people who in their work and in their lives have explored the relationship between the various peoples of the American West and the remarkable range of topography and geography that constitutes this loosely defined region.

This collection also demonstrates the vast range of the new field of environmental history. In the twenty years since the field emerged, it has gone through a series of evolutions. Preceded by the older political style of conservation history and, beginning in the early 1970s, the relatively newer field of wilderness history, environmental history began with a strong tinge of advocacy; many of its early practitioners saw themselves as among those who recognized the damage humans were doing to the physical world and felt an obligation to alert the public in their own way. By the mid 1980s, activism began to give way to analytical scholarship about the human impact on the physical world, assessing the ways in which human beings, their accoutrements, their "portmanteau biota," in the words of Alfred W. Crosby—the collection of animals, microbes, plants, and whatever else that accompanies humans as they move—affected the world around them. Yet this was confined to one realm, what Donald Worster, a contributor here, defined as the agro-ecological dimension. Environmental history found itself trapped in a narrow niche: it was largely devoted to the study of human relationships to physical nature in the nonurban world.

In the past decade, environmental history has come to embrace a wide range of new dimensions. Race, class, and gender have made their appearance in environmental history, as have urban and pollution studies, the concept of "environmental justice," and its corollary, "eco-racism." The Gaia theory has developed a presence, and environmental historians have begun to engage in a kind of self-criticism typical of academic disciplines but until now not present in this youthful field. The results include the more comprehensive dimensions of environmental history represented in this work as well as a post-ironic, post-industrial sensibility that reflects the issues of the approaching twenty-first century.

As the millennium approaches, the moment has come to move toward this "post-ironic history," a history that takes existing premises, refracts them, and reconstitutes them in a language that speaks to the world at large. The worlds of scholarship and public discourse have become separate; it is time to move beyond the obsession with irony that dominates academic historical writing and use the insights of the past generation to speak to a larger public. The authors here make a beginning in that direction. They construct lenses through which people can see the past. Place is perhaps the most important of these concepts, and in this collection William deBuys, Dan L. Flores, Stephen J. Pyne, and Mike Davis all describe places in a manner that the people who inhabit and have inhabited them would recognize. Donald Worster, Marguerite S. Shaffer, and I construct pasts that lead to the present, that address the problems of the moment in historical context, while Helen Ingram, Char Miller, and Robert Gottlieb take the choices, decisions, and practices of the past and make them coherent in a complicated present.

This is a geographically and conceptually broad collection that focuses on the Southwest but ranges elsewhere in the West. The themes of environmental history—the complicated and overlapping relationship between people and their places—are abundant, as are the concepts of western history, aridity, cross-cultural relationships, regionalism, and similar themes. The essays span the five hundred years since contact, even venturing a little into the time before Francisco Vásquez de Coronado brought his men up the Rio Grande and commenced the search for Cíbola. New themes such as the social cost of tourism and gaming, both explored here, emerge alongside older, more established subjects of inquiry. Under this rubric of the concept of "reopening," a range of conceptualizations link up in new and exciting ways. This is the legacy of the "Second Opening of the West" conference: these new linkages between existing fields, new depth added to old ones, and new areas of inquiry opened up to further scrutiny. They reopen a dialogue recently deemed closed, embracing the new, resuscitating the old, and moving forward toward the millennium.

Part 1

Places

William deBuys

Dreams of Earth

Come over a little farther. Climb this gravel terrace and scan the open, naked desert. You must squint to see the few scrawny shrubs that stipple these badlands, and you can't escape the sense of being cut off and alone. Feel how hard the ground is underfoot. Hear how the gravel crunches like oyster shells. Mexicans call this kind of land *pedregal*: it is a pavement of cobbles and pebbles from which the wind has lifted every grain of soil. Thus armored by subtraction, the barren ground has lain like this a thousand years. Barring skid marks or spinning tires, it might so lie a thousand more.

This is a sacred place. The broad circle etched in these gravels is the outline of a shaman's hut, long vanished from the site. And there, the curling path that doubles back on itself and comes twisting round again marks where the shaman's people danced, year after year the same pattern, until their feet hammered a discernable trail into the dark, sun-varnished ground. They also sang here. And they recited tales that took a week of nights to tell—weird, convoluted tales that never really ended and would not fit our idea of what a story is, tales with passages that were little more than recitations of the names of place after place: canyon, butte, hill, and plain, scattered over hundreds of desert miles.[1] The tales' obsession with geography exceeds even the obsession of the tribes of Israel with genealogy, which produced the tedious "begats" of the Old Testament. Clearly the stories recited on this barranca helped teach their listeners the tangled paths of the people's mythology. It is tempting to believe they also helped teach paths of geography, so that among a people who ranged far and wide across the deserts, the right song or story might hold clues enough to guide a person where he might never have been—all the way to the Hopi mesas, say, or westward to the sea.

They came also to this spot to dream, and they put great stock in dreams, as much as any people ever have. They believed that all things worth knowing were to be learned through dream and that little of importance might be learned in any other way. The most powerful among them said they could dream their way back into the actual primordial enactment of the events of the mythic tales and songs they recited, back into the decisive moments in the lives of their gods, back even to the earliest moments of creation. At such a place as this gravel terrace, dreamers sought those dreams or, sleeping elsewhere, traveled here in dream, or thought they did, for purposes beyond the limits of our ken.

If ever you would contemplate the dreams of those who wished not to reclaim the earth, only to inhabit it, absorb this place in your mind. You may be sure *they* did. Look there: the outline of a lizard, ten yards long, lies embedded in the pedregal. They shaped the body by removing the desert gravel to bare the clay beneath, and they bermed the lifted gravel around the edges of the figure to emphasize its outline. The lizard's legs they made a different way, beating the gravels deeper in the clay, much like the path of the dance pattern.

And over here. Come on, though it's a fair walk. Now see what they scraped and tamped in the gravels. The bison on the walls of Lascaux are not more beautiful than this snorting, coiled-neck horse with flowing mane and a luxuriant fountain of a tail. This beast might haunt the dreams of anyone, including us. It is the soul of this place and the heart of our story, which is the story of the greatest encounter in the history of these lands—or of any lands on the continent. This story, repeated with variation everywhere in North, Central, and South America, is the bizarre and only half-articulated story of first encounters between the native people of this hemisphere and the emissaries of Europe.

We will soon speak more of the horse of the pedregal. But for now look south and see the patrol roads of the international border. If distances do not deter you and you've the constitution of a fit camel, you might walk from here to a place of comfort, close by the Colorado River, where cottonwoods will shade you. Allow a day for the trek, unless you undertake it unprepared in the full sun of high summer; in which case, allow eternity.

We'll not further suggest the location of this place. Precise information is inessential to our story, and divulging too much invites danger. A kind of X, a crossing of trails, marks this spot where treasures lie, and these treasures, if generally known, would attract attention from barbarians.

Perhaps you hear them on the wind. The grating, flatulent complaint of their motors breaks the silence of the desert: looking for the sound, you see a clot of them, in the padded suits and hard-shell headdresses of their own bizarre tribe, fleeing their dust cloud across a far barranca. Their boots, tires, and blindness could in moments destroy the gifts and art that lie embedded at our feet. These gifts are the property of no one. They belong to the memory of the continent.

The trails that cross here proceed to the cardinal directions. Westward lies the ocean, which drew many past this place. Some who passed by belonged to tribes, local or distant: others were Spanish, including, in 1776, a long caravan of colonists bound for the new settlement that became San Francisco; later, and far more numerous, came an army of invading *norteamericanos*, soon followed by legions of gold-mad fortyniners, both gringo and Mexican. Outsiders had less interest in the trail that ran north and south through this place. This was a trail considered sacred by the people who used this place for dreaming. They said their ancestors followed it when they journeyed downriver from Avikwame, Spirit Mountain, far to the north, where the gods had made them. Since then, the people of innumerable generations have used the trail for war and commerce and also to travel to Avikwame, in body or in dream, there to reenter the continuous and unending moment of original Time. They called the trail *xam kwacan* and took their name from the second of those strange words: Quechan (kweh-tsan´), the people who came down.[2]

By the time Juan Bautista de Anza crossed the Colorado in 1774, searching out the route (along trails well known to the Quechan) by which he would lead colonists from Sonora to Alta California, the Spanish had learned a good deal about the Quechan and other Yuman-speaking tribes who dwelled beside the river. The honor of first contact on the European side belonged to Hernán de Alarcón, who commanded a fleet in support of Francisco Vásquez de Coronado's northbound land expedition of 1540. Alarcón had sailed to the head of the Gulf of California and anchored his ships, then ascended the Colorado in launches, perhaps as far as Yuma Crossing. Though he failed to rendezvous with Coronado, he found occasion to share the corn, beans, and squash of the river people, which they grew in the floodplain of the river, and he tasted the bread they made from ground beans of the honey and screwbean mesquites.[3] He also drew from them all the news he could of Coronado's violent arrival at Zuni two months earlier, in July. The Indians were well informed on this, though Zuni, or Cíbola as the Spanish then knew it, lay more than the breadth of Arizona away.[4] Alarcón quickly realized that the people of the river were not isolates. They traded far across the deserts that enfolded them, and their world was large.

In 1604, Juan de Oñate struck west from the Hopi pueblos, descended the Bill Williams Fork to the main stem of the Colorado, whence he continued downstream to the gulf, contacting numerous Yuman tribes from the Mohaves in the north to the Cocopas at the river's mouth. One village chief regaled the dour Spaniard with tales of still other tribes, farther along, "with ears so large they dragged on the ground," and of a one-footed people who slept under water, and of still others who slept in trees or standing upright with burdens on their heads, or others who subsisted solely on the odor of their food, or others—most shocking, in the teller's view—entirely bereft of hair. Francisco de Escobar, Oñate's Franciscan chronicler, expressed skepticism that "there should be so many monstrosities in so short a distance," but, reflecting that the Almighty might produce freaks if He so chose, acknowledged that "since He is able to create them, He may have done so."[5]

It remained for the Italian Jesuit Eusebio Francisco Kino, in the course of three visits to the junction of the Gila and Colorado Rivers, to fix the understandings of his adopted countrymen in tighter focus. When he approached the confluence in 1699, Kino encountered the

Quechan people well settled there. Evidently the Quechan, whom Kino called Yumas, had migrated downriver and wrested control of the area since Oñate's time. Lieutenant Juan Mateo Manje, who accompanied Kino not so much to protect the padre as to serve as secular witness to his discoveries, described the Yuma as "a well-featured and large people," adding that "their women are pretty, and much whiter than those of any other nation of Indians known in New Spain."[6] Manje was able to observe both sexes directly and without the interference of clothing, for they went about entirely naked, save that the women wore skirts made of strands of willow bark, which rustled as they moved.

Kino recorded little of his first contact with the Quechan. What most fired his imagination was a gift the Indians made him of large blue abalone shells, which, so far as he understood the provenance of such things, seemed likely to have come from the Pacific. This was disconcerting, for Kino then believed, as all of Europe did, that California was an island, which lay separated from the continent by the as-yet unlocated and much sought after Straits of Anian, which were presumed to connect with the head of the Gulf of California. The blue shells, however, suggested that a land route to California might exist and that to reach it one need only cross the thousand-foot-wide, skin-brown waters of the Colorado, a feat which the Quechan, masterful swimmers, accomplished almost daily. Further assertions by the Quechan that clothed white men were known to dwell beyond the deserts to the west lent support for a new geography. Those whites might be the Spanish of the coastal missions at San Diego and San Gabriel.

But what was one to make of such tales? The tellers, after all, were related to the same naked and painted people who had beguiled Escobar with preposterous yarns and who even now spoke of a white woman, clothed head to foot in blue, who years ago had visited the river people bearing a cross and speaking unintelligibly. Kino and Manje were neither so gullible as to wholly believe such tales, nor so rash as to dismiss them out of hand. In those days of early contact between whites and Indians, the hot sun of history may have been at the Europeans' backs, but myth still lay like dew on the new lands, and its vapors scented every breath that anyone, white or Indian, might draw.

For the Quechan the physical world of known trails that stretched from the Pacific coast to (probably) the Rio Grande and from the Sea of Cortez to sacred Avikwame was not disjunct from the mythic, dreamtime plane where Kumastamxo, their foremost deity, and the first people forever dwelled in the moment of creation. The buttes, mountains, spires, and sentinels that marked their heat-soaked home-land were not separate from the monsters and heros who, according to myth, the landforms formerly had been. In the Quechans' view of the world, which remains foreign to those of us who were born to the chiaroscuro of history, things mythological and empirical might exist together and without conflict, with no epistemological Straits of Anian separating one class of knowing from another.[7]

So too for the creole Spaniard Manje, born in the New World, and the Italian Kino, who did God's work in Spain's name. For both, the Almighty was an immanence, not an idea. They traveled always in His presence and prayed daily for such guidance, blessing, and favorable intervention as He might bestow. Like Escobar, they acknowledged that for Him all things were possible, and so the mysteries of strange lands and stranger people (like the Quechan, whose men wore sticks in their noses and whose women, like the men, painted their bodies most outlandishly) contained nothing that could not be contained by Him. As to the Lady in Blue, Manje and Kino allowed that, notwithstanding the greater likelihood that God would have given her the power of tongues in order to communicate with the natives, "perhaps the visitor was the Venerable María de Jesús de Agreda," who in the year 1630 through the medium of heavenly transport "preached to the heathen Indians of this North America and the borders of New Mexico."[8]

Kino, true son of both his holy faith and knowledge-hungry time, bridged the worlds of myth and history. In 1700 he returned to the confluence of the Colorado and Gila, carrying with him a telescope. From a summit in the Gila Mountains east of present-day Yuma, he descried the head of a large body of water on the southwest horizon. Another year passed, and he returned a third time, intent upon de-scending the Colorado to the bay he had seen and confirming that neither it nor any other barrier of water separated the deserts of famil-iar Sonora from the fabled coast of California. Manje was not with him; the lieutenant had been called away to chastise "sorcerers" else-where in Sonora. As Kino passed downstream on the east side of the river, having never crossed to the far bank, his small retinue of Indian servants was soon swallowed amid a gathering throng of several hun-dred Quechan and Pimas.

The tumult of so many savages—for surely from a Spanish point of view that is what they were—was too much for Kino's sole white companion, a servant whose name is lost to history. As the ragged pro-cession departed Quechan land and arrived downstream at the first village of the Quíquima,[9] the Spanish servant contrived to fall behind. Seizing a moment when he was little noticed, he turned his horse and spurred for Sonora. Kino, hearing the news, dispatched two Indian boys on fast mounts to catch the deserter, but in vain. The panicked servant had too great a lead. Though worried by this abandonment, Kino pressed on. He paused to treat for peace between the Quechan and their Quíquima enemies (with temporary success), then continued southward, the river always on his right.

There followed, two days later, a spectacle that must have been one of the most extraordinary sights human eyes have witnessed in North America. The natives who had followed Kino, together with gathering bands of Quíquima, and all of them turned out in their painted best—stripes, say, on the torso, dots across the face, an arm red, a leg black or white, and everyone different—crowded both banks of the river. The Quíquima cut a path through the jungled thickets to the water's edge for Kino and his horses, but the horses mired in the river mud and could not pass. Never mind. With Kino's encouragement the natives lashed cottonwood logs together to make a raft, and a great reed basket, waterproofed with pitch, was placed upon it. The black-robed Jesuit then climbed into the basket while crowds on either bank made "dances and entertainments after their fashion."[10] From our van-tage, centuries later, we may forever wonder whether Kino next spread his hands and smiled, or prayed for strength and grimly eyed the turbid river with its dark relentless flow. We know only that at last, installed in a basket atop his tippy raft, the padre committed himself to the current and to the care of at least a score of Quíquima swimmers, who surrounded his unlikely and unseaworthy craft and pushed it toward the farther shore. Thus was Eusebio Kino, with all the fanfare the Colorado delta in 1701 could muster, ferried to the land that by then he knew to be most surely California.

Kino's geographical discoveries made possible, three quarters of a century later, the pathfinding of Juan Bautista de Anza, from whom we begin to learn in detail of the Quechan, their neighbors, and the river world of delta and desert which they inhabited.

Had there been at crucial times a few more men like Anza, the history of northern New Spain and Mexico might have been different. Sam Houston was lucky to face only Santa Ana at San Jacinto and not a leader like Anza, and Brigadier General Stephen Watts Kearny, in the Mexican War, had similar good fortune that only Manuel Armijo then served as governor of New Mexico. Anza, his stern eyes glowing from a face otherwise masked by a thick, pointed beard, was a man of extreme discipline and unquestionable courage, who by one estimate may have traveled twenty thousand miles in the saddle.[11] No wonder he died a little short of reaching fifty. Like Kino, he lived almost always in motion, rarely resting, but unlike the padre, he was a native son of Sonora and a warrior. Born in 1736 at the presidio of Fronteras, which his father commanded, Anza enlisted at the age of sixteen and fought Apaches, Seris, and other desert tribes for most of the next thirty years. His greatest military achievement came in 1779 when he delivered the beleaguered province of New Mexico, which he served as governor, from the thrall of the Comanches. His victory in pitched battle over the Comanches' most redoubtable chief, Cuerno Verde, laid a foundation for the closest thing to peace New Mexico had known in a century.[12]

Anza, however, earned his greatest fame in two expeditions to Alta California a few years earlier. The first was a journey of exploration in 1774 to find a route across uncharted deserts and mountains; the second, in the winter of 1775–76, constituted a veritable migration of 240 soldiers and colonists, plus a thousand head of livestock, along that route to San Francisco Bay. Crucial to both expeditions was Anza's cultivation of good relations with the Quechan, who controlled the vital crossing of the Colorado near its confluence with the Gila. From an encampment near the river, Anza wrote to Viceroy Bucareli in Mexico City:

The people who live on this Colorado River are the tallest and the most robust that I have seen in all the provinces, and their nakedness the most complete; their weapons are few, as I have informed your Excellency on another occasion; their affability such as is never seen in an Indian toward a Spaniard; and their number must run into thousands, for in a league and a half which I have travelled on both rivers I have seen about two thousand persons, notwithstanding that they are afraid of us because of our color and our clothing, which seem more strange to them than their entire nakedness to us. As a result of the inundations, their lands are so fertile that they yield grain in the greatest abundance.[13]

Anza had discerned the key to the natives' tall physical stature and, indeed, to much of their culture: it was the generosity of the river. Nearly every year the Colorado and the Gila flooded in spring, depositing fresh silt on their alluvial plains, which the rivers also braided with sloughs and twisting ponds. In some areas the plains stretched a mile or more back from the river. In spring when the floods receded and the drying silt began to crack, the Quechan, like the other river Yumans, moved down from their winter villages in the uplands at the desert's edge and spread out, family by family, in *rancherías* scattered along the floodplain. They planted maize, tepary beans, and various cucurbits (squashes and pumpkins) in the drying mud, and nature did almost all the rest. In most years no additional irrigation was necessary, for the water table was high and the soils held moisture well, but if the crops began to wilt, the Quechan filled clay pots from the brown river and watered them by hand. The river gave abundantly of fish, too—mainly the humpback sucker and several species of minnows, some up to three feet long. The natives shot them with arrows in the shallows or caught them any way they could: bare-handed, with baskets, nets, or weirs, or with thorn hooks baited with grasshoppers.[14]

They also planted a grass known today as Sonoran panicgrass (*Panicum sonorum*), that was like wild millet. They filled their mouths with seeds and blew them onto moist soil, mainly in places too boggy for corn.[15] And they hunted rabbits and other small game and gathered the beans of the mesquite, both honey and screwbean, which grew on the river terraces a level or two above the floodplain. When the river flooded too much or too little, the protein-rich mesquite beans helped carry them through times of want.

With food generally plentiful, the river Yumans may have been as well nourished as any native people on the continent. They lived, to be sure, at the mercy of their environment, but it was an environment more reliable and predictable than nearly any other, which may partly explain their character. Certainly, compared to the Arizona Hopis and the Puebloans of New Mexico, who relied no less on agriculture but depended on rainfall that was famously capricious in timing and amount, the river world of the Yumans epitomized regularity and security.

One can argue that a variable environment helped engender the Puebloans' elaborate ritual, dance, and cosmography—much of which was directed toward guaranteeing a needed but too often interrupted orderliness within the cosmos. An underlying idea was to persuade the supernatural inhabitants of creation not to interfere with the cycles of life but to allow the seasons to change, the rain to fall, the animals to reproduce, and all other elements of change to proceed according to their inherent regularity. In this way, abundant crops and game might be ensured.[16]

But for the river Yumans, such assurance need not have been so assiduously sought, for the Colorado and the Gila already, in most years, gave it freely. The point here is not to argue for environmental determinism, only to say that in the case of the Quechan, the forgiving character of the environment in which they dwelled helped sustain the outward, if superficial, simplicity of their tribal lives.

This simplicity pleased Spanish missionaries like the fussy Pedro Font, a Franciscan who accompanied Anza on his second expedition. With customary condescension Font noted in his diary the kinds of shamans who would have presided at the gravel terrace where the horse was etched: "There are some wizards, or humbugs, and doctors among them, who exercise their offices by yelling, blowing, and gestures."[17] But there were no full-fledged priests commanding the day-to-day obedience of the people. Nor was there much evidence of effigies, icons, sacrifices, or intricate ritual. For a man like Font the scarcity of such things was reassuring: it meant less to erase, less to overcome in the course of bringing such heathens to the Christian fold. Yet still he found much to dislike about them—their "disorderly and beastlike" ways of living, their body painting and self-piercings, and their many repugnant personal habits, including a penchant for dust-raising flatulence, which Font described in passages so detailed that a century and a half later his circumspect American translator elected to leave them, for propriety's sake, in the original Spanish.[18]

Font also detected among the Quechan what he felt to be a troubling combativeness. He knew little of their habits of warfare and had he inquired might have learned that, indeed, they were fond of fighting and campaigned, in alliance with the Mohave and other groups, almost yearly against the downstream Cocopas and the Maricopas, who lived some distance up the Gila. The Quechan disdained attacking the enemy from a distance, Apache-style, with the kind of long-range bow Anza might have better respected. Their way, like that of all the river Yumans, was to close with the enemy in organized ranks and batter them, hand to hand, with maces and stabbing clubs until one side or another held sole command of the corpse-littered battlefield. Indeed, as Font suspected, they were not a docile people, and their way of combat was no mere chest beating. (One reason the Quechan and Mohave did not more stoutly resist U.S. forces in the late 1850s and 1860s was that the ranks of their warriors had been thinned—to the point, for the Quechan, of virtual annihilation—by a disastrous battle with the Maricopa in September 1857, which left some 140 of their number dead.)[19]

But Font, while acknowledging the need for a large presidio to answer the Quechans' truculence, looked on the bright side: "Thus, it is seen that these people are greatly disposed to enter the Holy Church as soon as provision may be made for it, and that they are not repugnant to subjection to the law of God and of our sovereign, for they say they will be glad when Spaniards and fathers come to live with them. It seems to me that a great Christendom may be won among these tribes."[20]

In 1779 Spaniards and fathers duly came to stay, and gradually, as more colonists continued to arrive, their numbers swelled, though the band of troops protecting them did not. The error was fatal. Too many times did Spanish soldiers molest Quechan women, and too many times did their livestock trample Quechan crops. By July 1781 the Quechan had had enough of Christendom. They rose up and systematically destroyed the two small Spanish settlements at Yuma Crossing, killing four priests and fifty-five male settlers. They took the women and children captive, releasing many of them a few months later. In spite of various attempts to bring them to heel, never again would the Quechan submit to Spanish control.[21]

Thus, in anger, ended almost two and a half centuries of intermittent, friendly contact between the *adelanteros* of New Spain and the people of the river.

American history was born in incompleteness. Its most profound moment—that of first contact between Europeans and Native Americans—we know almost exclusively from only one side of the encounter. The other left comparatively little record of what it felt, thought, and experienced.

And what a void this silence leaves. After hearing from Alarcón, Kino, Anza, and their like, we still know relatively little of those first cultural temblors along the Colorado—or anywhere else. In that moment of early contact, whole societies of native people, encompassing complete and unduplicated ways of seeing the world and being in it, apprehended the perfect foreignness of the European, his animals, plants, and weapons, and perforce thought long and hard about the obdurate strangeness of them. But sadly for all posterity, those thinkers, for want of means if not desire, laid up no comments against the ages. A few legends have come down, only a few, and time has greatly blurred their images. The moment of contact, induplicable in every instance yet endlessly replicated across an entire continent, band by clan by tribe by nation, comes to us only by half.

No doubt in many early episodes of contact, the actors scarcely knew the import of their actions. Natives may have thought that the newly arrived strangers would soon go away and never, if prayers be answered, come back. And for many Europeans, one native group no doubt seemed little different from any other. They rarely grasped the extraordinary diversity of the societies through which they cut their path.

It is not just history we are missing, but also literature. European accounts of first contact, whether by friar, soldier, or journal-keeping wanderer, give us the author's view well enough, though usually tailored to please the viceroy or *custos* or commanding general to whom the writer reported. But while such narratives help establish who said what to whom and when, they seldom suggest what, from the natives' point of view, might have been the *feel* of events.[22]

We will never truly know the counsels of the tribe, the vying of factions within it, the calculations of trust and mistrust, the assessments of power, each side measuring the other, man by man, weapon by weapon—nor the shock of ideas or fear for the old order's crumbling, reactions that probably came later, with reflection. More immediately, there was the envy of possessions like knives and colored cloth; astonishment at the frightful energy of gunpowder; the exhilarating sensation of the first taste of wheat flour or dried apricot; the odd entanglement of curiosity and contempt as the natives pondered the Others' beards, clothes, and modesty or lack of it; and not least their amazement at the strangers' lack of women, soon followed, we may assume, by wariness and jealousy as the eyes of the new men took in the women of the tribe and as the women, their minds equally consumed with assessment, reacted to that.

In the absent native literature of first contact there would have been as much marvel and mystery, as much horror and tragedy, as in all the rest of the literature of the world. Even then, it would have been incomplete, for the truest first contacts were often not perceived as such. These would have been the terrible first epidemics of European diseases, which in many cases preceded the arrival of the Europeans themselves. For want of understanding the biological cause of these irruptions, blame would have been fixed on whatever fault of gods or ritual or human error was most readily observed. Perhaps such a dynamic explains the following dread recollections, by an old Mohave, who in turn heard the story from the Kamía, concerning the Alakwisa, a river tribe long presumed to be extinct when the story was recorded:

There was a small pond from which the Alakwisa used to draw their drinking water, and which had never contained fish. Suddenly it swarmed with fish. Some dug wells to drink from, but these, too, were full of fish. They took them, and, although a few predicted disaster, ate the catch. Women began to fall over dead at the metate or while stirring fish mush, and men at their occupations. They were playing at hoop and darts, when eagles fought in the air, killed each other, and fell down. The Alakwisa clapped their hands, ran up, and gleefully divided the feathers, not knowing that deaths had already occurred in their homes. As they wrapped the eagle feathers, some of them fell over dead; others lived only long enough to put the feathers on.[23]

Such fragments are the little we have of the missing literature of America: a few tales warped by time, some scraps of codexes, a smattering here and there of petroglyphs and pictographs. Each relic sharpens our hunger for that which was lost. In the land of the Colorado desert, none more fiercely hones that appetite than the image in sun-darkened gravels of the snorting, coiled-neck horse.

The pedregal crunches underfoot as you approach. In this place, outside the hut whose outline is preserved here, Quechan elders in the time of Kino and Anza, as well as elders of the predecessor tribes who held this ground in the time of Oñate and Alarcón, would have pondered the identity and intentions of the bearded white-skins who arrived from afar.

This much was obvious: the foreigners knew hunger and thirst the same as the people of the tribe. They knew suspicions and fears. They had a language, albeit an unintelligible one. They had the same audacity to impose their will on others. And to do so, they had swords and guns, which were equivalent, if superior, to the weapons of the people. One thing which they had, however, was utterly incomparable. More than the strangers' weapons, their clothing, their odd foods, or their fixation with the symbol of the cross, more than the outlandish-looking strangers themselves, the beasts the Spanish rode were of an order that the people of the river had never seen before on earth.

Those who squatted on the gravel barranca and surveyed the trails the Spanish traveled must have long pondered such matters. Among them, perhaps foremost among them at some indeterminate time, was the artist who executed, alone or with others, what we shall call the horse intaglio.

He had no doubt seen other four-legged creatures: deer in the bosques by the river, desert bighorn in the canyons toward the Mohave country. If he had ever joined a trading expedition to Hopi, where the river people bartered for cotton blankets, he might have seen elk among the forests and prairies of what is now Arizona. And although he might not have seen the beasts for himself, he surely spoke with others who had seen bison on the plains far to the east of the Zuni; the Indians of the delta described such creatures to Alarcón in 1540 and showed him war shields made of their nearly impenetrable hide.[24]

But none of those creatures possessed the feature that so distinguished the horse. None of them had a long, flourishing, abundant tail, which is the most pronounced characteristic of the horse intaglio. The artist rendered it with evident fascination. The narrow stump of the earthen tail bursts into a cascade of hair that falls nearly to the horse's heels. Not that the tail is excessive. Like every other detail of the intaglio, it is properly proportioned to the whole.

The image exceeds twenty feet in length from the rearmost curve of the tail to the tip of the creature's nose, and its features are true: the bend of the rear hocks, the arch of the neck, the poise and carriage of the head. The creature captured here is an intelligent and vital horse, rendered by methodical removal of desert-varnished cobble and pebble. The artist scraped out the stones to a depth of one or two inches, piling most of the material around the outline of the image. He etched ears where ears should be and an eye where an eye should be. He made four long, strong legs by wetting the ground and tamping the gravels into separate relief from the gravels around them. No doubt when the intaglio was fresh, one could tell the beast had hooves—solid hooves, not split like those of a deer. Strangely, though, the legs are straight and static, while the rest of the animal seems enlivened with motion.

There are other uncommon touches: at the withers and continuing forward to the throat, the artist removed less of the cobble, so that an indistinct dusky area remained. And in the space between the front knees and the muzzle—the domain of breath and vocal sound—the reverse exists: here the artist made a shallow, separate excavation, not quite as deep as the basin of the body. Was water offered here, or grain? Or something that surpasses facile logic? It is easy to imagine, perhaps too easy, that through use of this minute depression the artist and shaman (it is impossible to believe they were not the same person) attempted connection to, if not mastery of, the spirit of the powerful, enviable, and quintessential horse.

It is useless to attempt saying what the horse intaglio "means." One can no more say what is meant by the cave paintings at Lascaux, or by Botticelli's Venus or Andy Warhol's soup cans. We are better advised to think of the intaglio as exploration more than statement, as quest more than achievement.

What little we know of it comes from understanding the context of the work, rather than the work itself. First, it is unique—at least now. Cocopa lore includes mention of a second horse intaglio paired with this one. The presumed site of the second, however, is now a dusty void—part of the pit of a gravel quarry.[25] Certainly the diggers of the pit, as they proceeded, never would have thought to seek the advice of the Quechan before they tore into the site and would have had no idea what they destroyed. Considering that the U.S. Bureau of Reclamation never consulted the tribe before building the All-American Canal across Quechan land in 1938,[26] a road builder or cement producer can hardly be held to a higher standard on land outside the reservation.

Second, intaglios and other forms of "earth art" lie scattered far and wide across the deserts of the lower Colorado. Traditions of sand painting (known to the Quechan, Cocopa, Navajo, and others) probably attach to the same deep cultural root that produced these extraordinary forms. Many of the desert earth figures—"geoglyphs" in the parlance of archaeologists—depict abstract shapes or stylized humans. Some are hundreds of feet long; only a few are as realistic as the horse. Although dating is difficult, most geoglyphs substantially predate European contact, some possibly reaching back to the arrival of the area's earliest people thousands of years ago.[27] Virtually all are at risk to vandals.

Third, the river Yumans would have first encountered horses in the winter of 1540–41, when Melchior Díaz, in command of a third division of Coronado's expedition, journeyed to the Colorado delta in search of news either of his general or of Alarcón, who had departed the area a few months earlier. Horses next arrived in the possession of Oñate in 1604, but there is no evidence that the Quechan kept horses of their own until they picked up strays from Kino—and most of these they appear to have eaten or returned.[28] In subsequent years, through intermittent contact with Sonora, they acquired other horses which they refrained from eating, so that when Anza passed through in 1774 he could observe, with just a hint of jealous contempt, that "the horses kept by the Yumas, however it may be, are seen to be fat in the extreme."[29] Anza's hard-used mounts, we may assume, showed plenty of rib, while the Quechan horses did little but loaf and graze.

Fourth, in keeping with the themes of their cosmology, the river Yumans undoubtedly sought to come to terms with the horse through dreaming. They believed deeply in the power of dream. In his encyclopedic and authoritative *Handbook of the Indians of California*, the usually restrained Alfred Kroeber makes this categorical observation: "There is no people whose activities are more shaped by this psychic state, or what they believe to be such, and none whose civilization is so completely, so deliberately, reflected in their myths."[30]

The Yuman people believed that all knowledge and power, skills and understanding a person might possess were acquired through an extraordinary process of prenatal dreaming. While still in the womb, the spirit of the individual dreamed its way back to Avikwame, where in the presence of Kumastamxo such gifts were conferred as the unborn being might in life enjoy. At birth, this dream was forgotten, but in adolescence the individual might begin, through dreaming, to reenter that earlier dream and to recapture the gifts with which he or she had been endowed.[31] Approached this way, the river Yumans saw learning not as a process of acquisition, let alone of study, but of recovery— a return to an earlier, more complete state. The means for this return was "proper" dreaming, supplemented and reinforced by the telling of dreams, which was a tribal obsession. Elders listened carefully to the dream stories of those who aspired to possess influence within the tribe, and the seasoned old ones would judge whether the dreams of the young might be classed as merely ordinary or as "great" dreams, which brought power. They further judged whether in life the dreamer's actions validated the claims he made for his dreams.[32]

Such a dynamic of knowledge would not easily have accommodated new information. Dreams, passed down through generations, became myths. Those myths and dreams coalesced into song cycles, which were the core of the tribe's shared knowledge and religious understanding. The telling of any one of them might last all night, night after night for a week or more, and still not be exhausted. How puzzling the horse must have been. How difficult to find a place in a universe, already deemed complete, for a creature that had never before existed but was now so clearly manifest, tangible, and redolent of power.

It is not hard to imagine that the artist and shaman who created the horse intaglio would have strived to dream a dream by which to integrate the horse with the store of tribal knowledge. One wishes that all the problems resulting from contact between Europeans and Native Americans had been as philosophically pure and incorporeal.

Except in their taste for war, the river Yumans contrasted as much with Europeans as any people on the continent. Their idea of the character of knowledge and how it might be transmitted was utterly ascientific and unrational—a barbarous worldview from the perspective of the heirs of Descartes and Galileo. Differences ran no less deeply in the approach of natives and Europeans to tangible things. Though the Quechan and other river Yumans possessed the means, through the generosity of the Colorado, to amass material wealth, they disdained accumulation. When a member of the tribe died, they burned not just the body, but all the decedent's possessions, including his house.

It comes as no surprise, then, that the first Europeans who found their way to Yuma Crossing considered the natives so variously amusing, appalling, and astounding. So would we, who trouble with writing and reading books like this one, if we had trod in Kino's or Anza's shadow. It should come as still less a surprise that the litany of damages ensuing from contact with Europeans included for the Quechan and other Yumans the same sequence of disease, dispossession, and dependency that has afflicted virtually every other tribe and band on the continent. For them, as for natives throughout the Americas, the dawn of history wakened them to conditions more nightmarish than they had ever dreamt.

It may be useless to wish that things had been different, yet to wish is as natural as dreaming. Imagine, for a moment, if by dream or any other means we might reenter those earlier times. Imagine being present at the creation of the horse intaglio or at the birth of any other expression of those days. Imagine going back to reinhabit those moments of first contact, armed with knowledge of the promise and threat that they held. Imagine discovering the means to steer a different course across the sea of intervening years and to land here on the shore of the present with a full continental cargo, still intact, of people, ideas, and understandings.

Notes

A version of this chapter will appear in *Salt Dreams: Reflections from the Downstream West*, to be published by the University of New Mexico Press.

1. A. L. Kroeber, *Handbook of the Indians of California* (New York: Dover, 1976), pp. 755–785. See also Jack D. Forbes, *Warriors of the Colorado: The Yumas of the Quechan Nation and Their Neighbors* (Norman: University of Oklahoma Press, 1965).

2. Robert L. Bee, in *Handbook of North American Indians* (Washington, D.C.: Smithsonian Institution, 1983), vol. 10, p. 97; Bee, *The Yuma* (New York: Chelsea House, 1989), p. 13; Stephen Trimble, *The People* (Santa Fe: School of American Research, 1993), pp. 393, 410–415. Avikwame is Newberry Mountain, near the extreme southern tip of Nevada. For more information on Yuman groups, start with Kenneth M. Stewart, "Yumans: An Introduction," in *Handbook of North American Indians,* vol. 10. The most thoroughgoing attempt to trace the shifting territories and allegiances of Colorado River tribes is in Forbes, *Warriors of the Colorado.*

3. Carroll L. Riley, *The Frontier People* (Albuquerque: University of New Mexico Press, 1987), p. 141.

4. George P. Hammond and Agapito Rey, *The Coronado Narratives, 1540–1542* (Albuquerque: University of New Mexico Press, 1940), pp. 146 ff.; see also Riley, *Frontier People,* p. 149.

5. Herbert Eugene Bolton, *Rim of Christendom: A Biography of Eusebio Francisco Kino, Pacific Coast Pioneer* (Tucson: University of Arizona Press, 1936, 1984), pp. 416–417.

6. Bolton, *Rim of Christendom*, p. 414.

7. Kroeber, *Handbook of the Indians of California*, p. 784.

8. Bolton, *Rim of Christendom*, p. 418.

9. Later accounts would identify the Quíquima as the Halyikwamai, who became incorporated among the Maricopa along with several other displaced Yuman groups; see Henry O. Harwell and Marsha C. S. Kelly, "Maricopa," in *Handbook of North American Indians*, vol. 10, p. 74.

10. Bolton, *Rim of Christendom*, p. 471.

11. J. N. Bowman and R. F. Heizer, *Anza and the Northwest Frontier of New Spain* (Los Angeles: Southwest Museum, 1967), p. 32.

12. Stanley Noyes, *Los Comanches: The Horse People, 1751–1845* (Albuquerque: University of New Mexico, 1993), chapter 7.

13. Bowman and Heizer, *Anza*, p. 111.

14. The literature on Yuman subsistence is extensive. See Kroeber, *Handbook of the Indians of California*, chapters 50, 52–53; Bee, *Yuma*, pp. 20 ff.; *Handbook of North American Indians*, vol. 10, passim; William H. Kelly, *Cocopa Ethnography*, Anthropological Papers of the University of Arizona no. 29 (Tucson: University of Arizona Press, 1977); Edward W. Gifford, *The Kamia of the Imperial Valley*, Bulletin 97 (Washington, D.C.: Bureau of American Ethnology, 1931).

15. The most detailed discussion of the use of Sonoran panicgrass is in Gary Nabhan, *Gathering the Desert* (Tucson: University of Arizona Press, 1985), pp. 151 ff.

16. William deBuys, *Enchantment and Exploitation: The Life and Hard Times of a New Mexico Mountain Range* (Albuquerque: University of New Mexico, 1985), p. 17; Alfonso Ortiz, ed., *New Perspectives on the Pueblos* (Santa Fe: School of American Research, 1972), pp. 3–6, 143.

17. Herbert Eugene Bolton, *Anza's California Expeditions*, vol. 4 (Berkeley: University of California Press, 1930), p. 101.

18. Bolton, *Anza's California Expeditions*, vol. 4, pp. 103 ff.

19. Kroeber, *Handbook of the Indians of California*, p. 753; Bee, *Yuma*, p. 53. See also Forbes, *Warriors of the Colorado*, pp. 291–292 and passim for discussion of intertribal conflicts.

20. Bolton, *Anza's California Expeditions*, vol. 4, p. 119.

21. Bee, *Yuma*, pp. 42–47.

22. A monumental exception is Álvar Núñez Cabeza de Vaca's *Adventures in the Unknown Interior of America* (Albuquerque: University of New Mexico Press, 1961, 1983).

23. Kroeber, *Handbook of the Indians of California*, p. 798.

24. Hammond and Rey, *Coronado Narratives*, p. 146. Font, among others, mentions that the Quechan were well supplied with Hopi blankets; see Bolton, *Anza's California Expeditions*, vol. 4, p. 103.

25. Boma Johnson, *Earth Figures of the Lower Colorado and Gila River*

Deserts: A Functional Analysis, Arizona Archaeological Society Publication no. 20 (Phoenix: Arizona Archaeological Society, 1986), p. 29.

26. Bee, *Yuma,* p. 94.

27. Johnson, *Earth Figures,* p. 14. see also *Imperial Valley Press,* 19 April, 1994.

28. Forbes, *Warriors of the Colorado,* p. 129; cf. Bee, *Yuma,* p. 38.

29. Bolton, *Anza's California Expeditions,* vol. 2, p. 175; Bee, *Yuma,* p. 38; Herbert Eugene Bolton, *Coronado, Knight of Pueblos and Plains* (Albuquerque: University of New Mexico Press, 1949, 1990), chapter 15.

30. Kroeber, *Handbook of the Indians of California,* p. 755 and chapter 51, generally.

31. The ethnographic literature is vague as to the extent to which Yuman women shared, if at all, in the potential for "significant" dreaming.

32. Stewart, "Yumans," p. 65; Kroeber, *Handbook of the Indians of California,* as in note 30.

Dan L. Flores

Environmentalism and Multiculturalism

In the year 1804 in the Orleans Territory—a time and geography far removed—a colorful and energetic New Englander named John Sibley arrived in the French city of Natchitoches on the Red River to assist in the transfer of Louisiana to the United States. Prolific in a number of ways (he had already started and abandoned two families by 1804), Sibley threw himself into his charge of writing an account of "Lower Louisiana" for the Jefferson administration. In a series of missives to the president, he described the Indian nations of the Spanish border-lands with such insight that Jefferson soon appointed him U.S. agent of the Indians of the region. Sibley's account of the Red River was done so well that Jefferson had the Sibley description printed along with some of the first dispatches sent back from the Lewis and Clark expedition.[1]

In a series of very telling passages, Sibley also described the creole natives of Louisiana. Although he had a Massachusetts Yankee's con-tempt for the backwardness of much of the Louisiana creole lifestyle (he claimed that there was neither plow nor ferry in the Natchitoches area until an Irish Pennsylvanian had introduced them "under similar opposition to the Copernican system"),[2] Sibley nonetheless mustered a grudging admiration for the lifeways of some of the rural residents.

One group that he particularly singled out for praise were the Euro-American residents of a little wilderness hamlet (located just south of today's Shreveport) called Bayou Pierre. Nominally led by a frontiers-man named Pierre Bouet Lafitte, the Bayou Pierre settlement comprised about forty families of intermarried French and Spanish settlers, the unintended result of the imperialist confrontation between the two Crowns in an area so remote that the Gauls and Iberians commonsensically were constrained to commit love, not war, on one another. Living among and evidently getting along famously with the Caddo Indians, the Bayou Pierre settlers were subsistence agriculturists and pastoralists who bartered cheese, butter, and bacon hams to the town-dwellers downriver. When they occasionally needed currency to operate in the cash economy, they drove herds of horses from the Indian villages on the plains to the settlements. By 1805 they had already lived in the Bayou Pierre region for three-quarters of a century, and despite his ethnocentrism even Sibley could see that their adaptation had enabled them to survive well, while recently arrived American cotton farmers were already depleting fields downriver.

Within half a century after Sibley's time, however, the Bayou Pierre settlements had been transformed. Despite the problems with declining fertility, the Red River Valley had been entirely converted into a monoculture of cotton plantations. Within a few decades after the arrival of the Americans, there was no room left in the valley for a stock commons or a barter-and-subsistence economy based on backwoods living.

I have reasons beyond merely the topic of my presentation for telling you this story. Pierre Bouet Lafitte had a daughter named Marie, and in 1820 she and a young neighbor, Pedro Flores, were married. Their son, named Pierre after her father, grew up speaking French, watched the Indians leave the country while he was yet an adolescent, ended up converting his Bayou Pierre pastures to cotton, lived long enough to see his slaves freed by President Lincoln. His son, John Valcoure Flores, spoke both French and English and married a local Bayou Pierre girl named Mary Lacobee: although they remained on the ancestral Lafitte land, eventually hard times forced John Valcoure to lease it out and open a butcher shop. His son, Bill Flores, was never taught French, let alone the subsistence lifestyle of the previous century, and he married a German girl whose entire family (Bill Flores excepted) converted to Mormonism.

Bill Flores's son—my father—was born on the old Lafitte *vacherie* two centuries after those creole families had founded Bayou Pierre, but except for the homestead and a cemetery, Pierre Bouet Lafitte's land-holdings were all gone by 1916. So, in my family, were the lyrical sounds of the Louisiana French language—to say nothing of Spanish. So was Catholicism, and so of course was any memory of the subsistence economy that Sibley had praised and that my forebears had once prac-ticed. My mother, an Anglo-Celt from the Arkansas Ozarks, took it upon herself to preserve a smattering of the cuisine of my Louisiana ancestors. But Louisiana squirrel gumbo doesn't amount to much of a culture. And watching my family's ancestral lands grow pine trees for Louisiana-Pacific is as much proof as I need that Bayou Pierre's eigh-teenth-century environmental adaptation has not merely been mar-ginalized, it has gone into the landfill.

I hope you will forgive me for personalizing this introduction to my essay on multiculturalism and the environment. But I didn't have to look far to find an example of what has happened when the arc of American history has confronted the kinds of small-scale adaptations that culturally diverse peoples have made on this continent. My family's history is a personal experience of what Carolyn Merchant has de-scribed as a transformation from the Colonial ecology of early America to the capitalist ecological revolution of the late eighteenth century.[3] Cultural and economic Americanization was the result. Perhaps that kind of assimilation has been a good thing. And yet I have to wonder how much of real importance was sacrificed, what information about living simply on the American land my ancestors knew that I never will.

A century after Jefferson's great purchase made my Louisiana an-cestors citizens of the United States, another American president—Teddy Roosevelt—was setting in motion the foundations of mainstream Ameri-can environmentalism. Roosevelt and his coterie of bureaucratic ex-perts, among them Gifford Pinchot of the Forest Service and Arthur Powell Davis of the Bureau of Reclamation, were little concerned with issues such as cultural adaptation to place. But they were extraordinar-ily effective in convincing the American people that conservation was itself a great democratic experiment. Examine the public pronounce-ments of these men and you'll be hard-pressed to find much evidence of the national drive for efficiency that historians now believe fueled early conservation. On the contrary, Roosevelt, Pinchot, and Davis consistently spoke the rhetoric of democratic opportunity. Forests, water, and wildlife had been exploited by powerful interests, they argued. Thus conservation was all about allowing the little man to share in America's cornucopia. It was all about creating "the greatest good for the greatest number over the longest time," as the conservationist slogan went.[4]

Then there was John Muir, the Scottish-American founder of the Sierra Club, promoter of national parks for spiritual and aesthetic reasons, and the father of a strain of environmental thinking known as preservation. For his part Muir referred to the mountain lands of the American West as "the people's temples."[5] Public retention of such lands as either national forests or, preferably, as national parks would accomplish a great and necessary good for all the American people, Muir believed.

Now fast-forward to 1991. In northern New Mexico two Hispanic men sitting on a corner bench stop talking and spit in the dirt as a Forest Service truck with the despised *floresta* logo on its doors drives by. In Washington the People of Color Environmental Leadership Summit assembles to try to call forth a new kind of American environmentalism that combines concern with nature and social justice. Attendees review the situation of the past decade: the Urban Environmental Conferences in 1976 and 1977, in which community leaders in ten cities had attacked environmentalism as a white-collar, middle-class issue more concerned with obscure animals than jobs for the poor and minorities; the situation of farm workers, still suffering from pesticide exposure long after the Environmental Defense Fund's successful suit to have DDT banned resulted in chemicals that were safer for wildlife but turned out to be worse for workers; the routine and ongoing environmental discrimination in hazardous waste sitings; and finally, the response to letters sent by two minority rights groups in 1990 to the CEOs of the ten major environmental groups, charging that the racism and whiteness of environmentalism is its Achilles' heel. The Sierra Club, whose polls in the 1970s had indicated that only 15 percent of its members strongly supported activity to help urban and minority poor, in 1990 had only one Hispanic and no blacks out of a national staff of 250. The Audubon Society had that year three blacks out of a national staff of 315. Stung by the racism charge, the National Wildlife Federation joyously reported that 23 percent of its staff was minority—until someone mentioned that it probably ought not count secretarial help and maintenance workers.[6]

The environmental community is familiar with the conservative and business mantra that environmentalists are nothing more than a pack of elitists. Can this charge be true? If we examine a select group of case studies from American history—case studies more specifically related to the environmental movement than the all-too-common experience that my ancestors went through, where the mainstream market-and-consumer economy overtook and overwhelmed a successful local adaptation—what are we likely to find?

What we are likely to find is troubling. Three significant episodes in environmental history exemplify that bad news: the racism and classism of the early wildlife conservation movement, the slaughter of sheep on the Navajo Reservation in the 1930s, and the conflict between Hispanos and the Forest Service in northern New Mexico. The growing involvement of urbanites and cohesive efforts by ethnic groups in more recent events may force environmentalists to cast a wider multicultural net than they have in the past.

From the perspective of cultural pluralism, the historical record of American environmentalism can be interpreted unfavorably. For instance, a number of contemporary environmental historians have recently reassessed some of our most cherished ideas about the origins of wildlife conservation. The story of American wildlife conservation has long been treated as a celebration. Standard historians have referred to the centralized state management of "game" animals (featuring turn-of-the-century laws regulating seasons, bag limits, hunting techniques, and age, size, and sex of the target animals) as crusades or triumphs of enlightened thinking. Both early sportsmen's groups and government experts pledged themselves to "save" American wildlife and to manage it democratically, efficiently, and with the long view in mind—or so the story goes.

In fact, if the work presently being done by Richard Judd and Louis Warren is indicative, American wildlife conservation may have murkier and more socially driven beginnings than we have thought.[7] In a mirror of contemporary human-wildlife issues in Africa, Alaska, and the Pacific Northwest, management that at first glance (or rhetorically) seemed to reflect a triumph of modern scientific thinking toward wildlife actually may have contained the seeds of class or social conflict.

In Judd's and Warren's versions, for example, nineteenth- and early twentieth-century laws protecting wildlife were in reality strategies aimed at regulating people, often specific groups of local people who used wildlife in ways that urban white elites deemed either undemocratic, unsporting, or a threat to huntable and fishable stocks of game species. At a time when immigration was pouring thousands of unassimilated Europeans into the Northeast every year, and when year-round and ceremonial hunting of wildlife by many Indian peoples continued in the West, urban elites began pressuring for state game boards that would restrict local and rural practices.

Many of our traditional champions of early wildlife conservation come across poorly in this environmental movement of almost a century ago. William T. Hornaday, the famous director of the New York Zoological Park who played a key role in early wildlife battles, was perhaps the most offensive of the group, charging in 1913 that the "lower classes of Southern Europe" were a "dangerous menace to our wild life."[8] Madison Grant, president of both the Boone and Crockett Club and the Save-the-Redwoods League, was another conservationist who spoke out against "the alien gunner." So did the Audubon Society. The state of Pennsylvania was even persuaded to pass a law prohibiting immigrants from killing wild game.[9] Expressing the perspectives of the aristocratic sportsman who hunted only for trophies and for manly immersion in the sport, Hornaday actually tried to get laws passed to stop those who would "sordidly shoot for the frying pan," as he put it. "Pot-hunting" and "pot-shot" became terms of opprobrium, carrying with them implications of class and ethnicity.[10] Evidently, some of the urban elites who pressed for wildlife laws convinced themselves that while it was "sporting" to use animals as live targets and symbols of wilderness prowess, ethnic immigrants, rural rednecks, and Southern blacks who hunted wildlife and fished for food were a threat and should be regulated.

Judd and Warren point out that groups such as rural Maine fishermen, Native Americans such as the Blackfeet and the Puebloans, and ethnic Americans such as the Italians, with their long tradition of small-game hunting for the pot, invariably lost these battles to more politically astute urban elites who had science, government experts, and certainly political clout on their side.[11] (Perhaps the most interesting exception to these urban victories over rural land-use practices has been the success of western stock raisers over grazing and predator issues in the twentieth century; intriguingly, most of these rural resource users have not been members of unassimilated ethnic groups.)[12]

I have already mentioned in connection with my own family history the widespread tendency for the market economy to transform localized adaptations to place. This transformative process was in many respects at the heart of national integration a century ago. Not only were immigrants to be rapidly assimilated into the national culture, so too were American Indians, so were Southerners after the Civil War, and so were Filipinos, Samoans, and Hawaiians after the Spanish-American War. And closer to home, so was another culturally diverse group—the Mormons, whose adaptations to the environment of the Mountain West had been so successful that they had led John Wesley Powell to base his land-use plan for the West on the Mormon model.[13] But as a price for Utah's admission to the Union, the Mormon West had to undergo a process of "Americanization"—not just on the polygamy question but with respect to resource privatization, as well—that one scholar has compared to Southern Reconstruction.[14] Judging from more recent Utah environmental history, that process has worked all too well.

Moreover, by the 1930s American conservationists had found reason to *blame* unassimilated groups when major ecological disasters struck. One example of this casting of blame is the time when the Navajos were said to have too many sheep.

The Navajo Reservation today sprawls across a large swath of northern Arizona and New Mexico and a strip of Utah, the result of several increases that trebled its size between 1876 and 1901. A country whose haunting beauty has finally come to be appreciated during this century, it was widely regarded a century ago as a wasteland, useful only for holding the rest of the world together. Yet on it the Navajo population grew from approximately 10,000 in 1876 to some 40,000 by 1930, built largely around a herding economy that had produced flocks of sheep and goats totaling somewhere between 1 million and 1.4 million animals by the beginning of the New Deal. The Navajos, Richard White has argued, were yet outside the mainstream of the American economy and culture, forging their own adaptation to their place.[15]

The Navajos had arrived in the Southwest soon after the abandonment of the region by the Anasazi—an abandonment now linked with drought and a severe episode of gullying that affected the Four Corners country in the twelfth and thirteenth centuries. Six centuries later, and simultaneous with the growth of the Navajo population and of their flocks, intense gullying once again began to afflict the Southwest. With no knowledge of prior gullying episodes, however, firsthand observers in the Southwest—Aldo Leopold, for example—linked the trenching they saw with the introduction into the southwestern landscape of domestic grazing.[16] In fact, although modern researchers do not underestimate the impact that grazing had—and can have—in transforming the sensitive Southwest, most geologists and climatologists now believe that the Navajo herd increases and the severe gullying episode of 1880–1940 were coincidental, that southwestern gullying was part of a larger pattern of climate shifts and was precipitated either by drought or by more-intense summer storms.[17]

But a larger historical pattern was at work, too. In the 1920s Los Angeles had first appropriated the waters of the Owens Valley to slake its thirst, and it soon began to look to the Colorado River. Secretary of Commerce Herbert Hoover sought and obtained congressional authorization for the Colorado River Project, whose main structure was to be Boulder Dam (renamed Hoover Dam).

As construction began, however, it became evident that siltation from several tributaries of the Colorado would soon and seriously undercut the dam's capacity. Seeking a cause for that siltation, the U.S. Geological Survey found it in the gullies that were slicing like buzz saws into the soft sediments of the Southwest. And seeking a cause for the gullies, conservationists and range experts in several bureaus found it in the Navajo herds. "The fact is," one report in 1931 read, "the Navajo Reservation is practically 'Public Enemy No. 1'" in causing problems for Hoover Dam, and California's thirst for water.[18]

To bring Navajo culture in line with scientific thinking about ecology—to save Boulder Dam, Los Angeles, the Southwest, and (so it was argued) the Navajos themselves—drastic herd reductions (54 percent in 1936, 58 percent in 1940) were forced on the Navajos. The result was not just Navajo bitterness and rejection of John Collier's Indian New Deal programs, but an end to the old way of life. Their herds slashed, most Navajos were soon forced to enter the American cash economy and to open the doors of the reservation to other problematic developments such as coal and uranium mining. Casting about for someone to blame for what now appears to have been nature's own retribution for the folly of plugging the Colorado River with concrete, once again the American conservation movement seemed to settle on safe, nonwhite culprits.

The last historical example is also a Southwestern one—the mountain villagers of northern New Mexico who found themselves, after three centuries of going native in the valleys of the Sangre de Cristo Mountains, confronted in the early twentieth century with uniformed conservationists representing Gifford Pinchot and the U.S. Forest Service.

This interplay between a people with a distinctively adapted culture and the agents of centralized, scientific conservation is, it seems to me, a very nice test of American environmentalism vis-à-vis multiculturalism. For generations—continuously since about 1610—New Mexicans colonizing the Sangre de Cristos from Taos and Santa Fe had used the southern Rockies as a commons where they cut firewood and shepherded small flocks of sheep and goats. The Forest Reserve Act of 1891, however, drew a boundary around peaks including Truchas, Wheeler, and Santa Fe Baldy, and proclaimed the area the Pecos Forest Reserve. When forest service rangers attempted to regulate villager use, violence broke out in Rociada (1901) and Cuba (1909). That early violence was a portent.

For the next three-quarters of a century the Forest Service waged a campaign to restore the Sangre de Cristos to ecological health by gradually reducing grazing permits for the Carson and Santa Fe National Forests. The number of permittees dropped from 2,200 in 1940 to fewer than 1,000 in 1970. In the 1950s, Forest Service studies showed the two forests capable of supporting 14,400 cattle and 25,200 sheep; actual permit figures ranged from 30 percent to 50 percent above those limits (21,600 and 32,200).[19]

As for the cultural traditions of local peoples (almost 95 percent of permit holders in the two forests were local Hispanos), the Forest Service at midcentury was sympathetic but essentially more interested in the health of the mountains.[20] William deBuys, the best historian of this episode, is convinced that the ecology of the Sangre de Cristos was in dire straits, although it may be that the catalyst for deterioration was provided by stockmen fleeing overgrazed ranges in Texas who poured their animals into the Sangre de Cristos during the 1880s. Yet in restoring the mountain meadows, the Forest Service essentially made war on the local culture. As permit numbers plummeted (the village of Cundiyo saw a 60 percent reduction in the early 1960s; Canjilon, near Abiquiu, lost 75 percent of its permits), the Hispano herders who remained found themselves abandoning their traditional goats and sheep for cattle, the only animals economically viable in such small numbers.[21] A 350-year-old pastoral and subsistence village life was in cardiac arrest.

In their desperation to protect themselves, the New Mexican villagers denied that the mountains were in trouble, and they evoked their long tenure to buttress their argument. "We are natives," one villager insisted. "We have dealt with grazing here all our lives. . . . We know the country."[22] When no one heard, the villagers resorted to action. The ensuing violent conflict between the villagers and the Forest Service in the 1960s was in good measure responsible for the rise of Alianza, with its insistence on traditional rights to the land. When the widespread violence had subsided, the Forest Service became more serious and more sensitive. A report entitled *The People of Northern New Mexico and the National Forests* became the basis of new management, a part of which was acknowledgment that both the mountains and the Spanish-American and Indian cultures had "unique values" and ought to be preserved by the Forest Service.[23]

Forest Service flexibility in New Mexico may point up the transition to more modern thinking, but it came at a price, and that may be instructive of the future. Over the past two decades, saving both the mountains and indigenous cultures has been a catch-22, and the only solution managers could devise was essentially to grow more mountains. The adoption of the Savory rotational grazing strategy has helped a little, but in the effort to save Hispano traditions, the most successful program has involved creating new mountain grasslands by letting Le Tourneau Tree Crushers (diesel-powered tree uprooters) loose on the piñon-juniper forests. Social justice, in other words, has meant environmental compromise.

This sort of solution—increasing the size of the pie—may answer democracy in the short term, but it involves us in the tightening noose of a dilemma in a finite world. I am reminded of an often overlooked passage in Lynn White's famous essay on the causes of our environmental problems: "Our ecologic crisis is the product of an emerging, entirely novel, democratic culture," White wrote. "The issue is whether a democratized world can survive its own implications."[24]

In two recent books, however—*Environmentalism and the Future of Progressive Politics* and *Forcing the Spring: The Transformation of the American Environmental Movement*—Robert Paehlke and Robert Gottlieb argue from separate perspectives that if environmentalism is to redefine American life and become a culture-shaping ideology, its most important late twentieth-century task is to make common cause with Americans of diverse cultures and local attachment to place, who have understandably been uneasy about the "whiteness" of environmentalism.[25] Since 1970 there has emerged—distinct from mainstream environmentalism—a local, participatory, alternative environmental movement whose issues most often have centered on toxic waste. One well-known criticism of Green party politics in Europe is that it has ignored "strong personal attachment to place," yet mainstream American environmentalism seems to be making the same mistake. Note that community-based grassroots movements, often led by women, have had everything to do with the protection of hearth and home. In toxic waste siting, of course, the corporate strategy invariably has been to find a location that is job-starved and poor, and often in rural areas that have a predominantly minority population. The practice finally led the Commission for Racial Justice of the United Church of Christ to publish *Toxic Wastes and Race in the U.S.* (1987), linking civil rights and environment and coining the phrase "environmental racism." Today the Earth Island Institute continues to publish a *Race, Poverty, and Environment* newsletter. Yet many of the affected groups, such as the blacks of Cancer Alley in Louisiana who are fighting the environmental fight, refuse to call themselves environmentalists and remain suspicious of the national environmental organizations.

Ignoring these kinds of discrimination may well turn out to be environmentalism's Achilles' heel if the movement really aspires to go beyond critiquing American life to the point of actually transforming it. Modern environmentalism has looked the other way as uranium mining has victimized southwestern Indians, leaving Indian country pocked with pits and tailings. Environmentalists ignored the radioactive tailings spill into the Rio Puerco on the Navajo reservation in 1979 while simultaneously turning Three-Mile Island into a worldwide event. And environmentalists, including Paul Erlich and Edward Abbey, seemed to think nothing about alienating nonwhites from the movement with their discussions about population and immigration.[26]

Fundamentally, what environmental racism and classism mean is that some people suffer disproportionately from environmental decisions while others benefit disproportionately. I have a friend, an African historian who works on conservation issues, who has long argued with my romance about the big East African wildlife parks. Saving African wildlife certainly does have long-term implications for the health of Africa—but to see African tribal groups displaced by game parks and denied hunting privileges in places they formerly frequented so that white European and American tourists can see lions and elephants is a troubling prospect for worldwide environmentalism. Hence the title of my friend's book manuscript: "White Hunters, Black Poachers."

I confess that I am impatient with social critics who tell us what we all ought to be doing. But I am going to indulge the impulse myself just this once. As long as environmentalists come across as concerned about nature but uninterested in the unique environmental relationships the human animal has forged, there is going to be a ready opening for groups like the Wise Use Movement, which despite its transparent fronting for industry is nonetheless acquitting itself rather well in the West these days. Thus I think that biocentrics are going to have to come to terms with what one would have thought Charles Darwin laid to rest long ago—that far from being "separate" from nature, human beings happen to be biological animals, too.

And finally, I would like to make this point: diversity in human culture just may be almost as important to adaptation and evolution on earth as we have long believed ecological diversity to be. In the best philosophical sense, choosing between humans and nature is a non sequitur.

Notes

1. John Sibley, "Historical Sketches of the Several Tribes in Louisiana . . . ," in Thomas Jefferson, *Message from the President of the United States Communicating Discoveries Made in Exploring the Missouri, Red River, and Washita, by Captains Lewis and Clark, Doctor Sibley and Mr. Dunbar* (New York: Hopkins and Seymour, 1806).

2. Sibley, "Historical Sketches," pp. 60–61.

3. Carolyn Merchant, *Ecological Revolutions: Nature, Gender, and Science in New England* (Durham: University of North Carolina Press, 1989).

4. See Gifford Pinchot, *Breaking New Ground* (New York: Henry Holt, 1947).

5. Frederick Turner, *Rediscovering America: John Muir in His Time and Ours* (San Francisco: Sierra Club Books, 1984), p. 312.

6. Robert Gottlieb, *Forcing the Spring: The Transformation of the American Environmental Movement* (Washington, D.C.: Island Press, 1993).

7. Louis Warren, *The Hunter's Game* (New Haven: Yale University Press, 1997); Richard Judd, *Common Lands, Common People: Society, Landscape, and Conservation in Northern New England* (Cambridge, Mass.: Harvard University Press, 1996).

8. William T. Hornaday, *Our Vanishing Wildlife* (New York: New York Zoological Society, 1913).

9. Gottlieb, *Forcing the Spring;* Warren, *Hunter's Game.*

10. Hornaday, *Our Vanishing Wildlife.*

11. Judd, *Common Lands, Common People;* Warren, *Hunter's Game.*

12. Thomas Dunlap, "The Coyote Itself: Ecologists and the Value of Predators, 1900–1972," *Environmental Review* 7 (spring 1983):54–70.

13. See John Wesley Powell, *A Report on the Lands of the Arid Region of the United States* (Boston: Harvard Common Press, 1983; facsimile of 1879 edition).

14. Gustave Larson, *The "Americanization" of Utah for Statehood* (San Marino, Calif., 1971).

15. Richard White, *The Roots of Dependency: Subsistence, Environment, and Social Change among the Choctaws, Pawnees, and Navajos* (Lincoln: University of Nebraska Press, 1983), pp. 236–249.

16. Aldo Leopold, "The Virgin Southwest" and "Pioneers and Gullies" in Susan Flader and J. Baird Callicott, eds., *The River of the Mother of God and Other Essays by Aldo Leopold* (Madison: University of Wisconsin Press, 1991), pp. 106–113, 173–180.

17. Yi-Fu Tuan, "New Mexican Gullies: A Critical Review and Some Recent Observations," *Annals of the Association of American Geographers* 56 (December 1966):573–597; William Denevan, "Livestock Numbers in Nineteenth-Century New Mexico and the Problem of Gullying in the Southwest," *Annals of the Association of American Geographers* 57 (December 1967):691–703.

18. Bureau of Indian Affairs, *Annual Report of the Navajo District* (Washington, D.C.: Government Printing Office, 1937), pp. 51–52.

19. William deBuys, *Enchantment and Exploitation: The Life and Hard Times of a New Mexico Mountain Range* (Albuquerque: University of New Mexico Press, 1985), p. 248 table.

20. DeBuys, *Enchantment and Exploitation,* p. 249.

21. DeBuys, *Enchantment and Exploitation,* p. 259.

22. Quoted in deBuys, *Enchantment and Exploitation,* p. 272. See also Paul Kutsche and John R. Van Ness, *Cañones: Values, Crisis, and Survival in a Northern New Mexico Village* (Albuquerque: University of New Mexico Press, 1981).

23. Jean Hassell, *The People of Northern New Mexico and the National Forests* (Albuquerque: U.S. Forest Service, Southwest Region, 1968).

24. Lynn White, Jr. "The Historical Roots of Our Ecologic Crisis," in David and Eileen Spring, eds., *Ecology and Religion in History* (New York: Harper, 1974), p. 19.

25. Robert Paehlke, *Environmentalism and the Future of Progressive Politics* (New Haven: Yale University Press, 1989); Gottlieb, *Forcing the Spring.*

26. See Paul Erlich, *The Population Bomb* (New York: Ballantine, 1968). Abbey was infamous in his last years for letters and remarks opposing immigration from Mexico, particularly; see, for example, his diatribe in his journal entry for July 31, 1983, in David Peterson, ed., *Confessions of a Barbarian: Selections from the Journals of Edward Abbey, 1951–1989* (Boston: Little, Brown & Co., 1994), p. 306.

Stephen J. Pyne

Pyre on the Mountain

Fire is a primordial Southwest presence, an environmental synthesis of mountain and monsoon. Rock, climate, storm, grass, and tree create an ecological strike-a-light, the tinder to catch its spark, the wind to fan its embers, and the fuel to propagate flame into free-burning fire. Its fires are as much a regional feature as saguaros, ponderosa pines, and coyotes; and like those others fire has evolved. Fire's regime has changed with its sustaining environment, its mountain smokes rising like telegraphic signals to update the message of those reformations. The fire bust of June 1990, erupting in the Dude Creek fire of Arizona, suggests the shape of the contemporary landscape in which the Southwest's inextinguishable pyre on the mountain threatens to become a postmodern exercise in environmental deconstruction.

In the Southwest, fire seasons follow a natural rhythm of wet and dry, a two-cycle engine for which lightning typically provides the spark. This interplay of wet and dry takes several forms. Part is topographic, in which the Southwest's fabulous terrain creates differentials between moisture and aridity. Slopes that face south or north betray different levels of moisture; so do plateaus that range from high to low; so does the contrast between peak and ravine. Someplace is nearly always dry, someplace else nearly always wet. The greater cause, however, is climatic: the summer monsoon. Surges of moisture from the south strike mesa and mountain, and thunderstorms tower like spumes from surf on a reef. Rain descends in veils, drying while yet in the air. Lightning kindles fires that flash from the peaks like beacons.

The process is spotty, like a handful of popcorn scattered on a skillet. One moment there is a deluge, the next a flood of desert sun. Ideally, there is enough storm to hurl lightning and wind, not enough to quench burning snags. Add to this, winds that splash out from thunderheads like water from an overturned bucket, spillage that makes for dust storms in the desert, fire storms in the mountains. Altogether it is one of the great ecological rituals of the region, and it accounts for the fact that the Southwest has the highest concentration of lightning fires in the United States.

The figures are astonishing. Between 1960 and 1974 there were 12 days in Arizona and New Mexico when more than 100 lightning fires started; on June 28, 1960, lightning kindled 143 fires. In 1970 lightning ignited 100 fires on July 18, and the next day brought 100 more. On June 24, 1971, 103 lightning fires burned 75,713 acres. The Southwest's national forests average more fires per year than any other region; they have the second highest rate of burned acreage, from both wild and controlled fires; and critical fire weather occurs here with greater frequency and persistence than anywhere else in the nation. Yet, despite the prodigious numbers of fires, there are few truly devastating burns. The sheer number of ignitions, plus the exquisite minuet between rain and fire, ensures a certain equilibrium that balances large numbers of fires with smaller individual fires. As the monsoon persists, the wet triumphs over the dry. The number of fires rises steadily from May to August, while the average size of those fires diminishes.[1]

But while fire busts are frequent, they are rarely immense and even more rarely fatal. The Dude Creek fire outside Payson, Arizona, in late June 1990 shocks because it was both. It took familiar elements—some ancient, some modern—and compounded them into an event that looked grotesque, alien, out of character. Perhaps it was. The conflagration savaged forests, houses, and a fire suppression organization.

The fire blew up on June 27, the hottest day ever recorded in Phoenix (122.5°F), which argued that it was an old story intensified. But it burned through a forest vastly different than that of presettlement times—through summer homes and trailer parks that had little historic precedent, through a society that had sought to eliminate fire of all kinds. Old and new had come together with as much force and fury as wet and dry. When a microburst of wind drove the fire through a squad of prison inmates trained as firefighters, killing six and hospitalizing four others, the Dude Creek fire prodded debate about how fire and American society could coexist here, which is to say, about what the character of each had become.[2]

That extraordinary fire load is not simply a product of natural processes. The real narrative of fire history in the Southwest belongs to its human firebrands, who have coexisted, if not coevolved, with the regional biota throughout the Holocene. For millennia humans have busily restructured the geography and seasonality of southwestern fire—sometimes complementing and sometimes countering the natural order. Lightning had to compete not only with rain but with aboriginal firesticks. Human inhabitants added other sources of ignition in the service of hunting, raiding, foraging, and horticulture, and as an inadvertent by-product of a seasonal nomadism whose routes became trails of smoke from camp fires, signal fires, and escaped fires of diverse origins.

"The most potent and powerful weapon in the hands of these aborigines," concluded S. J. Holsinger, of the General Land Office, at the turn of the century, "was the firebrand. It was used alike to capture the deer, the elk, and the antelope, and to vanquish the enemy. It cleared the mountain trail and destroyed the cover in which their quarry took refuge." Obviously burning on this scale "must have exerted a marked influence upon the vegetation of the country. Their fires, and those of the historic races, unquestionably account for the open condition of the forest. . . . The high pine forests were their hunting grounds, and the vast areas of foothills and plateau, covered with nut-bearing pines, their harvest fields." It is important to note that the aboriginal fire regimes were themselves metastable and transitional as peoples migrated or departed out of the region.[3]

There is an old adage in firefighting which says that the fine fuels drive the fire. Fine fuels include grasses, conifer needles, low shrubs: the portion of the fuelbed that reacts most quickly to changes in moisture and heat, that most readily combusts. It determines the ease of

ignition and the rapidity of fire spread. Under aboriginal rule, fine fuels blossomed, and the Southwest burned easily and often. Lightning
and firestick competed to see which would burn a particular site or in
what season. The density of that competition fashioned, like bees in a
hive, an intricate honeycomb of burned and unburned sites. In dry
years fires simmered for weeks, smoldering and flaring as the opportunity permitted. The principal check against conflagrations was simply
the magnitude of low-intensity burning on all sides.

There are eyewitness accounts to the burning, but the most compelling evidence was recorded in the land itself, the golden grasslands,
hillside montages of brush and forbs, and, most spectacularly, oak and
pine savannas. Early explorers spoke enthusiastically about the great
natural parklands of the region in which mature ponderosa pines
marched in majestic columns. In 1882 Captain Clarence E. Dutton,
exploring the Kaibab Plateau for the U.S. Geological Survey, exulted,
"The trees are large and noble in aspect and stand widely apart. . . .
Instead of dense thickets where we are shut in by impenetrable foliage,
we can look far beyond and see the tree trunks vanishing away like an
infinite colonnade. The ground is unobstructed and inviting. There is a
constant succession of parks and glades . . . the pines standing at inter-
vals varying from 50 to 100 feet, and upon a soil that is smooth, firm,
and free from undergrowth. All is open, and we may look far into the
depths of the forest on either hand."[4]

For his report on a prospective wagon road through northern Arizona, army surveyor Lieutenant Edward F. Beale wrote in 1858, "We
came to a glorious forest of lofty pines, through which we have traveled ten miles. The country was beautifully undulating, and although
we usually associate the idea of barrenness with the pine regions, it was
not so in this instance; every foot being covered with the finest grass,
and beautiful broad grassy vales extending in every direction. The forest was perfectly open and unencumbered with brush wood, so that
the traveling was excellent."[5]

The apparent explanation for the character of these semitended
savannas is that only a fraction of ponderosa pine seedlings survived
the regular onslaught of fire through bunchgrass. Great trees, toppling
over, ripped up the ground at their roots, creating pockets of grass-free

soil; so did the fallen trunks when, after a period of organic decomposition, they burned to white ash. In the critical years that followed, seedlings thrived and eventually reached a state in which they could survive routine surface fires. Around Flagstaff, for example, fire-scarred pines testify to fires that burned an average of every 1.5 years. Mature trees grouped oddly, clustered in ways that betrayed their origin in the churned-up soil of old root-holes, or aligned along the trend of fallen boles. The macrogeography of such forests depended on the microgeography of fire refugia.

The paradox that the land was both burned and forested baffled some observers, such as the Norwegian naturalist and explorer Carl Lumholtz, who witnessed an astonishing profligacy of aboriginal burning across the border with Mexico: "These Indians, the pagans as well as the Christians, keep up the custom of burning off the grass all over the sierras during the driest season of the year . . . [so that] fires are seen continually burning day and night all over the mountains up to the highest crests, leaving the stony ground, blackened and barren, but the forests stand green." That was the rub. Despite this fantastic amount of firing, Lumholtz became convinced that "the continuous, immense forests here could never be destroyed by the Indians" because, paradoxically, all this chronic burning inoculated the forests against wildfires; the periodic fires ensured the forests' "indestructibility."[6]

All this changed with the advent of European colonization. Settlers introduced some new ignitions and removed several old ones, but it was by utterly restructuring the regional fuel complex that they remade the fire regimes of the Southwest. Generally, European colonization made itself felt in the New World primarily through farming. This impact was muted in the Southwest, however. Regional aridity, hostile tribes, distance from major markets, the slow movement of westering Americans, the retarded admission of Arizona and New Mexico into statehood—all militated in the Southwest against the kind of pervasive agricultural settlement that had typified most of the American frontier. Logging and land clearing remained relatively local; farming concentrated on irrigation rather than lands fire-flushed for nutrients. Indians, sequestered onto special reservations, became inconsequential as a source of fire. When Gifford Pinchot visited Arizona in 1900, he watched a distant Apache setting "the woods on fire" to improve his hunting, trailing fire like a broken lance in the dirt.[7]

Settlement in the Southwest followed hoof, not axe. Pastoralism prevailed—first through Hispanics, then through partial adoption by select tribes of indigenes (such as the Navajo), and then, with mounting force, through Americans. Livestock were brought to the Southwest in immense numbers. Cattle and sheep (the sheep were "ten times worse," Pinchot insisted) hit the region like a shock wave, disassembling fire regime after fire regime in ways that may prove irreversible. Flocks roamed in the hundreds of thousands, pounding forests and grasslands, leaving clouds of biotic dust to blow in their wake. (Pinchot was wrong: the cattle were worse because sheep often browsed on tree seedlings and cattle did not, allowing arboreal reproduction to multiply unchecked.) When the big ranches collapsed, hundreds of smaller homestead ranches took up the slack. The epidemic of herds continued.

In the aboriginal Southwest, grass had infiltrated every landscape, and some it had dominated. In the Europeanized Southwest, exotic herbivores seized every blade and pursued the succulent grass into every niche. No place was spared. Rolling hills of oak, high desert grasslands, mountain meadows, slopes dappled with chaparral, open pine forests with their cathedral columns—the relentless hoofs and hungry teeth found them all. Thanks to his herds the reach of the rancher far exceeded his own numbers. He became the biotic conquistador of the Southwest. There was no sanctuary, no refuge from the conquest. The indigenous fires went the way of the grizzly bear and the mountain lion. Only on Indian reservations could fire survive in anything like its former state, and then only if tribes did not take up herding with the same ruthlessness evident elsewhere in the region. What had fed the flames of fast combustion came to stoke the slow combustion of metabolizing livestock. Well before systematic fire control, cattle and sheep cropped fire from the land, and they did so with a thoroughness that later engine companies, smokejumpers, and helitack crews could never equal.

The chronicle is written widely if complexly in the land. The finely bounded mosaic that had constituted the Southwest scene smeared; desert succulent, mesquite, juniper, and chaparral replaced grasses in desert basins and across high plateaus; brush congealed into jungles; open forests—once dappled with glades of sun and shadow—snarled with downed logs, dense tangles of understory, and young groves of pine and fir "as thick as the hair on a dog's back." In 1902 Holsinger observed that "in Arizona you will find no young forests of any considerable extent antedating a period of forty years, and almost all of the regrowth has sprung up within the last quarter of a century." Surveying southern Arizona in the early 1920s, Aldo Leopold reasoned that "one is forced to the conclusion that there have been no widespread fires during the past 40 years." Forty years later Charles Cooper mapped the peculiar age structure of Arizona pines and determined that the forest derived from a small number of cohorts, all of which became established during the favorable climatic periods of the early twentieth century but which survived because they were spared fires. Others have disputed the climatic argument for broadcast regeneration—1919 as an *annus mirabilis*, for example—but agreed with the outcome. What had been restricted to microsites and select meteorological moments began to thrive everywhere, year after year. Trees and brush multiplied like fruit flies in a jar of bananas. They spread, a scabby reaction to a vast ecological infection.[8]

If it is not everything, timing accounts for much of this condition. An interesting study has compared the forest structure on the Chuska Mountains in the Navajo Reservation to that elsewhere in northern Arizona. The Navajos acquired livestock from the Spaniards, and their herds soon swelled. Huge numbers of sheep and goats were introduced to the Chuskas by the 1820s. As the flocks advanced, fires receded. But the rapid reforestation that followed American grazing later in the century did not immediately occur here. Regeneration apparently had to wait for a favorable climate, which occurred through the region in the early decades of the twentieth century. The congestion of the Chuska forests thus came synchronously with that elsewhere in the Southwest, the product of a beneficent climate that promoted regeneration and the absence of fire-thinning made possible by intensive grazing.[9]

Grazing came with plenty of accomplices. Loggers aggravated the scene by culling whatever mature or old-growth timber they could reach.

Bark beetles, fungi, and dwarf mistletoe infested the thickets that, in the absence of bunchgrass and fire, sprang up in unnatural profusion. Droughts like that which gripped the region at the turn of the century magnified grazing's shock wave, further reducing the amount of light fuels needed to carry fire. So did the other instruments of settlement: the fire-breaked roads, the patterns of fixed land ownership that prevented the seasonal cycling of peoples and fires, the introduction of exotic flora, the mining and urbanization that created local markets for livestock and the railroads that bound herds to national markets, the reservation of public lands, and the establishment of professional forestry. All the different means, however, tended to lead to the same end: the suppression of light fire and the encouragement of fuel arrays that promoted intense fires.

The fine fuels—the grasses and forbs—that had carpeted aboriginal Arizona massed into three-dimensional jungles that readily transformed surface fires into crown fires. In places, thickets of young growth (two meters high and seventy years old) existed in a comatose state, unable to grow and unwilling to die, waiting until fire could shock them back to life. A century after Beale rejoiced in the open pinelands of the region, Wallace Covington and Margaret Moore estimated that tree density had exploded from 23 per acre to 851, tree basal area from 23 to 315 square feet per acre, and crown closure from 8 percent to 93 percent. Where Dutton had praised the wooden colonnades of the Kaibab, tree densities had ratcheted upward from 55.9 to 276.3 per acre, tree basal area from 44 to 245 square feet per acre, and crown closure from 16.5 percent to more than 70 percent. Herbage had correspondingly plummeted, from 1000 to 112 tons per acre in northern Arizona, and from 589 to 117 tons per acre on the Kaibab Plateau. On one site near Flagstaff, herbaceous plants that had covered 83 percent in 1876 covered only 4 percent in 1990. More ominously, fuel loads rocketed from 2 and 0.2 tons per acre, respectively, to 44 and 28 tons per acre. The land metamorphosed from a pine savanna to a forest entangled with dog-hair thickets. In recent years the woody invasion has also included houses. While the ultimate reasons for this biotic drama reside in the character of settlement, the immediate cause has been the elimination of free-burning fire.[10]

The march of woody weeds was only a beginning. Biodiversity

declined, and those creatures inimical to ranching or dependent on the old fire regime melted away. Worse, the land started to erode. In southern Arizona a spectacular cycle of arroyo-cutting began in eerie lockstep with the cattle invasion. Elsewhere there were landslides, debris flows, and garden-variety siltation on a bigger scale than had ever been known before. Alarmed, irrigation associations campaigned for forest reserves and grazing control. (To oppose overgrazing was not to promote burning, however. Humus remained the guarantor of watersheds, and it appeared as vulnerable to flame as to hoof.)

The cumulative outcome was a colossal degradation of the landscape for which the tree, elsewhere a talisman of land health, was ironically an emblem of decay. By the early 1920s the declination had reached its nadir. Even cattle and sheep could no longer thrive on the land and had to be shipped to feed pens for fattening. Economically, ranching depended for the most part on public subsidies, even as it remained a political power—that relationship not being entirely coincidental. The debate over the relative contributions of climate and anthropogenic activities continues, but clear-eyed observers of the day had no doubt about the chain of causality. In 1933 Leopold wrote epigrammatically that "when the cattle came the grass went, the fires diminished, and erosion began."[11]

By the time organized fire protection arrived, it had only to confirm the fire ban announced by overgrazing. Fire suppression was, at first, an exercise in regional mop-up. Aboriginal fires, those that remained, were banished to reservations. Livestock had perverted fuels and quelled the impact of lightning ignitions; fires had little to burn, or they burned amid open forests, where they were easily extinguished by pine boughs and blankets. Even ranchers who sought to "green up" spring pasture by burning found it difficult to do so. Arguments for "light burning" as the "Indian way" were dismissed by professional foresters as "Paiute forestry," and advocates were treated with the condescension normally reserved for perpetual-motion mechanics and circle-squarers.[12]

But of course fire could never be abolished. Tremendous extents of the Southwest were committed to public reservations for Indians, forests, parks, the military, wildlife refuges, and other purposes. These lands remained quasi-natural, persisting in forms that would not yield to farm or city. Something like the native fuels endured, though often leavened with pyrophytic weeds. Lightning too continued its restless foraging, eager to seize whatever fuels came within its strike. Fire endured.

As decades rolled by, however, the fires that escaped began to burn with unprecedented intensity and magnitude. Increasingly the saga of settlement moved from irony to tragedy. Fire had enhanced biodiversity; fire exclusion, through hoof and later shovel, destroyed it. Anthropogenic burning had improved fire control; fire suppression worsened it. Ranchers had sought to replace the wild with the domestic, and so they had done with grizzlies and cattle; but in the process they had also replaced the domesticated fire with the feral fire. If the land became less suitable for wild fauna, it became progressively more prone to wild fire.

That trend continued despite the New Deal's monumental investment in environmental reforms, including the Civilian Conservation Corps. Crown fires—large by virtue of their intensity as well as their size—increased from 10,127 acres per year in the 1940s to 15,117 acres per year in the 1980s, despite a massive commitment to high-tech firefighting. Fires that had rarely exceeded 3,000 acres in presettlement times routinely reached 10,000 to 20,000 acres as the twentieth century passed its midpoint. It became apparent that to remove fire was as powerful an ecological act as to introduce it. In 1972 the Tall Timbers Research Station mustered a task force that singled out the pine forests of the Southwest as a case study in the consequences of fire exclusion. Slowly, grudgingly, the fire establishment admitted that its successes, ever more costly, were self-defeating. The tragedy of American fire history, of which the Southwest was a robust subnarrative, was not that wildfires were suppressed but that controlled fires were no longer set.[13]

These concerns were not restricted to the Southwest, but when, some twenty-five years ago, the clamor for reform shook the national fire establishment, the Southwest responded quickly. For the new era this meant that somehow, in some form (preferably benign), fire had to be retained in the landscape. Where it had disappeared, it had to be restored. Prescribed fire for fuel reduction, for conversion of woodlands to pasture, for wilderness ecology, and for improved wildlife habitat became acceptable, if not commonplace. Excepting the South, the Southwest practiced more broadcast burning than any other region. But it was not enough.

Nowhere has anyone reintroduced fire as fully as it has been removed. Restoration failed to keep pace even with annual requirements, much less to make inroads in reducing a century's backlog of burning; those fires did little more than make the minimum payment on an ecological credit card charged to its maximum limits. Often the fuel situation has worsened, particularly as logging exploded throughout the region's national forests in the 1980s and slash proliferated. It is easy to fund a dramatic firefight, tough to justify the quiet burning which, if it is done properly, does not become a public spectacle. It is difficult to restore fire without restoring the other conditions that had helped sustain it. The end could only follow from the means; somehow those accumulated fuels had to be disposed of.

The new Southwest is a product of the old Southwest. Those fuel loads on public lands are a kind of environmental debt, like toxic dumps, that will take decades of determined action to clean up. It is not clear that either the resolve or the money is there to do it; the backlog is too great, and the requisite social consensus too elusive. The logging of large trees inflames environmentalists. The removal of small trees does not suit the economics of sawmill logging. Above all, air quality considerations increasingly regulate the pattern of open burning. Wood smoke must compete with industrial sources—smelters, coal-fired power plants, automobiles—for its share of the regional airshed. In 1975 and again in 1979, air-pollution alerts in Phoenix resulted, in part, from an overload of broadcast burning on the Mogollon Rim. It is hard to explain to residents of the seventh-largest metropolitan area that they can no longer burn fireplaces at will but that tens of thousands of acres of forest wildland need to be broadcast-burned. The cultural distinctions make no difference to regional airsheds or to lungs degenerate with emphysema.

And now exurban sprawl plasters the private lands within and around the public domain with houses—another woody weed—adding all the problems of a suburban environment but with few of its correctives. Exurbanites are reclaiming a rural landscape but without a rural economy, and so they increase the complexity (and expense) of fire protection without improving the prospects for fuel treatment, broadcast burning, or fire services. The developer is replacing the rancher: and summer homes and trailer parks and tourists are supplanting the throngs of sheep and cattle that once penetrated every meadow and forest pastures. A four-wheeled seasonal transhumance has replaced its four-hoofed predecessor. But the outcome for fire regimes remains unchanged. The fuel situation worsens, without a corresponding improvement in ignition.[14]

Like shots fired in the dark, sooner or later lightning will hit the right combination of fuel, wind, and terrain with perhaps fatal effects, particularly when lightning discharges, as it does here, with the scatter of a shotgun blast. Increasingly it appears that wildfire is the only legally and politically acceptable form of burning, as though drive-by shootings were the only sanctioned form of target practice. As drought seized the region in the late 1980s, wildfires increased. The Dude Creek fire was the new regime's climax, and its prophecy.

The character of southwestern fire reflects the changing character of its human occupation. The classic blaze in the Southwest is a trying fire that exposes and assays, sometimes with stark symbolism, sometimes with fatal finality, the relationship between the natural landscape and the humans who live on it. It is difficult to reconstruct the impact of early humans, whose firesticks coincided with the colossal climatic fluctuations that ended the last ice age. Probably the Southwest featured a diffuse geography of burning in which firestick and grass created a regime that always simmered but rarely boiled, the intensity of fires following the tidal surges of rain and drought, the human firebrands smoothing out the jerky rhythms of lightning and wind, the very ubiquity of the burning helping to dampen catastrophic eruptions.

It is easier to document the dramatic alterations that have accompanied European settlement. The landscape mosaic became coarser and more brittle, less able to absorb chronic disturbances. From some sites fire vanished—flooded into irrigable fields, paved into cityscapes, eaten away by livestock, or swatted out by determined fire crews. From others, fire receded temporarily, only to return in altered but reinvigorated form. Elsewhere it was kept in check only through ever-increasing investments in fire suppression. The slow growth rates in the semiarid Southwest bought time; decades might pass before the consequences of fire exclusion became apparent or irreversible.

That interdependence is again shifting. Whatever climatic changes may occur, human-inspired change is outstripping it. Overall, human activity is increasing the total number of fires even as it shrinks to a razor's edge the border between a controlled fire and a wildfire. Smaller numbers of fires break free, but these rage over larger areas and with greater ferocity. Like the interest on a compounding debt, wildfire threatens to claim an ever larger proportion of the region's fire economy. The rural landscape that had once served as a buffer between the urban and the wild continues to shrivel; in its place, houses insinuate themselves into every nook and cranny of private land. There is little slack, small margin for error. The gradient between the wild and the urban steepens, building like an electric charge. Eventually it will arc.

In southern California, the intermix fire is a familiar morality play, almost a distinctive art form. Certainly the environment is built to burn. Clearly, the construction of expensive wood-shingled houses in mountains bristling with decadent chaparral and exposed to Santa Ana winds is an act of hubris. But the worst fires typically begin with arson. This transforms an environmental dilemma into a simple parable of human madness or malice.

It is more difficult to interpret fire in the Southwest, where lightning, not arson, normally supplies ignition. The relationships are more complex and balanced, the ironies more subtle. The tensions between nature and humans are multiple, not readily decoded into simple dialectics. The region remains a fire-baked mosaic of history and geography. It is not clear, for example, whether the Dude Creek fire was a freak event, the fiery manifestation of a record-shattering heat wave, or the calling card for a new era in which, regardless of technological investments, the pressure of human population and the legacy of suppressed fires will combine to make a truly ungovernable fire regime. Is it the old amalgam, merely intensified? Or is it a new compound, as volatile as nitroglycerin, ready to explode at the first stumble? It seems to be both.

But neither is it obvious how to restore fire. However significant fire was to the presettlement Southwest, its removal was only one part of fashioning today's Southwest, and its reinstatement will not by itself restore that lost landscape. It is not apparent by what means fire should be reinstated, nor to what ends it should be applied. Hardest of all is the determination of an environmental standard. The existential Earth offers no absolutes, only the record of many pasts and the prospects of many futures. The privileging of ancient peoples and former landscapes speaks with no more authority. That anthropogenic fire has been an inextricable part of the Southwest's history does not declare how it might become a part of the Southwest's future. The one hard fact is that the existing scene has, for various reasons and to diverse groups, become unattractive, unacceptable, and in the broadest sense progressively uninhabitable. But however conceived, fire remains, an inevitable end, an unavoidable means.

Fire belongs in the mountainous Southwest, and unless the peaks flatten, the monsoon evaporates, the seasons homogenize, or the biota vanishes, those fires will continue. They ought to continue. The issue is how to relate to fire—how to keep it from destroying people and how to prevent people from transforming flame into a destroyer. Otherwise the border between the human and the natural will grind with greater and greater force, and out of that friction will come fire that no one wants and no one can control. The summer beacon will become a pyre on the mountain.

Notes

This chapter has been adapted from *World Fire: The Culture of Fire on Earth* by Stephen J. Pyne, © 1995 by Stephen J. Pyne. Reprinted by permission of the author and Henry Holt & Co.

1. Jack S. Barrows, "Lightning Fires in Southwestern Forests," unpublished report, Northern Forest Fire Laboratory (U.S. Forest Service, 1978); Thomas W. Swetnam, "Fire History and Climate in the Southwestern United States," in J. S.

Krammes, tech. coord., *Effects of Fire Management on Southwestern Natural Resources*, General Technical Report RM-191 (U.S. Forest Service, 1990), pp. 6–17. In the latter, see also L. F. DeBano et al., "Selected References: Fire Effects in the Southwest," pp. 255–293, for an excellent bibliography.

2. Eldon Ross et al., "Accident Investigation Report: Dude Fire Incident, Multiple Firefighter Fatality," unpublished report, Tonto National Forest (1990), obtained through the Freedom of Information Act.

3. S. J. Holsinger, "The Boundary Line between the Desert and the Forest," *Forestry and Irrigation* 8 (1902):23–25.

4. Clarence E. Dutton, *Tertiary History of the Grand Cañon District*, U.S. Geological Survey Monograph 2 (Washington, D.C.: Government Printing Office, 1882), p. 133.

5. E. F. Beale, "Wagon Road from Fort Defiance to the Colorado River," 35th Cong., 1st sess., Sen. Exec. Doc. 124 (1858). Cited in Lewis Lesley, ed., *Uncle Sam's Camels: The Journal of May Humphreys Stacey Supplemented by the Report of Edward Fitzgerald Beale (1857–1858)* (Cambridge, Mass.: Harvard University Press, 1929), p. 210.

6. Carl Lumholtz, in C. W. Hartmann, "Indians of Northwestern Mexico," *Congress International des Americanisters* (1897):115–136.

7. Gifford Pinchot, *Breaking New Ground* (Seattle: University of Washington Press, 1972; reprint), p. 179.

8. Holsinger, "Boundary Line," p. 22; Aldo Leopold, "Grass, Brush, Timber, and Fire in Southern Arizona," *Journal of Forestry* (1924):2–8; T. N. Johnson, "One-Seed Juniper Invasion of Northern Arizona Grasslands," *Ecological Monographs* 32 (1962):187–207; Charles F. Cooper, "Changes in Vegetation, Structure, and Growth of Southwestern Pine Forests since White Settlement," *Ecological Monographs* 30 (1960):129–164.

9. Melissa Savage and Thomas W. Swetnan, "Early 19th-Century Fire Decline Following Sheep Pasturing in a Navajo Ponderosa Pine Forest," *Ecology* 7, no. 6 (1990):2374–2378.

10. W. W. Covington and M. M. Moore, "Postsettlement Changes in Natural Fire Regimes: Implications for Restoration of Old-Growth Ponderosa Pine Forests," in Merrill Kaufmann et al., tech. coords., *Old-Growth Forests in the Southwest and Rocky Mountain Regions. Proceedings of a Workshop*, General Technical Report RM-213 (U.S. Forest Service, 1992), pp. 81–99.

11. Aldo Leopold, "The Virgin Southwest," in Susan L. Flader and J. Baird Callicott, eds., *The River of the Mother of God and Other Essays* (Madison: University of Wisconsin Press, 1991), p. 179.

12. See Stephen J. Pyne, *Fire in America: A Cultural History of Wildland and Rural Fire* (Princeton, N.J.: Princeton University Press, 1982), pp. 100–122.

13. Harold H. Biswell et al., *Ponderosa Pine Fire Management: A Task Force Evaluation of Controlled Burning in Ponderosa Pine Forests of Central Arizona*, Miscellaneous Publications no. 2 (Tallahassee: Tall Timbers Research Station, 1973).

14. See Frank Ronco, Jr., tech. coord., *Proceedings: Arizona Conference on Wildfire and the Urban/Wildland Interface* (Arizona State Land Department et al., 1991).

Mike Davis

Las Vegas Versus Nature

It was advertised as the biggest non-nuclear explosion in Nevada's history. On October 27, 1993, Steve Wynn, the state's official "god of hospitality," flashed his trademark smile and pushed the detonator button. As 200,000 Las Vegans cheered, the Dunes Hotel, former flagship of the Strip, slowly crumbled to the desert floor. The giant dust plume was visible from the California border.

Nobody in Nevada found it the least bit strange that Wynn's gift to the city that he so adores was to blow up an important piece of its past. This was simply urban renewal Vegas-style: one costly façade destroyed to make way for another. Indeed, the destruction of the Dunes merely encouraged other corporate casino owners to blow up their obsolete properties with equal fanfare: the Sands, of Rat Pack fame, came down in November 1996, while the Hacienda was dynamited at the stroke of midnight on New Year's Eve. Extravagant demolitions have become Las Vegas's version of civic festivals.

In place of the old Dunes, Wynn's Mirage Resorts is completing the $1.25 billion Bellagio, a super-resort with lakes large enough for jet-skiing, created using water that came from the allotments of the original Dunes golf course. Wynn's purchase of the Dunes solved his problem, but not that of other developers of resorts. Impresario Sheldon Adelson, who is building the $2 billion, 6,000-room Venetian Casino Resort on the site of the Sands, with gondolas along artificial canals, has not explained where his water will come from; neither has Circus

Circus Enterprises, which is transforming the old Hacienda into Project Paradise, "an ancient forbidden city on a lush tropical island with Hawaiian-style waves and a swim-up shark exhibit."[1]

In the five years since Wynn blew up the Dunes, $8 billion has been invested in thirteen major properties along the Strip alone. As a result, the Sphinx now shares an adjacent street address with the Statue of Liberty, the Eiffel Tower, Treasure Island, the Land of Oz, and, soon, the Piazza San Marco. And the boom, still breaking all records in 1997, shows every sign of continuing.[2]

By obscure coincidence, the demolition of the Dunes followed close on the centenary of Frederick Jackson Turner's legendary "end of the frontier" address to the World's Columbian Exposition in Chicago, where the young prairie historian meditated famously on the fate of American character in a conquered and rapidly urbanizing West. Turner questioned the survival of frontier democracy in the emergent epoch of giant cities and trusts (not to mention Coney Island and movies) and wondered what the West would be like a century hence.

Steve Wynn and the other robber barons of the Strip think they know the answer: Las Vegas is the terminus of western history, the end of the trail. As an overpowering cultural artifact it bestrides the gateway to the twenty-first century in the same way that Burnham's "White City" along the Chicago lakefront was supposed to prefigure the twentieth century. At the edge of the millennium, this strange amalgam of boomtown, world's fair, and highway robbery is the fastest growing metropolitan area in the United States. (It is also, as we shall see, the brightest star in the neon firmament of postmodernism.)

More than 30 million tourists had their pockets picked by its one-arm bandits and crap tables in 1996: a staggering 33 percent increase since 1990. (By the time you read this, Vegas should be hard on the heels of Orlando, Florida, which is, with 35 million visitors to Walt Disney World and Universal–MGM Studios, the world's premiere tourist destination.) While southern California has suffered through its worst recession since the 1930s, Las Vegas has generated tens of thousands of new jobs in construction, gaming, security, and related services. As a consequence, nearly a thousand new residents, half of them Californians, arrive each week.[3]

Some of the immigrants are downwardly mobile blue-collar families—the Californians are called "reverse Okies" by locals—desperately
seeking a new start in the Vegas boom. Others are affluent retirees
headed straight for a gated suburb in what they imagine is a golden
sanctuary from the urban turmoil of Los Angeles. Increasing numbers
are young Latinos, the new bone and sinew of the casino-and-hotel
economy. In spring 1995, Clark County's population passed the one
million mark, and anxious demographers predicted that it will grow
by another million before 2010.[4]

The explosive, and largely unforeseen, growth of southern Nevada has
dramatically accelerated the environmental deterioration of the American Southwest. Las Vegas long ago outstripped its own natural-resource
infrastructure, and its ecological "footprint" now covers all of southern Nevada and adjacent parts of California and Arizona. The hydro-
fetishism of Steve Wynn (he once proposed turning downtown's Fremont Street into a pseudo-Venetian Grand Canal) sets the standard for
Las Vegans' prodigal overconsumption of water: 360 gallons daily per
capita versus 211 in Los Angeles, 160 in Tucson, and 110 in Oakland.
In a desert basin that receives only 7–8 inches of annual rainfall, irrigation of lawns and golf courses (60 percent of Las Vegas's total water
consumption)—not to mention artificial lakes and lagoons—adds the
equivalent of another 20 to 30 inches of rainfall per acre.[5]

Yet southern Nevada has little water capital to squander. As Johnny-
come-lately to the Colorado Basin water wars, it has to sip Lake Mead
through the smallest straw. At the same time, reckless groundwater
overdrafts in Las Vegas Valley are producing widespread and costly
subsidence of the city's foundations. The Strip, for example, is several
feet lower today than in 1960, and sections of some subdivisions have
had to be abandoned.[6]

Natural aridity dictates a fastidiously conservative water ethic.
Tucson, after all, has prospered on a reduced water ration: its residents
actually seem to prefer having cactus instead of bermuda grass in their
front yards. But Las Vegas haughtily disdains to live within its means.
Instead, it is aggressively turning its profligacy into environmental ter-
rorism against its neighbors. "Give us your water, or we will die," de-

velopers demand of politicians grown fat on campaign contributions from the gaming industry. Las Vegas is currently pursuing two long-term and fundamentally imperialist strategies for expanding its water resources.

First, the Southern Nevada Water Authority is threatening to divert water from the Virgin River (a picturesque tributary of the Colorado with headwaters in Zion National Park) or steal it from ranchers in sparsely populated central Nevada. In 1989 the Authority (then called the Las Vegas Valley Water District) stunned rural Nevadans by filing claims on more than 800,000 acre-feet of surface- and groundwater rights in White Pine, Nye, and Lincoln Counties.[7]

This infamous water grab ("cooperative water project" in official parlance) brought together an unprecedented coalition of rural Nevadans: ranchers, miners, farmers, the Moapa Band of Paiutes, and environmentalists. Their battle cry has been "Remember the Owens Valley," in reference to Los Angeles's notorious annexation of water rights in the once-lush valley on the eastern flank of the Sierra Nevada: an act of environmental piracy immortalized in the film *Chinatown*. Angry residents of the Owens Valley blew up sections of the Los Angeles Aqueduct during the 1920s, and some central Nevadans have threatened to do the same to any pipeline highjacking local water to Las Vegas.[8]

Since 1966, the Authority, without abandoning its legal claims to central Nevada water, has put more emphasis on withdrawing Virgin River water directly from its terminus in Lake Mead. This conforms to its second, and more important, strategy of increasing Las Vegas's withdrawal of Colorado River water stored in Lake Mead or in downstream reservoirs. To circumvent the status quo of the Colorado River Compact, the Authority has teamed up with the powerful Metropolitan Water District of southern California in what most observers believe is the first phase of a major water war in the Southwest.

Las Vegas and the Los Angeles area want to restructure the allocation of Colorado River water away from agriculture and toward their respective metropolitan regions. In most scenarios, this involves a raid on Arizona's allotment, and Arizona's governor, J. Fife Symington III, retaliated by allying himself with water managers in San Diego and the Imperial Valley. (Major players in this anti–Metropolitan Water District coalition also include the billionaire Bass brothers from Fort Worth, who have bought up tens of thousands of acres of choice agricultural land in the El Centro area in order to sell their federally subsidized water allotments to San Diego.)[9]

Through one or another of these machiavellian gambits, the Authority's general manager, Pat Mulroy, has assured the gaming industry that Clark County will have plenty of water for continued breakneck growth over the next generation. Independent water experts, however, have criticized Mulroy's optimistic projections, and one of them, Hal Furman, caused a small sensation in February 1997 with his assertion that "southern Nevada will run dry shortly after the turn of the century." In the event of such a crisis, Las Vegas's last resort probably would be "to help subsidize the costly process of desalting Pacific Ocean water in exchange for some of California's Colorado River share." This, however, would almost certainly double the current, artificially low, acre-foot cost of water.[10]

Compounding the problem of future water supply is the emergent crisis of water quality in Lake Mead, which operates as both reservoir and wastewater sink for Las Vegas. Federal researchers in 1997 discovered that "female egg protein in blood plasma samples of male carp" was causing widespread reproductive deformation in the fish. This catastrophic endocrine disruption, with potential human genetic impact as well, is likely related to the large amounts of toxic waste, especially pesticides and industrial chemicals, that are discharged into the lake.[11] In 1994, moreover, thirty-seven people, mostly with AIDS, died as a result of a lethal protozoan, *Cryptosporidium parvum*, that experts from the national Centers for Disease Control surmised was carried in tap water drawn from Lake Mead. Public health researchers have become alarmed by the coincidence of these two outbreaks at a time when hypergrowth is overwhelming regional water and waste treatment capabilities. As one biologist recently asked on the op-ed page of the Las Vegas *Review-Journal*, "Will more people die from *Cryptosporidium* contamination of our drinking water when we put more wastewater back in the lake?"[12]

Finally, to return to yet another *Chinatown* parallel, watchdog groups such as the Nevada Seniors Coalition and the Sierra Club are increasingly concerned that the Southern Nevada Water Authority's $1.7 billion water delivery system from Lake Mead, currently under construction, may be irrigating huge speculative real-estate profits along metropolitan Las Vegas's undeveloped edge. For example, one major pipeline (the so-called South Valley Lateral) runs through an area near the suburb of Henderson where private investors recently acquired huge parcels in a complicated land swap with the Bureau of Land Management, which controls most of Las Vegas's desert periphery. This is the same equation—undervalued land plus publicly subsidized water—that made instant millions for an "inside syndicate" when the Los Angeles Aqueduct was brought to the arid San Fernando Valley in 1913.[13]

Southern Nevada is as thirsty for fossil fuels as it is for water. Most tourists naturally imagine that the world's most famous nocturnal light show is plugged directly into the turbines of nearby Hoover Dam. In fact, most of the dam's output is exported to southern California. Electricity for the Strip, as well as for the two million lights of downtown Las Vegas's new (and disconcerting) "Fremont Street Experience," is primarily provided by coal-burning and pollution-spewing plants on the Moapa Indian Reservation northeast of the city, and along the Colorado River. Only 4 percent of Las Vegas's current electrical consumption comes from "clean" hydropower. Cheap power for the gaming industry, moreover, is directly subsidized by higher rates for residential consumers.[14]

Automobiles are the other side of the fossil fuel problem. As Clark County's transportation director testified in 1996, the county has the "lowest vehicle occupancy rate in the country" in tandem with the "longest per person, per trip, per day ratio." Consequently the number of days with unhealthy air quality is dramatically increasing. Like Phoenix and Los Angeles before it, Las Vegas was once a mecca for those seeking the restorative powers of pure desert air. Now, according to the Environmental Protection Agency, Las Vegas has supplanted New York as the city with the fifth highest number of days with "unhealthy air" (as measured from 1991 to 1995). Its smog already contributes to the ochre shroud over the Grand Canyon and is beginning to reduce visibility in California's new East Mojave National Recreation Area as well.[15]

Las Vegas, moreover, is a major base camp for the panzer divisions of motorized toys—dune buggies, dirt bikes, speed boats, jet-skis, and the like—that each weekend make war on the fragile desert environment. Few western landscapes, as a result, are more degraded than the lower Colorado River Valley, which is under relentless, three-pronged attack by the leisure classes of southern Nevada, Phoenix, and southern California.

In the blast-furnace heat of the Colorado River's Big Bend, Las Vegas's own demon seed, Laughlin, has germinated kudzulike into an important gambling center. Skyscraper casinos and luxury condos share the west bank with the mega-polluting Mojave Power Plant, which devours coal slurry pumped with water stolen from Hopi mesas hundreds of miles to the east. Directly across the river, sprawling and violent Mohave County, Arizona—comprising Bullhead City and Kingman—provides trailer-park housing for Laughlin's nonunion, minimum-wage workforce, as well as a breeding ground for antigovernment militias. (It was here that Timothy McVeigh worked as a security guard while incubating his *Turner Diary* fantasies of Aryan vengeance.)

The Las Vegas "miracle," in other words, demonstrates the fanatical persistence of an environmentally and socially bankrupt system of human settlement and confirms Edward Abbey's worst nightmares about the emergence of an apocalyptic urbanism in the Southwest. Although postmodern philosophers (who don't have to live there) delight in the Strip's "virtuality" or "hyperreality," most of Clark County is stamped from a monotonously real and familiar mold. Las Vegas, in essence, is a hyperbolic Los Angeles—the Land of Sunshine on fast-forward.

The historical template for all low-density, resource-intensive southwestern cities was the great expansion of the 1920s that brought two million midwesterners and their automobiles to Los Angeles County. This was the "Ur" boom that defined the Sunbelt. Despite the warnings of an entire generation of planners and environmentalists chastened by the 1920s boom, regional planning and open-space conservation again fell by the wayside during the post-1945 population explosion in southern California. In a famous article for *Fortune* magazine in 1958, sociologist William Whyte described how "flying from Los Angeles to San Bernardino—an unnerving lesson in man's infinite capacity to mess up his environment—the traveler can see a legion of bulldozers gnawing into the last remaining tract of green between two cities." He baptized this insidious growth-form "urban sprawl."[16]

Although Las Vegas's third-generation sprawl incorporates some innovations (casino-anchored shopping centers, for example), it otherwise recapitulates, with robotlike fidelity, the seven deadly sins of Los Angeles and its Sunbelt clones such as Phoenix and Orange County. Las Vegas has (1) abdicated a responsible water ethic; (2) fragmented local government and subordinated it to private corporate planning; (3) produced a negligible amount of usable public space; (4) abjured the use of "hazard zoning" to mitigate natural disaster and conserve landscape; (5) dispersed land uses over an enormous, unnecessary area; (6) embraced the resulting dictatorship of the automobile; and (7) tolerated extreme social and, especially, racial inequality.[17]

In mediterranean California or the desert Southwest, water use is the most obvious measure of the environmental efficiency of the built environment. Accepting the constraint of local watersheds and groundwater reservoirs is a powerful stimulus to good urban design. It focuses social ingenuity on problems of resource conservation, fosters more compact and efficient settlement patterns, and generates respect for the native landscape. In a nutshell, it makes for "smart" urbanism (as seen in modern Israel, or the classical city-states of Andalucia and the Maghreb), with a bias toward continual economies in resource consumption.[18]

Southern California in the early Citrus era, when water recycling was at a premium, was a laboratory of environmental innovation, as evinced by such inventions as the bungalow (with its energy-efficient use of shade and insulation), solar heating systems (widespread until the 1920s), and state-of-the-art sewage and wastewater recovery technologies. Its departure from the path of water rectitude, and thus smart urbanism, began with the Owens Valley aqueduct and culminated in the 1940s with the arrival of cheap, federally subsidized water from the Colorado River. Hoover Dam extended the suburban frontier deep into southern California's inland basins and in the process underpriced traditional water conservation practices such as sewer-farming and stormwater recovery out of existence.

Unlike Los Angeles, Las Vegas has never practiced water conservation or environmental design on any large scale. It was born dumb. Cheap water has allowed it to exorcise even the most residual semiotic allusion to its actual historical and environmental roots. Visitors to the contemporary Strip, with its tropical islands and Manhattan skylines, will search in vain for any reference to the Wild West (whether dude ranches or raunchy saloons) that themed the first-generation casinos of the Bugsy Siegel era. The desert, moreover, has lost all positive presence as landscape or habitat; it is merely the dark, brooding backdrop for the neon Babel being created by Wynn and his competitors.

Water profligacy likewise dissolves many of the traditional bonds of common citizenship. Los Angeles County is notorious for its profusion of special-interest governments—"phantom cities," "county islands," and geographical tax shelters—all designed to concentrate land use and fiscal powers in the hands of special interests. Clark County, however, manages to exceed even Los Angeles in its radical dilution and dispersal of public authority.

The Las Vegas city limits, for example, encompass barely one-third of the metropolitan population (versus nearly half in the city of Los Angeles). The major regional assets—the Strip, the Convention Center, McCarran International Airport, and the University of Nevada, Las Vegas (UNLV)—are located in an unincorporated township aptly named Paradise, while poverty, unemployment, and homelessness are disproportionately concentrated within the boundaries of the cities of Las Vegas and North Las Vegas.

This is a political geography diabolically conceived to separate tax resources from regional social needs. Huge, sprawling county electoral districts weaken the power of minorities and working-class voters. Unincorporation, conversely, centralizes land-use decision making in the hands of an invisible government of gaming corporations and giant residential and commercial-strip developers.

In particular, the billion-dollar corporate investments along the

Strip—with their huge social costs in terms of traffic congestion, water and power consumption, housing, and schools—force the fiscally malnourished public sector to play constant catch-up. This structural asymmetry in power between the gaming corporations and local government is most dramatically expressed in the financing of the new public infrastructures to accommodate casino expansion and the growth of tourism. A classic example is the Southern Nevada Water Authority's new water distribution system, whose bonds are guaranteed by sales taxes—the most regressive means available, but the only significant source of undesignated state revenue in Nevada.[19]

Contrary to neoclassical economic dogmas and trendy "public choice" theory, corporate-controlled economic development within a marketplace of weak, competing local governments is inherently inefficient. Consider, for example, the enormous empty squares in the urbanized fabric of Las Vegas, dramatically visible from the air, that epitomize the leapfrog pattern of development that planners have denounced for generations in southern California because it unnecessarily raises the costs of streets, utilities, and schools. Crucial habitat for humans (in the form of parks), as well as for endangered species such as the desert tortoise, is destroyed for the sake of vacant lots and suburban desolation.

Similarly, both Los Angeles and Las Vegas zealously cultivate the image of infinite opportunity for fun in the sun. In reality, however, free recreation is more accessible in older eastern and midwestern cities that cherish their parks and public landscapes. As long ago as 1909, experts were warning Los Angeles's leaders about the region's looming shortage of parks and public beaches. Although the beach crisis was partially ameliorated in the 1950s, Los Angeles remains the most park-poor of major American cities, with only one-third the usable per capita open space of New York City.[20]

Las Vegas, meanwhile, has virtually no commons at all: just a skinflint 1.4 acres per thousand residents, compared with the recommended national minimum of 10 acres. This park shortage may mean little to the tourist jet-skiing across Lake Mead or lounging by the pool at the Mirage, but it defines an impoverished quality of life for thousands of low-wage service workers who live in the stucco tenements that line the side streets of the Strip. Boosters' claims about hundreds of thousands of acres of choice recreational land in Clark County refer to car-trip destinations, not open space within walking distance of homes and schools. One is not a substitute for the other.[21]

Some of the most beautiful desert areas near Las Vegas, moreover, are now imperiled by rampant urbanization. Developers are attempting to raise land values by privatizing natural amenities as landscape capital. The local chapter of the Sierra Club, for example, has recently mobilized against the encroachment of Summerlin West, a segment of the giant Summerlin planned community that is the chief legacy of Howard Hughes, upon Red Rock Canyon National Conservation Area—native Las Vegans' favorite site for weekend hikes and picnics. The project, as endorsed by the Las Vegas City Council (which was subsequently allowed to annex the development), encompasses 20,000 homes, two casinos, five golf courses, and nearly 6 million square feet of office and commercial space. As one local paper put it, most environmental activists were "less [than] enthused about the possibility of lining one end of Red Rock Canyon, one of the valley's most pristine landmarks, with casinos, businesses and homes."[22]

The recreation crisis in Sunbelt cities is the flip side of the failure to preserve native ecosystems, another consequence of which is the loss of protection from natural hazards such as floods and fires. The linkage between these issues is part of a lost legacy of urban environmentalism espoused by planners and landscape architects during the City Beautiful era. In 1930, for example, Frederick Law Olmsted, Jr., the greatest city designer of his generation, recommended "hazard zoning" to Los Angeles County as the best strategy for reducing the social costs of inevitable floods, wildfires, and earthquakes. In his sadly unrealized vision, development would have been prohibited in floodplains and fire-prone foothills. These terrains, he argued, were best suited for preservation as multipurpose greenbelts and wilderness parks, with the specific goal of increasing outdoor recreational opportunities for poorer citizens.[23]

Las Vegas is everything Olmsted abhorred. Its artificial deserts of concrete and asphalt, for example, have greatly exacerbated its summer flash-flood problem (probably the city's best-kept secret, except on occasions, as in 1992, when unsuspecting tourists drown in casino parking lots). Like Los Angeles, Clark County has preferred to use federal subsidies to transform its natural hydrology (the valley literally tilts toward the Colorado River) into an expensive and failure-prone plumbing system rather than use zoning to exclude development from the arroyos and washes that should have become desert equivalents to Olmsted's greenbelts. (The recent declaration of a desert wetlands park in the Las Vegas Wash riparian corridor is a belated half-measure.)[24]

Los Angeles was the first world metropolis to be decisively shaped in the era of its greatest growth by the automobile. One result was the decentralization of shopping and culture and the steady atrophy of its downtown district. Recently a group of theorists at the University of California at Irvine have suggested that we are seeing in Orange County, and other "edge cities," the birth of a "postsuburban metropolis" where traditional central-place functions (culture and sports, government, high-end shopping, and corporate administration) are radically dispersed among different centers.[25]

Whether or not this is truly a general tendency, contemporary Las Vegas recapitulates Orange County in an extreme form. The gaming industry has irresistibly displaced other civic activities, with the partial exception of government and law, from the center to the periphery. Tourism and poverty now occupy the geographical core of the metropolis. Other traditional downtown features, such as shopping areas, cultural complexes, and business headquarters, are chaotically strewn across Las Vegas Valley with the apparent logic of a plane wreck.

Meanwhile its booming suburbs stubbornly reject physical and social integration with the rest of the city. To use the nomenclature of the futuristic movie *Blade Runner*, they are self-contained "off worlds," prizing their security and social exclusivity above all else. Planning historian William Fulton has recently described suburban Las Vegas as a "back to the future" version of 1950s southern California: "It is no wonder that the Los Angeles homebuilders love Las Vegas. Not only can they tap into a Los Angeles–style market with Los Angeles–style products, but they can do things the way they used to do them in the good old days in L.A." As Fulton points out, while southern California homebuilders must now pay part of the costs of the new schools and water systems, Vegas developers "pay absolutely no fees toward new infrastructure."[26]

The most ambitious of Las Vegas's "off worlds" is Summerlin. Jointly developed by Summa and Del Webb corporations, and named after one of Howard Hughes's grandmothers, it boasts of complete self-sufficiency (it's "a world within itself," according to one billboard slogan) with its own shopping centers, golf courses, hospitals, retirement community, and, of course, casinos. "Our goal is a total community," explains Summerlin president Mark Fine, "with a master plan embracing a unique lifestyle where one can live, work, and play in a safe and aesthetic environment." (Residents rather than the corporations pay for key infrastructural investments, such as the new expressway from Las Vegas, through special assessment districts.) When Summerlin is finally completed in the early twenty-first century, a population of more than 200,000 living in twenty-six income- and age-differentiated "villages" will be hermetically sealed in Las Vegas's own up-scale version of Arizona's leaky Biosphere.[27]

The formerly gritty mill town of Henderson, southeast of the Strip, has also become a major growth pole for walled, middle-income subdivisions, and it is becoming Nevada's second-largest city. (For optimal advantage in its utility and tax obligations, Summerlin is divided between the city of Las Vegas and unincorporated Clark County.) On the edge of Henderson is the larval Xanadu of Lake Las Vegas: a Wynnian fantasy created by erecting an eighteen-story dam across Las Vegas Wash. "The largest privately funded development under construction in North America," according to a 1995 brochure, Lake Las Vegas (controlled by the ubiquitous Bass brothers of Fort Worth) is sheer hyperbole, including $2 million lakefront villas in a private gated subdivision *within* a larger guard-gated residential community. The Basses' grand plan envisions the construction of six major resorts, anchored by luxury hotels and casinos, as well as five world-class golf courses, in addition to "restaurants and retail shops that will be the upscale alternative for Las Vegas."[28]

Las Vegas's centrifugal urban structure, with such gravitationally powerful edge cities as Summerlin and Henderson–Lake Las Vegas, reinforces a slavish dependence upon the automobile. According to trendy architectural theorists such as Robert Venturi and Denise Scott Brown, whose *Learning from Las Vegas* has been a founding text of postmodernism, Las Vegas Boulevard is supposed to be the apotheosis of car-defined urbanism, the mother of strips. Yet the boom of the last decade has made the Strip itself almost impassable. Las Vegas Boulevard is usually as gridlocked as the San Diego Freeway at rush hour, and its intersection with Tropicana Road is supposedly the busiest street corner in the nation.[29]

As a result, frustrated tourists soon discover that the ride from McCarran Airport (immediately adjacent to the Strip) to their hotel frequently takes longer than the plane flight from Los Angeles. The Brobdingnagian scale of the properties and the savage summer heat, not to mention the constant assault by hawkers of sex-for-sale broadsheets, can turn pedestrian expeditions into ordeals for the elderly and families with children. The absence of coherent planning for the Strip as a whole (the inescapable consequence of giving the gaming corporations total control over the development of their sites) has led to a series of desperate, patchwork solutions, including a few new pedestrian overpasses. In the main, however, the Nevada Resort Association—representing the major gaming corporations—is relying on new freeways and arterials to divert cross-traffic from the Strip and a proposed $1.2 billion monorail to speed customers between the larger casino-hotels.

For most of the 1990s, contemporary Las Vegas has been one vast freeway construction site. Nothing has been learned from the dismal California experience, not even the elementary lesson that freeways increase sprawl and consequently the demand for additional freeways. When completed, the new Las Vegas freeway network will allow most local commuters to bypass the Strip entirely, but it will also centrifuge population growth farther into the desert, with correspondingly high social costs for infrastructure and schools.

Meanwhile, the Nevada Resort Association has concentrated its overwhelming political clout to ensure that a proposed increase in the 8 percent hotel room tax is spent exclusively on its own Resort Corridor Transportation Master Plan (the monorail). Having engineered the financing of the new water delivery system with regressive sales tax increases, the gaming industry has opposed all efforts by desperate Clark County School District officials to divert part of the room tax increase to school construction. As in previous tax fights, school and welfare advocates are strictly outnumbered by the resort association's hired guns. Nevada is the most notoriously antitax state in the country, and gaming industry lobbyists, their coffers swollen with the profits of the boom, dominate the legislature in Carson City. The recent flood of retirees to Las Vegas's suburbs has only reinforced the antitax majority. (Paradoxically, the Clark County electorate is aging, while the actual median age of the population—thanks especially to young Latino immigrants and their families—is declining.)[30]

One index of the extraordinary power wielded by the resort association is the fact that the relative contribution of gaming taxes to state revenue actually declined during the *annus mirabilis* of 1995 when hotel-casino construction broke all records. Yet the industry, shaken by the local "Rodney King" riots in spring 1992, is not unconscious that eroding education quality and social services will eventually produce social pathologies that may undermine the city's resort atmosphere. Their calculated solution, after months of top-level discussion in the winter of 1996–97, has been to volunteer the room tax increase—which is directly passed on to tourists and then spent exclusively on the Strip monorail—as a "heroic" act of social responsibility. This reduced the tax heat on the casino owners while conveying the clear message, scripted by resort association lobbyists, that the time had come for homebuilders and small-business owners to make a contribution to school finance. As columnist John Smith pointed out, "By coming out first, they shift the focus away from a potential gaming revenue tax increase [which would come out of their pockets] and raise the question of responsibility of Southern Nevada's developers and shopkeepers."[31]

In the meantime, the previous decade's hypergrowth without counterpart social spending has increased economic inequality throughout Clark County. Despite the feverish boom, the supply of jobless immigrants has far outpaced the demand for new workers in the unionized core of the gaming economy. The difference translates into a growing population of marginal workers trapped in minimum-wage service jobs, the nonunion gaming sector, the sex industry, and the drug economy. According to one estimate, Las Vegas's homeless population increased 750 percent during the superheated boom years of 1990–1995. At the same time, a larger percentage of Las Vegans lack health insurance than the inhabitants of any other major city. Likewise, southern Nevada is plagued by soaring rates of violent crime, child abuse, mental illness, lung cancer, epidemic illness, suicide, and—what no one wants to talk about—a compulsive gambling problem that is a major factor in family pathologies.[32]

This obviously provides a poor setting for the assimilation of Las Vegas's new ethnic and racial diversity. Despite consent decrees and strong support for affirmative action from the Culinary Workers Union, the gaming industry remains far from achieving racial or gender equality in hiring and promotions. In the past, Las Vegas more than earned its reputation as "Mississippi West." While African-American entertainers such as Sammy Davis, Jr., and Nat King Cole were capitalizing the Strip with their talent, blacks were barred from most hotels and casinos, except as maids, through the 1960s. Indeed, a comparative study during that period of residential discrimination across the United States found that Las Vegas was the "most segregated city in the nation."[33]

More recently, persistent high unemployment rates in the predominantly black Westside precipitated four violent weekends of rioting following the Rodney King verdict in April 1992. Interethnic tensions, exacerbated by a relatively shrinking public sector, have also increased as Latinos have replaced African-Americans as the valley's largest minority group. Indeed, black leaders have warned of "creeping Miamization" because some casino owners prefer hiring Latino immigrants instead of local blacks. Latinos, for their part, point to overcrowded schools (Latinos now constitute 40 percent of the elementary school population in the city of Las Vegas), police brutality, and lack of representation in local government.[34]

Let's return, once again, to Las Vegas and the end of western history. In his apocalyptic potboiler, *The Stand* (1992), Stephen King envisioned Las Vegas as Satan's earthly capital, with the Evil One literally enthroned in the MGM Grand. Many environmentalists, together with the imperiled small-town populations of Las Vegas's desert hinterlands, would probably agree with this characterization of the Glitterdome's diabolical *zeitgeist*. No other city in the American West seems to be as driven by occult forces or as unresponsive to social or natural constraints. Like Los Angeles, Las Vegas seems headed for some kind of eschatological crack-up (in the King novel, Satan ultimately nukes himself).

Confronted with the Devil himself, and his inexorable plan for two-million-plus Las Vegans, what can the environmental community do? The strategic choices are necessarily limited. On one hand, environmentalists can continue to defend natural resources and wilderness areas one at a time against the juggernaut of development: a purely defensive course that may win some individual victories but is guaranteed to lose the larger war. On the other hand, they can oppose development at the source by fighting for a moratorium on further population growth in the arid Southwest. Pursued abstractly, however, this dogmatic option will only pigeonhole Greens as enemies of jobs and labor unions. Indeed, on the margins, some environmentalists may even lose themselves in the Malthusian blind alley of border control, by allying themselves with nativist groups that want to deport hardworking Latino immigrants whose per capita consumption of resources is only a small fraction of that of their native-born employers.

A better approach, even if utopian in the short- or medium-run, would focus comprehensively on the character of desert urbanization. "Carrying capacity," after all, is not just a linear function of population and the available resource base; it is also determined by the social form of consumption, and that is ultimately a question of urban design. Cities have incredible, if largely untapped, capacities for the efficient use of scarce natural resources. Above all, they have the potential to counterpose public affluence (great libraries, parks, museums, and so on) as a real alternative to privatized consumerism, and thus cut through the apparent contradiction between improving standards of living and accepting the limits imposed by ecosystems and finite natural resources.

In this perspective, the most damning indictment against the Sunbelt city is the atrophy of classical urban (and pro-environmental) qualities such as residential density, pedestrian scale, mass transit, and a wealth of public landscapes. Instead, Los Angeles and its postmodern clones are stupefied by the ready availability of artificially cheap water, power, and land. Bad design, moreover, has unforeseen environmental consequences, as illustrated by southern Nevada's colossal consumption of electric power. Instead of mitigating its desert climate through creative design (e.g., proper orientation of buildings, maximum use of shade, minimization of heat-absorbing "hardscape," and so on), Las Vegas, like Phoenix, simply relies on universal air-conditioning. But, thanks to the law of the conservation of energy, the waste heat is merely exported into the general urban environment. As a result, Las Vegas is a scorching "heat island" whose nightly temperatures are frequently 5 to 10 degrees hotter than the surrounding desert.

Fortunately, embattled western environmentalists have some new allies. In their crusade for the New Urbanism, Peter Calthorpe, Andreas Duany, and other young, environmentally conscious architects have reestablished a critical dialogue between urban designers and mainstream environmental groups, particularly the Sierra Club. They have sketched, with admirable clarity, a regional planning model that cogently links issues of social equity (economically diverse residential areas, recreational equality, greater housing affordability through elimination of the need for second cars, and a preferential pedestrian landscape for children and seniors) with high-priority environmental concerns (on-site recycling of waste products, greenbelts, integrity of wetland ecosystems, wildlife corridors, and so on). They offer, in effect, elements of a powerful program for uniting otherwise disparate constituencies—inner-city residents, senior citizens, advocates of children, environmentalists—all of whom are fundamentally disadvantaged by the suburban, automobile-dominated city.

The New Urbanism has had many small successes in northern and central California, the Pacific Northwest, and other areas where preservation of environmental quality commands a majority electoral constituency. In the Southwest, by contrast, the Summerlin model—with its extreme segregation of land uses and income groups, as well as its slavish dependence upon cheap water and energy—remains the "best practice" standard of the building industry. (Only Tucson, with its self-imposed environmental discipline, constitutes a regional exception.) The West, in other words, is polarizing between housing markets where the New Urbanism has made an impact and those where 1960s southern California templates remain hegemonic. In the case of Las Vegas, where the contradictions of hypergrowth and inflexible resource demand are most acute, the need for an alternative settlement model has become doubly urgent.

The New Urbanism by itself is a starting point, not a panacea. A Green politics for the urban desert would equally have to assimilate and synthesize decades of international research on human habitats in drylands environments. It would also have to consider the possible alternatives to a regional economy that has become fatally dependent upon a casino–theme park monoculture. And it would need to understand that its major ally in the long march toward social and environmental justice must be the same labor movement (particularly the progressive wing represented by unions such as the Las Vegas Culinary Workers) that today regards local environmental activists with barely disguised contempt. These are the new labors of Hercules. Creating a vision of an alternative urbanism, sustainable and democratic, in the Southwest is an extraordinary challenge. But this may be the last generation even given the opportunity to try.

Notes

1. Dave Berns, "Venice in Las Vegas," *Las Vegas Review-Journal*, 27 November 1996; Gary Thompson, "Paradise to be Part of Vegas Strip," *Las Vegas Sun*, 19 November 1996.

2. Michael Hiltzik, "Stakes Raised Ever Higher in Las Vegas Building Boom," *Los Angeles Times*, 24 December 1996.

3. Darlene Superville, "L.V. Grew Fastest in Nation," *Las Vegas Review-Journal*, 2 October 1995; "Nevada No. 1 in Job Growth," *Las Vegas Review-Journal*, 13 February 1996.

4. Hal K. Rothman, *Devil's Bargains: Tourism and Transformation in the Twentieth-Century American West* (Lawrence: University Press of Kansas), forthcoming; Ed Vogel, "Growth Figures Revised," *Las Vegas Review-Journal*, 4 November 1995.

5. Data from telephone interviews with metropolitan water authorities.

6. *Annual Report, 1992–1993* (Las Vegas: Clark County Flood Control District, 1993).

7. Jon Christensen, "Will Las Vegas Drain Rural Nevada?" *High Country News*, 21 May 1990.

8. See Jon Christensen, "Betting on Water," in Mike Davis and Hal Rothman, eds., *The Grit beneath the Glitter: Tales from the Real Las Vegas* (Berkeley: University of California Press, forthcoming).

9. William Kahrl, "Water Wars about to Bubble Over," *San Bernardino Sun,* 4 February 1996; Mike Davis, "Water Pirates," *Los Angeles Weekly,* 23–29 February 1996.

10. Susan Greene, "Water Outlook Revised," *Las Vegas Review-Journal,* 20 February 1997.

11. Frank Clifford, "Lake Mead Carp Deformed," *Las Vegas Review-Journal,* 19 November 1996.

12. Larry Paulson, "Leading the Charge against Growth," *Las Vegas Review-Journal,* 17 January 1997.

13. Paulson, "Leading the Charge."

14. Jay Brigham, "Lighting Las Vegas," in Davis and Rothman, *Grit beneath the Glitter.*

15. Data provided by the Environmental Protection Agency. See also Keith Rogers, "Scientists Tackle Dirty Air in L.V.," *Las Vegas Review-Journal,* 15 January 1996.

16. Mike Davis, "How Eden Lost Its Garden," in Allen Scott and Edward Soja, *The City* (Berkeley: University of California Press, 1997).

17. Davis, "How Eden Lost Its Garden."

18. For a first-rate discussion of the principles of sustainable urban design, with particular application to southern California case-studies, see John Tillman Lyle, *Design for Human Ecosystems* (New York: Van Nostrand Reinhold, 1985).

19. For an authoritative discussion of Las Vegas's "tax scissors" (i.e., exploding social needs versus artificially constrained tax capacity), see Eugene Moehring, "Growth, Urbanization, and the Political Economy of Gambling, 1970–1996," in Davis and Rothman, *Grit beneath the Glitter.*

20. Davis, "How Eden Lost Its Garden."

21. *Parks and Recreation Master Plan, 1992–1997* (Las Vegas: Clark County Parks and Recreation Department, 1992).

22. Mike Zapler, "Huge Project OK'd Next to Red Rock," *Las Vegas Review-Journal,* 28 January 1997.

23. *Parks, Playgrounds, and Beaches for the Los Angeles Region* (Los Angeles: Olmsted Brothers and Bartholomew, 1930), esp. pp. 97–114.

24. Letters in *Las Vegas Review-Journal,* 1 February 1996.

25. Stuart Olin et al., *Postsuburban California* (Berkeley: University of California Press, 1992).

26. William Fulton, *The Reluctant Metropolis: The Politics of Urban Growth in Los Angeles* (Point Arena, Calif.: Solano Press, 1997), pp. 307–308.

27. Sam Hall Kaplan, "Summerlin," *Urban Land* (September 1994):14.

28. Adam Steinhauer, "Lake Las Vegas Resort Planned," *Las Vegas Review-Journal,* 13 December 1996.

29. Robert Venturi, *Learning from Las Vegas: The Forgotten Symbolism of Architectural Form* (Cambridge, Mass.: MIT Press, 1977).

30. Lisa Bach, "Panel Hears Mass Transit Options," *Las Vegas Review-Journal,* 7 February 1997; Susan Greene, "Schools, Roads Plan Nears," *Las Vegas Review-Journal,* 25 February 1977.

31. John Smith, "Gaming Industry Hits PR Jackpot with Hotel Tax Proposal," *Las Vegas Review-Journal,* 27 February 1997.

32. Robert Parker, "The Social Costs of Rapid Urbanization in Southern Nevada," in Davis and Rothman, *Grit beneath the Glitter.*

33. Mike Davis, "Racial Cauldron in Las Vegas," *The Nation,* 6 July 1992.

34. Davis, "Racial Cauldron."

Part 2

Pasts

Donald Worster

The Legacy of
John Wesley Powell

Westward-moving pioneers, creaking along the Oregon and Santa Fe
Trails of the last century, came into a country of raw, hard physical
nature, a country less softened by the forces of life than on the eastern
side of the continent. The sheltering forests thinned out, then disappeared over most of the terrain. Many felt themselves exposed, like
Adam and Eve, but there were no fig leaves growing in the neighbor-
hood to hide their movement.

Beyond the Missouri River the landscape was shockingly bare. It
was not a cleared space at all, shaped and controlled by human labor,
but wild and primeval, a landscape vividly expressing the power of the
inorganic: a burning sky, swift-moving clouds, wide-swinging rivers,
rugged buttes and mountains, vast desiccated plains, all expressions of
geophysical forces that could easily dominate the kingdom of plants
and animals, or even of human technology and culture.

The western lands were not only big, brown, bare, and imposing;
they also confronted the traveler with a timescale that was older than
anyone had supposed possible. By the mid nineteenth century, scientists had begun talking about a Cambrian period of geology, a Precam-
brian period, and closer to the present, a Carboniferous, a Triassic, a
Jurassic, a Cretaceous period. Life had appeared only in the later phases
of that history.

Western travelers familiar with the revolutionary new geology had
to realize that this new country was not new at all. From a wagon seat,

a pioneer looked out on loessial plains of dust blown in at the end of the last ice age. He or she peered into canyons cut through layers of rock deposited during those unimaginable eras of the past; faced mountains uplifted by tectonic powers that we have begun to understand only in the last few decades; passed over hidden seas and rivers buried hundreds of feet underground, their signature written in gravel and limestone beds that only modern deep drilling rigs can actually touch, that humans have never seen.

No nineteenth-century pioneer could have grasped just how immensely old the western lands really were. But surely a few must have sensed now and then that they had entered a place where time extended back before any civilization anywhere had appeared. They must have sensed, whatever their scientific training, that living organisms, and human communities too, had been highly vulnerable to those mighty physical elements. The age of the great trek westward was an age beginning to discover deep time, time beyond the mythology of Genesis, an age preparing to displace humans from the center of creation.

Among the many Americans who looked with intense interest and expectation toward the opening of the West was John Wesley Powell of Bloomington, Illinois. He had been born in 1834 in Mount Morris, New York, to English immigrant parents and was raised on a series of farms in Ohio, Wisconsin, and Illinois.[1] He read about the western lands from that rambling military man John Charles Frémont, and, increasingly bored with his life as a natural history teacher, he itched to be out among those magnificent rocks.

In the summer of 1867, Powell was at last on his way west, guiding a group of undergraduate students and small-town amateur naturalists along the Platte River, the route of the pioneers. They passed wagon trains filled with rural folk looking for productive homesteads. Powell, however, was heading in a different direction: to the Badlands of Dakota, where the White River has cut deeply into fine white clay sediments intermixed with thin sandstone layers, a place no farmer could love. Powell must have seen in such a sterile but strangely beautiful place the possibilities of a good crop of scientific discovery.

But at Fort Laramie, discouraged by reports of growing Indian resistance to white travelers, the party changed their minds and turned south into Colorado, heading for Pike's Peak. It was a momentous adjustment, of course, for during that summer in the Colorado high country, Powell first heard about the unexplored plateau country of the Colorado River, where erosion had worked on the grandest scale anywhere, where the river was reputed to disappear into vast subterranean conduits, where waterfalls larger than any ever seen by humans might thunder. What had begun as a college outing abruptly led to a new ambition to explore that fabled river through its canyons, whatever the risk, and add dramatic new knowledge to the American mind. During the winter of 1867–68 Powell prepared for that next, bigger expedition.

In late May 1869, at one o'clock in the afternoon, Powell and nine other men set off on the mission that would make his name legendary. Had the Sioux been a little less resistant to interlopers, he might have been digging away in the Badlands or clambering around the Black Hills before Custer got there and discovered gold. Instead, by the working of circumstance and ambition, he and his companions became the first Americans to navigate successfully the shadowed, dangerous labyrinth of the Colorado's canyons. They came out of the labyrinth on August 30 at Grand Wash Cliffs, and Powell returned to the settlements a national hero.

In that same decade of the 1860s the American West began to emerge for the first time as a distinctive region of the country. For a long while it had been as mysteriously located as heaven or hell. West had referred to a compass direction, a general trend of movement, a fantasy land rather than to a particular place with a particular past. After the Civil War, however, the vagueness began to disappear, and for the first time the West took shape as a major region of the United States. The West would be like neither the North nor the South; it would offer a new way of being American. It promised a new unity, a new geography of hope, a new beginning for a bankrupt nation.

Wes Powell was painfully aware of what the country had just been through. He had grown up in an abolitionist family and enlisted to fight as a private in the Illinois volunteer infantry before the war had really begun. A company officer at the battle of Shiloh, Tennessee, he was struck on the right arm by a Minié ball, which broke the bones and embedded itself in the flesh so deeply that it could not be removed. A war surgeon amputated Powell's arm just above the elbow. For the rest of his life Powell would suffer frequent, intense pain in that stump of an arm, reminding him again and again of those fierce battlefields, the heavy smell of gun smoke, the groans of other wounded men lying in hospital beds.

A few years later he was going down the Colorado River, the stump still throbbing, the trauma of sectional conflict a long way away but never to be forgotten. With others of his generation, he was seeking a country beyond fratricide, at once familiarly American in its ambitions yet a comparatively better America than all that had gone before.

Today, John Wesley Powell's name is widely connected with the West; but what was his true role in its development? Despite several good biographies of the man, and a thousand brief acknowledgments of his importance, Powell remains widely misunderstood. He is everybody's hero, the intrepid pathfinder of the West's most charismatic river, a paragon of rational, scientific planning, and so forth. But his most significant legacy remains obscure and even forgotten. That legacy was a set of ideas pertaining to the American people's relationship to the western lands, ideas that were more radical, more sweeping than we have appreciated or ever tried to apply.

What made this western region strikingly different from the eastern part of the country, Powell concluded, was its aridity. "The eastern portion of the United States," he wrote, "is supplied with abundant rainfall for agricultural purposes, . . . but westward the amount of . . . precipitation diminishes . . . until at last a region is reached where the climate is so arid that agriculture is not successful without irrigation."[2]

If Powell found the unifying reality of the West in its aridity, he also came to understand the economic realities that were sweeping into the West, as they were sweeping across the entire nation, in the 1870s. Men of wealth and power were everywhere looking for resources to exploit, stuffing into their pockets as much as they could grasp. The challenge, as he saw it, was to save the West for the people before it was permanently lost to the greedy. If science could reveal the secrets of the natural environments, perhaps it could also reveal how to build a permanent democracy in the land.

Powell's *Report on the Lands of the Arid Region*, published in 1878, provided a scientific argument for a new kind of social order. A familiar document to most western historians, its central theme is that the nation's land laws must be reformed; the public domain must not continue to be carved up into 160-acre parcels of private property.

All these facts are common knowledge among western historians. What has not been stressed is that after Powell's failure to get his reforms adopted, he worked them over into an even more radical proposal, a master plan for the West that has never been sufficiently understood.

In the early months of 1890 Powell ran a seminar for politicians and the public on understanding the West. The House Select Committee on Irrigation of Arid Lands held hearings on a bill to turn the arid lands over to the states and territories, the first of many such efforts by western politicians. As the foremost authority on those lands, Powell repeatedly testified, each time taking new maps to place on the wall. He intended to teach the congressmen the logic of the western landscape, valley by valley, and to suggest how a brand-new political system might be based on that logic. He wanted his audience to know the country as he knew it, both from high up on the canyon rims and from down on the river, and to understand its patterns of water, climate, and geology that had been interacting over so long a time. He wanted them to realize how little of the country could ever grow crops—at most there was water available to irrigate a mere one out of nine acres, and even that would require a considerable investment in storage reservoirs. He wanted the men in the hearing room to appreciate the conflicts that were already brewing in western valleys, as upstream developers diverted the water on which downstream farmers had come to depend. Above all, he wanted them to see that all the natural resources of the West were connected in a single integrated whole, so that what was done to the mountain forests affected the lowland streams, and that the lands without water were intricately related to those with water.

Powell was arguing, without bluntly saying so, that he did not think it wise to surrender any part of the public domain to the states and allow them to dispose of it as they pleased. Instead, Powell would create a completely new set of governmental units for the West based on what he called "hydrographic basins," or watersheds, reaching from one divide to another. "My theory," he explained, "is to organize in the United States another unit of government for specific purposes, for agriculture by irrigation, for the protection of the forests which are being destroyed by fire, and for the utilization of the pasturage which can only be utilized in large bodies; that is, to create a great body of commonwealths. In the main these commonwealths would be like county communities in the States."[3] Their purpose would be to plan and conserve the natural resources within their borders.

Powell had plotted on his maps the outlines of 140 such units in the West, though he thought 10 or so might be added, each approximately the size of two average counties. Within each unit a small part of the land would be turned into private property, mainly the irrigated farms, but much would remain communal property—for example, the dry grasslands and the mountain forests. Title to them would remain in federal hands, but the local people would have the use of them and would make all the rules for their management. "If they want that timber destroyed," Powell said, "if they want to sell it, if they want to destroy it and wipe out irrigation, they are responsible for it, and let them do as they please."[4]

Let them do as they please? That sounds suspiciously like turning the West over to the grabbers and gougers. But the "them" Powell had in mind was not the "them" of laissez-faire America, where individuals were encouraged to pursue their self-interest in disregard of the welfare of others. His "them" was local people gathered into meaningful communities. Powell also emphatically rejected the alternative, already being debated, of giving the federal government the main control over western resources. The government, he felt, should not cede its lands to the states, but neither should it set up a centralized, national bureaucracy to guard the forests (it would soon become "a hotbed of corruption," he warned) or to finance water development. "I say to the Government: Hands off! Furnish the people with institutions of justice, and let them·do the work for themselves."[5]

Four years after offering his blueprint, Powell resigned from the directorship of the Geological Survey, ostensibly because of the continuing pain from his wound; but in truth he was driven out of office by budget cuts and by general opposition to his ideas. In 1902 he died of a cerebral hemorrhage at his summer house on the coast of Maine, far from the West he had come to know better than anyone else of his generation.

The leading figures in burying Powell's blueprints for the West six feet deep were the homesteaders who continued to look for a piece of land they could fence in from their neighbors and manage on their own, along with the railroad corporations, mining companies, and cattle outfits invading the public domain, none of whom could see much merit in so many collective commonwealths getting in their way. But not least among those opposed to Powell's blueprint were President Theodore Roosevelt and his chief forester, Gifford Pinchot, who dominated the Washington community's thinking about the West and its natural resources during the first decade of the twentieth century.

For Roosevelt, the burning issue of the day was how to make the American nation-state the dominant force on earth, greater than England, Germany, Japan, or Russia had ever been or ever would be. America must be first in industry, military might, population, and moral influence. The most important means to that end, he repeatedly thumped home, was a national program of conserving natural resources. The point of conservation, he believed, was to promote a nationalist instead of an individualist ethos in America.[6]

The label we commonly attach to this Rooseveltian school of thinking is "progressivism," and it was progressivism that created the first national conservation movement. The essence of progressive conservation was, in Samuel Hays's words, "rational planning to promote efficient development and use of all natural resources."[7] Because the West was still largely in the public domain, it offered the best opportunity for strong good men, filled with moral idealism and technical expertise, to come out from Washington and show what they could do to achieve the common good. They were men imbued, writes Hays, with "the technological spirit," which identifies the conquest of nature as humankind's highest goal, but they wanted to put themselves in charge of the conquest.

John Wesley Powell was, to a point, one of them—but not wholly

so. Like them, he believed in rational planning of natural resource development. Like them, he believed in the promise of science and technology. Unlike them, he would have made the federal government a
giver of advice to western communities, but he would have left the
final decisions about how to use the land to the people who would
have lived most directly with the results of their management or mis-
management. He did not care whether western forests or rivers might
make the United States the leader among the world's nations; rather, he
thought of how those natural resources might best contribute to the
growth and cohesion of small communities. Unlike the progressives,
however, he did not look much beyond the local and regional scales. So
he became irrelevant to an age of reformers who had their eyes on
grander national goals.

Because of his nonconformity with progressive thinking, Powell
soon slipped into the shadows of American conservation thinking. Then
in the middle of the twentieth century he began to make a second coming, finding more and more admirers, especially after a series of biographies and other studies appeared in the 1950s, the most important of
which was Wallace Stegner's *Beyond the Hundredth Meridian: John
Wesley Powell and the Second Opening of the West*. Yet even his new
admirers were sometimes too eager to honor Powell by claiming that
his ideas had triumphed in the federal government and its land policies. "On any composite map showing the modern use and management and reclamation of western lands," declared Stegner, "it would
appear as if almost every suggestion Powell made has been finally
adopted, and every kind of western land is being put to the kind of use
Powell advocated."[8]

But that same composite map of the West would not show 150
new units of government, those resource-managing commonwealths
that Powell wanted and thought were vital to democracy. Nor would
the map indicate that environmental policy in the West has been dominated by local people acting as the grassroots in their own long-term
collective interest. The modern West is not, in environmental terms,
anything like the West that John Wesley Powell had in mind. Something critical is missing, and it is the very essence of Powell's blueprint

for the West: the idea of those cooperative commonwealths making the vital decisions about land and natural resources.

Of course, Powell would be a bewildered old fellow if he came back to look at the West we have been making since his death: a West that is now the home of 40 million people, ranging from Korean shopkeepers in Los Angeles to African-American college students in Las Vegas, from Montana novelists and poets to Colorado skiers, from Kansas buffalo ranchers to Utah prison guards. He might wonder again how to make a coherent regional whole of all that diversity, how to make an effective democracy of so many differences. So, Powell might ask us, how will you modern westerners enable all the people, the farm workers as well as the owners, the racial minorities as well as majorities, the illiterate as well as the informed, to exercise a voice in and learn responsibility for the decisions that affect their lives and the lives of their children? This is the ethical question that he would want us to consider today.

We might start with what we still have in common, despite all the demographic and economic changes that have gone on: we still hold the land in common, particularly the publicly owned portion of western land. Perhaps the most distinctive feature of the West, after aridity, is the fact of continuing and extensive public ownership of so much land, hundreds of millions of acres in all, a feature that ties the past to the present. In Arizona the federal government owns 43 percent of the land, in Utah 64 percent, in Nevada 82 percent, though in Kansas it owns only a little more than 1 percent.[9]

Some westerners persist in trying to alter that situation to their private advantage, just as they were doing in Powell's day. In 1979, for instance, the Nevada legislature passed a resolution demanding the transfer of federal lands to the states, ostensibly to give local people greater control of their own destiny—allowing them to decide what should be wilderness and what should not, to determine how many cows a family can graze or how many mines a company can dig—though the rest of the country understood that the real, controlling purpose behind that resolution was to give the more aggressive entrepreneurs more freedom to develop land and make money.

Those western public lands are simply not going to pass into private ownership ever. Say it loudly and clearly so the diehards will have to hear. The public lands are going to stay public. Both the nation and the region are moving in the direction of public ownership, or at least more public control, of more and more land. Other nations took that course a long while back and have placed extensive rules and restrictions on the rights of individuals to develop any land, public or private. We are moving in the same direction—toward communalizing land in America, though we are moving slowly and with much litigation, more slowly often than the developers are moving to turn land into shopping malls and housing estates. Anyone who resists that trend is fighting a lost cause. Because of that general historical trend, much of the West will remain in public ownership. It is far easier to apply rules and restrictions on development when land is already in public ownership than after it has been privatized, and that is why the West will have to live with extensive federal title for a long time to come.

Westerners, however, would feel much better about this situation if the controls over land were placed closer to home. Here is the point where John Wesley Powell, the Powell of reality rather than of myth as nearly as I can discern him, may still have some useful suggestions to make. Remember his maps divided along watershed lines, stretching from divide to divide, encompassing the lowlands and the highlands, including all the key renewable resources the land has to offer. Remember his notion that all the people who live within those watershed regions should have a voice in their conservation and development. Does that idea still have any practical possibilities in the West of today? Can some part of it be revived and realized? Could a West organized along those lines offer an example of environmental democracy to the old North and South, regions where the main challenge today is to re-create a public commons where so much land was so thoroughly privatized a long time ago?

Powell's ideal of the body-politic would have all the farm owners living within each watershed acting together as a single community. That is obviously not an adequate base for democracy in the West today, where only a tiny minority of the population are farm or ranch owners (in California, to take an extreme example, agriculturists con-

stitute less than 1 percent of the state's population). Massive urbanization has left most westerners with no direct relationship to the land or
the natural world that supports them, yet they too have a stake in how
the land fares. Today, Powell's commonwealths could not call themselves democratic if they left out that majority of people, but including
them in a meaningful way, as informed, capable, interested participants
in land- and water-use decisions, will not be easy.

The fact of the matter is that they are systematically left out of
land-use decisions, more left out then ever before. Whenever the Bureau of Land Management official sits down with lessees, the Bureau
of Reclamation official with water clients, the Forest Service official
with timber executives, or any of the above with lawyers from the leading environmental organizations, the vast majority of westerners are
left out of the conversation. So Powell's commonwealths, though they
still may be easy to draw on a map, must face the dilemma that all
institutions today confront: how to enable all the people—the farm
workers as well as the farm owners, the racial minorities as well as the
majorities, the illiterate as well as the informed—to have a voice in and
a responsibility for the decisions that affect their lives and the lives of
their children. Powell gave us an outline of what environmental democracy requires, but only we can adapt it and make it real for this
age.

Another change has come to the West over the last century: a growing awareness that the region holds treasures of natural beauty and
biological diversity that should be preserved against all threats of development or use, whether local or national. The federal parks and
wildlife refuges of the region, the greatest anywhere in the world, express that awareness, however haltingly. I cannot find in Powell's writings, nor in his commonwealth idea, any room for that awareness. Had
such treasures been given over to local irrigation communities, what
would have been their fate? The history of the West strongly suggests
that rural landowners have been among the slowest to accept the need
for ecological preservation. Their notion of conservation, if it exists at
all, is to preserve the capacity of the watershed or the soil or the forest
to furnish resources for their future consumption. Perhaps broadening
the electorate included in those commonwealths, bringing into the de-

cision-making process more urban environmentalists, backpackers, campers, and hunters, would broaden the conservation ethic implied in Powell's blueprint. But the problem is not merely one of narrow views needing enlightenment. Local communities cannot be expected to bear all the economic burdens of saving wildlife, wilderness, Yosemite Valley, or the Grand Canyon; such work is necessarily the responsibility of a larger population, of the entire nation, of the world, indeed of the human species.

Powell's blueprint, therefore, needs to be revised and updated in several ways. It needs to allow for a continuing federal role in the West to safeguard what local people cannot safeguard effectively, and it needs to allow far more people—urban people—to share in the commonwealth idea. But with those revisions added, the blueprint still looks pretty good after a hundred years of change.

If taken seriously today as the guiding political ideal, Powell's ideas could lead to a land ethic shaped by local citizens as well as agency professionals. They could suggest a way out of the old, weary standoff between cowboy capitalists, on the one hand, and federal bureaucrats, on the other, that has so long dominated western politics. They could encourage the growth of a more distinctly regional culture as western people learn who they are by assuming responsibility for the great brown land around them.

We are still exploring the American West, its physical contours and its hidden secrets. We are still inventing the region. We have not yet discovered all the institutions we will ever need to live successfully in this place. John Wesley Powell is now behind us in the canyons of the past, yet we can hear a few echoes from him that bear heeding: Learn where you are. Learn the limits of the earth. Learn to do more for yourself rather than depend always on the nation-state or on corporate capital. Learn to work together if you want to endure.

Notes

A version of this chapter appears in Donald Worster, *An Unsettled Country: Changing Landscapes of the American West* (Albuquerque: University of New Mexico Press, 1994). Reprinted by permission of the author.

1. The earliest biographical sketch was by M. D. Lincoln, "John Wesley Powell," *The Open Court* 16 (December 1902):705–715. I have also profited from reading James Aton's "Inventing John Wesley Powell: The Major, His Admirers and Cash-Register Dams in the Colorado River Basin," Distinguished Faculty Lecture no. 9, Southern Utah State College, December 1, 1988.

2. John Wesley Powell, *Report on the Arid Lands of the United States* (Washington, D.C.: Government Printing Office, 1878), p. 1. This book, according to Samuel Trask Dana and Sally K. Fairfax (see their *Forest and Range Policy: Its Development in the United States,* 2nd ed. [New York: McGraw-Hill, 1980], p. 39], "contends with [George Perkins] Marsh's work for the distinction of being the most significant document in American conservation history."

3. Select Committee on Irrigation of Arid Lands, *Ceding the Arid Lands to the States and Territories,* 51st Cong., 2nd sess., House Report No. 3767 (Washington, D.C.: Government Printing Office, 1891), pp. 133–134.

4. John Wesley Powell, "Institutions for the Arid Lands," *Century Magazine* 40 (May 1890):113.

5. Select Committee on Irrigation, pp. 133–134.

6. *Theodore Roosevelt: An Autobiography* (New York: Macmillan, 1916), pp. 408–436. In the sole mention of Powell, Roosevelt lauds him for his early leadership in western irrigation development but then dismisses him for failing to see "the need for saving the forests and the soil" (p. 408). That was, of course, a distortion of Powell's position; he opposed a strong federal role in conservation. For background on Roosevelt's conservation thought, see G. Edward White, *The Eastern Establishment and the Western Experience: The West of Frederic Remington, Theodore Roosevelt, and Owen Wister* (New Haven, Conn.: Yale University Press, 1968), chap. 8.

7. Samuel P. Hays, *Conservation and the Gospel of Efficiency: The Progressive Conservation Movement, 1890–1920* (Cambridge, Mass.: Harvard University Press, 1959), pp. 2–3.

8. Wallace Stegner, *Beyond the Hundredth Meridian: John Wesley Powell and the Second Opening of the West* (Cambridge, Mass.: Houghton Mifflin, 1954), p. 357. Stegner did acknowledge that Powell might see a few dangers in the federal idea of stewardship. "He might see, as many conservationists believe they see, a considerable empire-building tendency within the Bureau of Reclamation, an engineer's vision of the West instead of a humanitarian's, a will to build dams without due regard to all the conflicting interests involved. . . . He might join the Sierra Club and other conservation groups in deploring some proposed and 'feasible' dams such as that in Echo Park below the mouth of the Yampa [Utah]" (p. 361).

9. U.S. Department of the Interior, Bureau of Land Management, *Public Land Statistics: 1990* (Washington, D.C.: Government Printing Office, 1990), p. 5.

Hal K. Rothman

Pokey's Paradox
Tourism and Transformation
on the Western Navajo Reservation

In novelist Christopher Moore's *Coyote Blue*, a Lakota medicine man
named Pokey Medicine Wing—"lit up with liquor and firelight"—offers a commentary on the impact of tourism on Native American communities. "They are building that dam on the Bighorn River," he says
of a development in his home country. "They tell us that we will pros-
per from all the people who will come to the reservation to fish and
water-ski on the new lake. That's what they told us when they put the
Custer Monument here, but whites opened stores and took all the money.
This time we will get our share. We'll grow worms and sell them for
fishing."[1] Pokey Medicine Wing, representing all Indian people, faced
a paradoxical conundrum. He did not want to see people fishing and
water-skiing on his sacred lake, but he could not stop them from coming; nor could he directly capitalize on their appearance, for the conve-
nience stores and boat docks, the hotels and the restaurants, the real
money-makers, would also belong to whites. Pokey Medicine Wing
had to negotiate to preserve his position in a world that included tourists, with their $500 fishing rods, who were entirely ignorant of the
historical and mythical meaning of the place. Outright resistance was
futile; unabashed capitulation was unthinkable. The only possible response was to fashion an all-Indian economic vector within tourism, to
have Indians behave like the whites who had come to enjoy their land.
Pokey's choice of growing earthworms fit, but even he, excited in the

firelight, recognized its limits. In this paradox, none of the available choices could save the integrity of native life when faced with the on-slaught of the outside as manifest in tourism.

Pokey Medicine Wing offers the latest view of tourism. Scholars in a range of disciplines have become critical of the impact of tourism on communities; they approach tourism in a declensionist mode, positing a one-way street from a pure, so-called traditional past to a fouled present, fueled by the greed of entrepreneurs and catering to the whims of middle-class white Americans. Tourism is another form of exploita-tion, these authors say, another of the ways in which avaricious main-stream society consumes the virtues of distinctive cultures in its midst.[2]

Outside of this often-arcane scholarly discourse, tourism contin-ues to be perceived as a panacea for dislocated workers and economi-cally disenfranchised communities in a changing economic world. The employment it offers promises the potential to transcend the end of the industrial economy, to provide a way for the mass of unskilled and semiskilled workers to earn the sort of living that they hope can de-cently sustain their families. In the American West in particular, state governments and local leadership have plugged into this idea as a way to counteract the disappearance of long-term employment possibilities in traditional rural industries such as mining, agriculture, and ranch-ing. To many in areas in decline, tourism has become the logical expli-cation of the service economy. Marketing a place and its heritage has become standard western fare, as typical as the biscuits and gravy served across the region.[3]

Weakness in some industries and the demise of others have made western regional leaders turn to tourism as an easy-to-develop indus-try. Tourism rarely demands the investment of vast sums of local or state government money; more often, handy local attractions simply require packaging, and when needed, entrepreneurs can be recruited by the prospect of profit. As in Pokey Medicine Wing's formulation, often the federal government will contribute much of the funding for the creation of roads and other necessary infrastructure. Nor does tour-ism require a computer-literate skilled labor force, tax abatements, or other common development strategies. It does not necessitate import-ing a managerial class, huge quantities of machinery and equipment, or other industrial amenities. Best of all, it seems to encourage westerners to culturally remain westerners; they can, in time-honored fashion, "grow earthworms" and succeed. What the West is selling is itself, obviating the need for anything more than an understanding of the importance of the region in a wider American mythology. No wonder tourism has broad appeal.

The economic problems of Indian reservations have exacerbated the demand for tourist-oriented development. The anemic state of economic conditions in Indian country has made tourism an easy choice for tribal leaders and activists. Although tourism-based jobs are not always high-paying, to many Indian people, tourism seems less destructive than natural resource extraction, less transformative than clock punching and lunch-pail carrying. Yet Pokey Medicine Wing's problem looms large. Too often, it seems, from the development at Cochiti Lake in New Mexico to the Black Hills, poorly paid Indian labor in tourism leads to profits for Anglo traders and storekeepers even as it mythifies Indian people. In the process, the coveted wages do little to stem the social, cultural, and personnel deterioration that accompany the poverty of reservation life.[4]

Tourism in Indian country is far more complicated than either a simple declensionist construction or the Shangri-la view it is replacing. Tourism involves variations on the primary themes of modern economic life on the reservation, a middle position in the triangle of traditional economic practices, state- or tribal-supported poverty, and wage work in mines and industrial plants or on the railroad. In a world where stasis is impossible, tourism is an easy choice. Instead of the increased marginality and mounting poverty of the status quo, tourism offers potential salvation buried within the transformation that accompanies it. Its embrace embodies differing degrees of involvement with the institutions of the dominant culture, different goals and strategies than those of people who make other economic and cultural choices, and as Pokey Medicine Wing notes, its potential to save is truly limited. In some instances, tourism becomes a destructive force as local people remake their lives to meet its demands; in others, individual Indian people are able to use the cloak of federally supported tourism such as national park areas to fashion a life that provides them with an income but permits them to engage in the maintenance of tribal customs and traditions. In Indian country, tourism almost always involves accepting the paternalism provided by the federal government, but given the dearth of choices on most reservations, it offers alternatives—many more than are otherwise generally available to native people.

In areas with institutions too weak to replace faltering economic activities, tourism has often come to play an important role in the regional economy. Facilitated by transportation networks—in particular, paved roads—and supported by a limited but evidently extant institutional structure, tourism often becomes both a panacea and a fall-back position. Tourism is and will remain a devil's bargain for such places. Its transformative traits are rarely discussed as the implementation strategy takes place, and people often find that the changes tourism brings outweigh the material advantages that accrue from its presence. Tourism remakes people and communities on the terms of the visitor, even when significant barriers to that transformation, such as national parks or local resistance to incoming culture, exist and are vibrant. Its economic rewards, however limited, are often the best to which that region has access. Tourism is a devil's bargain, a choice between change and the remaking of sociocultural lines or stasis and the on-going poverty and marginality that accompany the lack of strategies for change.

The key to understanding the role of tourism in rural economies is to track the development of dominant cultural institutions. This is particularly true on Indian reservations, where the patterns of the formation and development of such institutions and their inherent weakness often dictate later reliance on tourism and other manifestations of a service economy. In this sense, tourism is a trap, a sink to which places fall, an end-of-the-road option chosen above few others: often it is the only option, hardly a choice but an economic necessity that communities and regions have little opportunity to resist.

One area where people experienced the many variations of this process of transformation was the Shonto region, in the heart of the western Navajo reservation. There the rise of tourism paralleled the decline of extant economic systems: the grazing of sheep, which was largely eliminated by the stock reduction edict of the 1930s, and off-reservation railroad work, something many Navajo eschewed and that began to decline in the 1960s. Faced with the need to make a living, Navajo men had to choose between tourism and extractive resource industries. These choices dictated the terms of many Navajo lives.

Until the coming of paved roads during the 1950s and 1960s, Shonto remained one of the most remote places on the reservation. Located in District Two—southeast of Navajo Mountain, southwest of Kayenta, and west of the Hopi reservation—the region evinced the localized differences that were so distinct among the Navajo. The people of the region had a long and proud history; they considered themselves apart from the experiences of their neighbors. They were not part of the ultimate moment in Navajo subjugation and humiliation, the forced expulsion to the Bosque Redondo in southeastern New Mexico in the 1860s, labeled the "Long Walk." Instead the people who lived in the Shonto area fled the American military. They found the area around Navajo Mountain far enough from the reach of the cavalry, and there they settled, retaining independence, autonomy, and a penchant for the very kinds of predatory behavior that Kit Carson sought to quell.[5]

The result was a regional culture isolated from the encroaching industrial world and its material by-products, less receptive to Anglo-Americans than other parts of the reservation. Trading posts came later and were fewer and farther between on the western reservation. Nor was their influence as pervasive before the stock reductions of the 1930s. On the western reservation, people had a different history than the Navajos who had been part of the Long Walk, lending a fierceness and insularity that waves of nineteenth-century Anglo-Americans found hard to pierce.

The Shonto area remained largely devoid of Anglo encroachment into the first decade of the twentieth century. As new trading posts began, spreading from rivers and railroads into the Navajo heartland, contact between Navajos and outsiders became increasingly common. In the vicinity of Shonto, John Wetherill's trading post, which opened in 1906 at Oljato, near the Utah-Arizona border, was the first perma-nent Anglo abode in the area. In March 1906, Wetherill, his wife, Louisa Wade Wetherill, and Clyde Colville settled there after a feast John Wetherill prepared to assuage the fears of Hoskininni and his son

Hoskininni-Begay, who led the Navajo people in the area east of Navajo Mountain. From the door of their "jacal" home of posts and mud
and the adjacent one-room trading post, it was more than 150 roadless
miles to the nearest railway stop in Gallup, New Mexico, and nearly as
far to Flagstaff, Arizona.[6]

This enterprise was an outpost, far from any ties to industrial society. Staffed by members of a family that had greater ties to the ethos of
the nineteenth century than its twentieth-century successor, the trading
post offered some of the advantages of industrialization but was not a
hegemonizing force. Like his more famous brother, Richard, John
Wetherill was consumed with the prehistory of the region. Louisa Wade
Wetherill spoke fluent Navajo and became a recognized expert on Navajo culture. Clyde Colville was a quiet man, out of sorts with the
world from which he came. Although the traders often pressed area
people to conform to the rules of American society on issues such as
polygamy, they also valued the freedom of living on the border between cultures, among people only peripherally exposed to the double-
edged wonders of the age of the dynamo.[7]

Much of the rest of the early-twentieth-century Anglo traffic in the
Shonto region consisted of surveys by scientists and government officials. Byron Cummings, a professor at the University of Utah and later
the University of Arizona who became a noted archaeologist, led field
surveys to the region beginning in 1906, and the famous Alkali Ridge
survey, on which Alfred V. Kidder and Sylvanus G. Morley began their
archaeological careers in 1908 under the loose guidance of Edgar L.
Hewett, also brought more activity to the area. The focus on Laguna
Creek and Tsegi Wash that dated from Richard Wetherill's excavatory
work in 1897 garnered more attention for the Shonto region. By 1908,
U.S. Department of the Interior Examiner of Surveys William Boone
Douglass had come to the area to assess reports of untrammeled archaeological ruins.[8]

In the United States early in the twentieth century, archaeological
ruins enjoyed vast cultural significance. As the regulatory society gathered momentum and with conservation as one of its focuses, preserving the remains of prior cultures developed a wide following among
the American elite. The efforts of John Wesley Powell and the Bureau

of American Ethnology further boosted the growing popularity of the subject, and as American social science became professionalized, control and protection of the places that contained archaeological ruins became a crucial part of regulatory strategy. The threat of unauthorized excavation—"depredation" in the parlance of scientists of the day—remained strong.[9]

To government officials and professional archaeologists, the appeal of the ruins of Tsegi Wash was that they had not yet been plundered. Elsewhere, farmers found prehistoric ollas, or pots, and if they could not find a buyer, simply smashed them. Avaricious individuals dug in unprotected ruins and made collections that they sold to museums and others, in the process often destroying walls and structures in search of artifacts and burials. Though there was little that overburdened government officials in Washington, D.C., could do about areas where such depredation had taken place, they could make a concerted attempt to protect places where it had not.[10]

This process came together in the summer of 1909 in the Shonto region. Douglass requested the establishment of Navajo National Monument sight-unseen in March 1909, and the new area, encompassing more than sixty square miles of the Navajo reservation, came into being. Douglass's goal was to protect the ruins from unsanctioned excavation. Cummings and other archaeologists sought to dig, bringing more Anglo-American influence to the region. Others such as J. Walter Fewkes, a zoologist-turned-archaeologist, followed, performing surveys and mapping the region. Because of the growing numbers of archaeologists and his personal interest, in the fall of 1909, John Wetherill moved his trading post to Kayenta, about twenty miles across the canyons to Tsegi Wash.[11]

The creation of the monument and the relocation of the trading post brought two institutions reflecting the values of American society into the heart of a region that actively resisted previous encroachment. The national monument was reduced greatly in size in 1912, but it remained a symbol of the expanding power of centralized authority in the United States. Wetherill's trading post in Kayenta contained a post office—the farthest from a railroad of any in the nation. After they moved the trading post to Kayenta, Wetherill and Colville worked to improve the road to Marsh Pass. Fewkes's survey cut a small road from the pass south of Kayenta into Laguna Creek toward Betatakin and Keet Seel, two of the primary ruins in the monument. One worker recalled that Fewkes ordered them to use a mule-pulled grader because his wife was "not one to walk." The improvements made it only slightly easier to reach the region.[12]

Pokey Medicine Wing might have approved of this initial economic incarnation in Navajo country, for it augmented the local economy without exerting significant influence on its culture. This first institutional presence had little impact on the people of the Shonto region. The kinds of transportation lifelines that sustained such outposts had not reached the area. The national monument existed primarily on paper; though John Wetherill served as its volunteer custodian, even the most rudimentary support system for it was absent. The archaeologists hired Navajo guides and laborers, providing capital that local people could use to purchase goods at the Wetherill-Colville trading post. Its operators did not seek to acculturate their neighbors. Instead they had a healthy respect for the Diné and their way of life, supported by the evident resistance to the influences of Anglo society by local leaders such as Pinietin of the Inscription House area, Hoskininni, and Hoskininni-Begay.

In this context, archaeologist Neil Judd's assertion that in 1909, when he encountered a war ceremony sing attended by several hundred Navajo, he was the first white that any of the men in their twenties had seen seems less preposterous than it appears. Although after nearly fifty years of being adjacent to a borderland most young Navajo probably had had prior contact with traders, miners, or Mormon settlers, they had been little influenced by this contact except to learn resentment of Anglo-Americans. The Shonto area people were the ones who escaped victimization, and they carried their independence proudly. Judd's observation was probably incorrect, but his feeling that he was intruding in a foreign world unwilling to yield to him because of the color of his skin and the type of clothes he wore rings true.[13]

Despite the presence of two different kinds of institutions—the national monument and the trading post—further development and concomitant acculturation proceeded slowly. Even the establishment of a new trading post at Shonto around 1915 did little to begin the process of acculturation of the Shonto Navajo. John Lee and John

Wetherill founded the post in 1914–15, and Hubert and C. D. Richardson, two well-known traders, followed in succession. In the 1920s, the trading post changed ownership many times, suggesting that it was a place on the periphery that offered weak cultural influence as well as little profit. A number of traders came and went during the Babbitt Brothers' ownership there, doing little more than trying to balance the books.[14] Despite pronouncements of the suitability of the area for visitors, and a growing parade of archaeologists and archaeology buffs, the institutions of the region provided material accouterments but relatively little cultural contact for area Navajos. The lack of access to the region protected it from the full brunt of railroad-transmitted industrial culture.

In the late 1920s, new ownership of the trading post at Shonto began to change its orientation. Tourism at the Grand Canyon, about 130 miles away, had become a major industry, prompting the construction of a railroad spur from Williams in 1903. By the 1920s, the process of institutionalization of tourism had proceeded rapidly. The Fred Harvey Company was a primary force, and its Indian Detours program attracted all kinds of visitors. The new owners at Shonto, Harry and Elizabeth C. Rorick, sought to capitalize on the American public's ever-growing interest in Indians when they arrived in 1929.

The development of even a nascent tourist industry required some infrastructural development. The first trading post had been a one-room affair, quickly replaced with an L-shaped stone building with living quarters on the east end. This was adequate for a trader but insufficient for overnight guests, the constituency that the Roricks sought to attract. With the help of area Navajos such as Bob Black and Cap Wolf, the Roricks built hogan-style stone guest cabins complete with cement floors for the visitors they planned to bring to nearby Navajo National Monument.[15]

But to achieve the Roricks' objectives, the trading post needed better access. The first step was some sort of road to the outside world. Existing trails had been scraped with pick and shovel across the canyons, and the grades were so steep that cars went up and down the hills in low gear, if at all. The Roricks began a single-handed campaign of road improvement. They engineered a road from the trading post west

toward Begashibito, which was soon washed out by unusually bad flood-
ing in the fall of 1930. Harry Rorick had some road surveying experience, and together with a crew of Navajos and some equipment bor-
rowed from the Indian agent in Tuba City, he built a new road to the
east that went near Betatakin and linked up with the main road to
Flagstaff. Via Shonto, there was a new way to reach Navajo National
Monument.[16]

Again a middle ground existed, a time in which the outside in-
truded but in limited and often advantageous ways for local people.
Harry Rorick's roads were supposed to carry tourists to the Betatakin
ruins; mostly they put cash in Navajo pockets that could later be used
at his post. There was a kind of reciprocity involved, an unspoken but
understood agreement that this was a joint endeavor in which everyone contributed to the ultimate economic health of everyone else.

The Roricks' tourist enterprise accelerated the impact of Anglo-
American institutions on the Shonto region. Government agencies had
little prior impact; loaning equipment to people such as Harry Rorick
constituted the federal presence. But the jobs Rorick created offered
considerable opportunity to earn wages, and the construction of roads,
buildings, and trails began the long process of eliminating barriers to
access and consequently to influence.[17] Although wage-earning did not
supplant livestock as the primary source of sustenance for area Navajos, it was a harbinger of changing economic and environmental conditions.

After drought and depression accentuated existing problems in the
regional economy, the reform-minded New Deal bureaucracy dramatically altered the economic and cultural climate of the Navajo reservation. An institutional structure at Shonto became apparent as a result
of the New Deal. A day school opened there in 1934, adding another
influence on the area. The day school was different from the trading
post and the monument, for the school had a characteristically
hegemonizing affect. Students there were exposed to decidedly non-
Navajo influence, structure, and ways of thinking and living. In 1937,
Shonto became the headquarters site for the newly formed Land Management District Two, and a corral, dipping tanks, and a horse pasture
were added.[18]

The four institutions—the day school, the national monument, the district headquarters, and the trading post—had a growing amount of influence in the region but less of an impact on most of its people. Each institution had a limited sphere and generally operated independent of the others. The school and the monument only peripherally addressed the economic issues of people in the region. The trading post added a dimension to local economics, but its owners were more concerned with profits than with the condition of the Navajo. They did not work to assimilate the Navajo, but rather to perpetuate Navajo lifestyles and culture, which in turn would sustain the trading post. The wage labor offered by government programs represented adaptation rather than acculturation, serving as a replacement economy while generally leaving existing cultural institutions intact.[19]

Poverty remained the rule for most Navajos. The economic climate of the 1930s accentuated the inherent economic weakness of the Navajo. Off-reservation Navajo were forced back onto the reservation, and the population soared as mortality declined and fertility increased. District Two, in which Shonto was located, experienced a 34.1 percent increase in population between 1936 and 1940 alone. At the same time, dire economic conditions affected the entire Navajo people. Wool dropped to five cents a pound, and many Navajos had to pawn the silver dime or quarter buttons they favored on their clothing. The Roricks were little help, for they failed to exploit new economic opportunities and by the early 1940s maintained only a shell of a trading post.[20] Pulling Navajos into the institutional sphere was relatively easy, but the apparatus to support such a transformation—business, transportation infrastructure, and similar necessities—remained weak. As a result, programs designed to help Navajos were inconsistently applied, ending Navajo control of their economic destiny and clearing the way for challenges to cultural autonomy. In the remote Shonto area, Navajos could no longer avoid contact with Anglo institutions. The trading post had become an economic staple, the various programs provided wages, and the school began an incomplete process of acculturation.

But Anglo-American institutions also had a negative effect on Indian life. No more devastating decision could have been made than the Bureau of Indian Affairs' well-intended enforced stock reduction program of the 1930s. Dependent on the herds but possessed of a limited and declining range that was asked to support a growing population of humans and animals, the Navajo faced a Malthusian conundrum. The limits on the expansion of their land caused by Anglo stock interests forced them to address the issue of surplus population. Despite the fledgling tribal council structure, the Navajo did not recognize a need to make reservationwide policy. In their prior experience, no such decision-making structure had been necessary.[21]

The stock reduction program was a major cultural shock in relatively autonomous places such as the Shonto area, where Navajo decisions held, Anglo influences were comparatively meager, and the people had a tradition that stressed their cultural independence. Bob Black, a landholder and respected person even as a young man, encountered the power of the law as a result of the stock reduction program. Caught running more sheep than was permissible, Black served thirty days in jail. After his release, he never ran sheep again. His first impression of the power of Anglo institutions was that they had an unmatched ability to disrupt his life.[22]

Black faced a dilemma. His land, previously used to graze the animals that supported his family, could no longer be used for that purpose without great risk. At best marginal for grazing, the land had little potential for other use. For Black, few options existed. But he had previous experience with wage labor: he had worked for the Roricks building the cabins at Shonto Trading Post. He also had a reputation as an honest, dependable, hard-working man and had a cordial relationship with John Wetherill, who continued to serve as custodian for the monument. With available Emergency Conservation Work funds, Wetherill was able to hire Black as a seasonal laborer in the summer of 1935. Black began a long career with the Park Service by building a ranger cabin on the rim of Betatakin Canyon.[23]

Bob Black's story was a microcosm of the changes Shonto area Navajos experienced as a result of the New Deal. As a result of decisions made outside of the region and enforced by institutions unfamiliar to the Navajo people, one form of economy replaced another: the first autonomous, independent, and largely devoid of currency as a medium of exchange, the successor paying in cash, dependent, and seasonal. While Black was well insulated by maturity, experience with Anglos, and reputation, others did not fare as well. Some lacked Black's flexibility, others his willingness to participate in wage-based activity.

Most simply did not have the proximity to opportunity that living next to the national monument offered.

Black's story highlighted the lack of ability to enforce Navajo cultural and economic decisions regarding land use. The people of the Shonto region were caught between Navajo custom or common law and tribal code, closely patterned after Anglo-American law. Navajo people recognized the authority of both, but the lack of officials to enforce tribal law in the community meant that common law held first, with tribal law as backup.[24] Tribal or federal officers to enforce outside law were uncommon in Shonto, so in all but the most serious cases, community custom was first applied. Yet this system, which led people to see Navajo ways as the ultimate authority in the community, failed, for in the face of stock reduction edicts, community standards had no bearing. The stock reduction was imposed, leaving area Navajo confounded by bifurcated jurisdiction.

As a result, despite the primacy of Navajo custom in day-to-day affairs, the mechanisms that existed for Navajo self-determination involved imposing a Euro-American structure on Navajo ways of living. Predictably, the system failed the Navajo, for it did not take into account the nature of Navajo culture and familial ties, much less economic and environmental relationships. By superimposing a system based on "foreign" law on people unfamiliar with such practices, the New Deal devalued local custom and practice under the guise of offering assistance. The result was disastrous.

Self-imposed systems of cultural and environmental regulations have maintained communities in some condition of environmental stasis. Törbel, a Swiss-German livestock farming community in the province of Valais, offered a prime example. Limited by a short growing season, altitude, and mediocre soils, the community was able to use an intricate system of restrictions and covenants of land ownership and transfer and particularly the substantial out-migration of young people to maintain a relative balance of resource demand, population, and wealth over a 700-year period. Törbel exported its excess population to Swiss cities and held firm against newcomers; only three new family names were entered in church landholding records in a 300-year period. This community survived the vagaries of environment, political change, and modernization by recognizing the limits of the physical environment and legislating boundaries on behavior.[25]

Although the Navajo system offered equal regulation of behavior, it had no successful mechanism to control ingress and egress of population and concomitant demand on natural resources. With sheep as their primary resource, Navajos needed a great deal of room. Population growth pushed many off-reservation, where they lacked protection from the demands of Anglo and Hispano livestock interests. Limited by grazing reduction rules on the reservation, those who remained within the boundaries faced similar privation. Promises of extension of the reservation seemed a solution, but in scope, the proposals of the 1930s fell far short.

Unlike the people of Törbel, Navajos could not make their worldview hold. Their customs did not supersede American law, and in fact the imposition of Anglo law robbed the Navajo of control of their fate. In a world with boundaries that seemed fixed but were easily redefined in practice—usually where Anglo or Hispano cattle or sheep interests had encroached—this lack of control over the law effectively terminated Navajo determination of the character of resource use. While Navajos could choose to defend their land from physical encroachment, they could not protect themselves from an invisible enemy that imposed an order in which they had no say.

The Navajo people and their animals together made up a livelihood unit—a measure of sustenance—and they learned that the area needed for each household unit to sustain itself was greater than the area over which they collectively exerted any measure of control. This led to enforced "bargains" such as the stock reduction program, an ostensibly well-intentioned program that ultimately proved culturally and economically disastrous.

The result for the Navajo was increased dependence on Anglo institutions and a need for a new form of economy. Again the infrastructure of Anglo institutions in the Shonto area was too flimsy to support new ways of survival dictated by Anglo culture, and Navajos needed to look to the outside. World War II became the catalyst that made wage-earning as important as more traditional forms of economic subsistence. Young Navajos entered the military, gaining exposure to the cultural world that had been encroaching upon them for more than a generation. The reverence for the warrior in Navajo tradition inspired some; others joined for more temporal reasons. Hubert Laughter, a young man from the Shonto area, signed up because one winter, he saw a Navajo he knew in the wool uniform of the military and the young man appeared well fed. In awe of the warrior tradition and recognizing that the stylish uniform would keep him warm and the army food would fill his belly, he enlisted, a process of decision making that left him aghast more than forty years later.[26]

The war broadened Navajo horizons in a fashion similar to the experiences of other minorities and many from rural areas elsewhere in the United States. In the Shonto area before the war, few Navajos had much exposure to the outside world; a man like Stanley Yazzie, who had been to the Blue Canyon School in the 1890s and spoke some English, was considered worldly. After more than two years of active duty and with a purple heart to his credit, Hubert Laughter returned a changed person. He had seen the world and recognized greater possibilities than the boundaries of the reservation could offer.

But for Laughter, as for many Navajos, the ties of home were as strong as the allure of the modern world. Eschewing a job as an airplane mechanic in Winslow, Arizona, he returned to the Shonto area. His wife's family, the Begishies, wanted him to herd sheep, but after Bob Black offered him seasonal employment at Navajo National Monument, Laughter was able to remain in the area with a more dependable source of income than livestock would allow. The availability of work at the monument allowed him to live in the traditional world of the Shonto Navajo and also derive what he needed from the modern world.[27]

Nor was Laughter's experience unique among his peers. Seth Bigman from Monument Valley, also a decorated veteran, was the first Navajo ranger at the monument to interpret the ruins to visitors. Bigman used the opportunity as a step toward a career in the federal service. Again, the option of wage labor permitted some young Navajos to remain in the vicinity instead of searching for work elsewhere.[28]

But for most of the people in the area, the institutions were insufficient to fill the gap in the economy left by stock reduction. Strategies for survival on the western reservation were few and far between, and an out-migration, especially of younger people, began. Some were forced to urban areas by the limitations on stock raising and the lack of other economic opportunities in the area. Others continued to reside in the area but worked seasonally for the railroads, living among other Navajos and working in an Anglo world.

By the 1950s, the railroad had become a crucial source of income for Shonto Navajos. At the age of twenty-one, men were expected to leave home to labor. Between 1945 and 1955, only one Shonto area man reached maturity without applying for railroad work. This kind of seasonal migratory employment was different only in degree from other forms of migrant and indentured labor in which other American minorities engaged.[29]

The experiences of Delbert Smallcanyon were typical. Born around 1920 in the Navajo Mountain area, he tended sheep for his family well into adulthood. He first left the reservation to work for the railroad during World War II, and later went from place to place, working for the railroad in Montana, Salt Lake City, Chicago, and elsewhere in the West. This kind of labor was seasonal and paid well, but it worked a hardship on Smallcanyon and his family. The outside world he inhabited was narrow and totally lacking in the virtues that a traditional Navajo sought. The wages were necessary, but Smallcanyon recalled the price of separation from family and culture as far exceeding the advantages of the paycheck.[30]

Yet for the upwards of 100 households and extended family units that made up the Shonto area by the end of the 1950s, the economic opportunities available in the region were insufficient. A series of economies had been formed and replaced since the 1870s, culminating in the stock reduction program, but in its aftermath, nothing substantial emerged. Stock raising as a viable means of sustaining a kinship unit ceased to exist. By 1950, wage-earning provided more than 50 percent of Navajo income, but there was little work close to home. Without a system of roads and railroads in the region, the chance to develop any kind of integrated economy remained remote. Shonto was caught between the world of its past and the future.[31]

In a belated manner, the level of deprivation of life on the Navajo reservation attracted attention. In the heady postwar climate, when the modern infrastructure of the United States was being built, road construction became a top priority. Most of the existing roads on the reservation were more appropriately labeled trails. As the idea that an affluent nation could eradicate social problems gained credence and the natural resources of the reservation attracted attention, efforts to remedy conditions began. The Navajo/Hopi Rehabilitation Act of 1950 set aside $38 million for road construction, $10 million of which was designated for improvement of secondary roads on the reservation. The Atomic Energy Commission also built roads to facilitate the extraction of uranium. Its first rudimentary road stretched from Teec Nos Pos to Kayenta; additional roads stretched from Kayenta to Monument Valley and later to Tuba City. These dirt highways were critical to the development of an infrastructure on the reservation.[32]

During the 1950s, the Navajo Tribal Council began to invest in capital development on the reservation. With the wealth from its natural resource base, the tribe embarked on a number of programs. A network of roads became one of the most important. In March 1958, the Tribal Council appropriated nearly $1 million for road building as a means to combat an economic recession. Arizona's Senator Barry Goldwater arranged a similar amount from the U.S. Bureau of the Budget. Much of the money was earmarked for the western reservation area that included Shonto and Navajo National Monument.

The addition of all-weather roads on the reservation offered many benefits. Besides encouraging industry, the roads brought travelers to see the region and made the Navajo people more mobile. One of the first tracts paved was the trail between the Utah border and Kayenta, a little more than twenty miles through the canyons from Betatakin and slightly more to Shonto. Following closely was the implementation of a plan to link Kayenta and Tuba City by paved road. Although a difficult area in which to build, a road through the heart of the western reservation was essential if the leaders of the Navajo people were going to pursue a combination of development and tourism as strategies for the economic advancement of their people.[33]

Paved roads in the region had clear implications for Navajo National Monument. A road would end the isolation that had characterized the monument since its establishment in 1909, bringing many more visitors to the monument and intruding upon existing relationships between the Park Service and its neighbors in the Shonto area. The roads facilitated the implementation of MISSION 66, the Park Service's major capital development program of the 1950s and 1960s, at Navajo National Monument, leading to the construction of a visitor center, a paved approach road, and other amenities.

But Navajo National Monument was very small, and the development program could not begin until the Park Service reached agreements governing use of land in the region with the Navajo Tribal Council and individuals in the vicinity of the monument.[34] An exchange of land and services followed. In a complicated series of arrangements finalized in a document called the Memorandum of Agreement of May 8, 1962, the Tribal Council allowed the National Park Service to use an additional 240 acres of land as a headquarters area.[35] There was little doubt that the loan of land implied a greater institutional responsibility to the people of the Shonto region.

Paved roads to the monument also played a major role in changing the western reservation. A marked increase in visitation to the area followed the completion of each stretch of paved road. Prior to 1960, the Shonto area was a long trek, too far from "civilization," over which cars had to travel too many washboard roads. The construction of paved roads to within fifteen miles of Betatakin Canyon exponentially increased the number of visitors at Navajo National Monument. In 1959, recorded visitation totaled 3,053; two years later, the number reached 6,175. In 1963, visitation reached 10,832, only to nearly double again to 20,401 after the opening of the new paved approach road, U.S. 564, to the monument in 1965.[36]

Responding to the increase in visitors required tremendous growth in the previously limited service economy on the western reservation. More gas stations, motels, campgrounds, stores, guides, and a range of other amenities became essential. The monument needed more staff members to meet the demands of visitors. Navajos learned to regard the tourists as sources of income and in places began to evince the interactive, friendly behavior that tourists desired.

By 1962, a pattern of inclusion had developed at the monument. The Navajo people in its vicinity had become a significant portion of its labor force, recognized the monument as a source of economic support, and loosely but generally supported its objectives. The monument and its staff were able to reciprocate by offering employment and some of the accouterments of modern society to the people of the region. The maintenance and seasonal labor positions at the monument were filled by area Navajos, usually relatives of current employees, Bob Black, or one of the other Shonto kinship groups. Black used the grader to level the road to Shonto on a regular basis; in the winter, the monument's snowplow could be found clearing the way to various hogans in the region. A nascent new economy had begun, as some of the people of the Shonto region were able to use government work and tourism support to fill the economic gap left by the stock reduction program twenty-five years before.[37]

This was a new situation, one unfamiliar to most of the people from Shonto. Government work was not physically demanding, but it required adherence to a different set of rules than did Navajo life. The government required clock-driven punctuality. Despite the large number of Navajo men who served in World War II and the Korean Conflict, the uniforms of the Park Service were new and novel to many from Shonto. The requirement of engaging the public also meant bridging a cultural divide. Although Park Service work had the ability to provide sustenance close to home, it could be disorienting and sometimes alienating for Shonto area people. Despite its many advantages, working for the Park Service meant engaging in a range of behaviors that turn-of-the-century Navajos would not have recognized as part of their culture.

Others in the region were able to derive income from their position adjacent to monument boundaries. The trip from the visitor center to either Betatakin or Keet Seel ruin crossed private Navajo land. Eight miles distant, Keet Seel was easier to reach by horse than on foot. In 1952, area Navajos began to make horses available for guided tours to Keet Seel. Pipeline Begishie, the patriarch of a local family, organized the trips. Many of the people in the area allowed their horses to be used—for a fee—and Begishie, E. K. Austin, or one of the others close by guided the trips. The fee was ten dollars per day for the guide and five dollars for each horse. The animals they used were big and strong, one observer recalled, and the trips had real appeal for visitors.[38]

This arrangement posed myriad problems, for it highlighted the different cultural assumptions of local Navajos, Park Service representatives, and the traveling public. Under the strict control of the Park Service, service in the national park system was generally first-rate, but the agency had little control over neighboring landholders who controlled access to the detached sections of Navajo National Monument. The superintendent and staff could only hope for the best. Service to visitors was spotty: in some cases the independent guided tours went well, but generally they did not. One staff member remembered the Austins as "good capitalists." They delivered people to and from Keet Seel in relative safety, but the experience was not the "trip of a lifetime." Visitors expected some mythic connection from a horse trip with Indians, but the Navajo saw themselves as a delivery system instead of a guide service.[39]

The memorandum of agreement of the following decade gave the Park Service greater influence over the activities of the guided tour operation. The cooperative nature of the agreement enabled the Park Service to extend a helping hand to the Austins. The Park Service "loaned" horses to ensure higher-quality animals for visitors, took reservations, and in general sought to improve the quality of service whenever possible. But much of the change was cosmetic in nature, and the improvement in the quality of the tours was minimal.

The new level of Park Service involvement was a mixed blessing. By taking reservations and supplying horses, the staff at the monument exerted at least a little influence over the operation. Conversely, because the Park Service took reservations, visitors assumed that the agency had control over the tours. Used to the high quality of visitor service characteristic of Park Service endeavors, they often found the Keet Seel horse trip lacking. Many were angry about what they considered a lapse in responsibility by the Park Service.

Throughout the 1960s and early 1970s, complaints about the horse operation increased. E. K. Austin was a "rough customer," unpopular with his neighbors, one who knew him recalled, and others remembered him in a similar fashion. One former employee called him the "bully of the canyon"; another acquired the habit of calling him "Ed the Pirate" and recalled that he had to separate Austin and visitors on more than one occasion to prevent fisticuffs. One former superintendent recalled members of the Austin family getting into a fistfight with each other during a meeting with park rangers.[40]

Visitors were often dissatisfied with their trip with the Austins. "Half-starved" horses, poor service, sullen guides, and drunkenness headed the list of complaints. Many people went to the Park Service to express their dismay, in the hope that an agency that had built its reputation on service could act to stop what they regarded as a blemish on its record. The Park Service had a standard reply that frustrated both staff members and visitors: because the Park Service did not control the Austins' land, it had little influence on the horse operation. "Things here on the Navajo Reservation are not like other places," Superintendent Jack Williams wrote in response to one complaint. "We are faced with jurisdictional and political problems that only the Navajo Tribal Council can alleviate."[41] Combined with the growing number of visitors who wished to go to Keet Seel, the Park Service recognized that it had a potentially major problem.

By the early 1970s, a consistent pattern was evident. Because Navajo National Monument was essentially an inholding on the Navajo reservation, the kind of control to which Park Service officials were accustomed eluded them. Without any direct authority over private land and unable to reach one portion of the monument without the use of land Austin controlled, the agency had to deal with a difficult situation. The best alternative was to seek to co-opt the Austins: show them the potential economic and cultural advantages of the Park Service approach to visitor service.

The cultural difference between the Austins and the Park Service was vast. The Austins spoke only Navajo, and while some communication in English certainly occurred, for a topic as important as this, it was imperative to find someone who could communicate in the Navajo language. In April 1973, Clarence N. Gorman, a career Park Service official and veteran of the Korean Conflict from Chinle who served as superintendent at Wupatki National Monument, was called to Navajo National Monument to help bridge the gap. Issues such as the treatment of visitors, courtesy, safety, promptness, and communications with the Park Service were paramount. At a meeting, really a visitor service seminar conducted in the Navajo language, Gorman tried to convey techniques that would result in better service and fewer complaints. In the aftermath of Gorman's visit, conditions improved and the number of unhappy visitors declined.[42]

But a gulf remained. Navajo guides and Anglo visitors had different perceptions of the trip. The Navajos saw themselves as guides rather than interpreters; they perceived their responsibility as limited to the safe delivery of visitors to the ruin and back. With a more instrumental than romantic approach to their animals, the guides often seemed uninterested and cruel in the eyes of their customers. A constant stream of complaints continued, reflecting a difference between expectation and actuality that characterized cross-cultural relations. The Park Service still had little ability to exercise substantive oversight. Ironically, for many visitors, riding horses with Indians on their trip to the ruins had significant cultural meaning. Despite any shortcomings, the Austins were part of the monument, their horse business an important component for visitors who sought a sense of being in the wild.[43]

The transformation of the demography of the labor force at the monument also reflected the changing relationships between the Park Service and the Navajo. Because the monument had little funding, seasonal labor remained intermittent before the 1930s. Most of the Navajos who worked at the monument before the 1930s were associated with the various archaeological expeditions. The New Deal provided money for the first seasonal laborers, among them Bob Black, who began in a seasonal capacity in 1935 and remained at the park for thirty-one years. Navajo veterans of World War II made up the first group of rangers at the monument, and they were followed by an expansion in the number of Navajo as MISSION 66 provided both temporary labor and permanent positions.[44]

Typical of the laborers was Delbert Smallcanyon, the man from Navajo Mountain who had previously been a herdsman and a railroad worker. He first went to the monument in 1968 as a temporary stonemason on a trail construction project. The job had considerable appeal, particularly when it turned into permanent part-time work. A permanent job close to home seemed a wonderful opportunity that allowed him to maintain a distinctly Navajo lifestyle—with the exception of wearing a Park Service uniform and punching a time clock three days a week. Each day he drove nearly fifty miles from Navajo Mountain to the monument, returning after a full day's work. Employment there allowed him to remain in his homeland, live a lifestyle that resembled that of his parents, and support his family—economically sustained by his job at the park.[45]

With the signing of the memorandum of agreement and the expansion of the staff at the monument, opportunities increased for Navajos who sought work there. They soon recognized that permanent ranger positions were generally filled by career Park Service employees; this prompted a number of younger Navajos to enter the Park Service, Gorman among them. But maintenance positions were available for local people, as were a range of seasonal positions. By the middle of the 1960s, the maintenance staff was exclusively Navajo except for the maintenance supervisor. In the middle of the 1980s, John Laughter took over this position, the first Navajo in a permanent supervisory capacity at the monument. Prior to coming to the monument, Laughter worked for a general contractor as a heavy equipment operator. In 1974, he began to work on the monument's maintenance crew and remained there for a decade, taking all the Park Service training courses he could.[46]

Navajos of different generations appeared to hold different views of the monument and its workings. In the 1980s and 1990s, older Navajos expressed gratitude for having jobs at the monument. The combination of proximity to their homes and good pay made the positions desirable. They did their work well, seemingly unaware of the context in which they labored. Younger Navajos understood the mission of the monument more clearly than did their elders, and they recognized how important it was to the economy of the entire western reservation. They could see its many ramifications on their lives and their families.[47]

In this insight lay one of the important paradoxes of working at the parks. National Park Service employment provided economic sustenance for many families on the western reservation as the dollars earned by one employee worked their way through familial networks, but in the process, the individual who earned the paycheck became an employee, a decidedly non-Navajo way of looking at the self. Federal dollars sustained Navajo life, but the people who earned that money— despite the way it sheltered their extended families from the consequences of social and economic change—became different as a result of earning it. They punched time clocks, wore uniforms, and accepted directives; they were classified as civil service workers, with all the protections and guarantees that went with that status. As a result, work at the monument changed them as it simultaneously provided a way for them and their families to remain in the Shonto region without falling into abject poverty.

Until the middle of the 1980s, structural problems with the distribution of employment at Navajo National Monument remained. In 1982, five of the nine permanent employees at the monument were Navajo. Three Anglos worked at the park, along with one Hispano. Yet all of the Anglos and the Hispano had higher GS, or General Schedule, rankings than did the five Navajos, leaving a skewed structure that reflected the slow process of the changing patterns of leadership in the national work force, including the civil service. After John Laughter became maintenance supervisor and Clarence Gorman was appointed superintendent, the historic limitations ended. By 1990, the monument had eleven full- and part-time employees. Eight, including the superintendent, the head of maintenance, and the entire maintenance department, were Navajo. The monument staff more accurately reflected the demography of the area.[48]

Other employment opportunities for the Navajo came from the development of extractive natural resource–based industries. Development of the natural resources of the reservation had begun with an oil boom in the 1920s, but little growth followed. During the 1950s, oil production again increased dramatically. The combination of greater Navajo demand for services and the need for more oil fueled the expansion. In 1950, there were 51 producing wells on the reservation; a decade later, the number had grown to 860. This spurt helped further more comprehensive development programs, as federal legislation that promoted such goals became one of the cornerstones of the New Frontier and Great Society programs of the 1960s. In 1965, the Tribal Council decided to explore systematic development of the minerals of the reservation. Among the projects was the Peabody Coal Company's Black Mesa Mine, near Navajo National Monument.[49]

From its inception, Black Mesa Mine was controversial. In 1964, the Peabody Coal Company negotiated a lease with the Navajo Nation for 40,000 acres on the reservation; two years later, an agreement with the Navajo and Hopi tribes added 25,000 acres of the Joint Use Area that the two shared. Black Mesa was a sacred place to the Navajo and Hopi peoples, but the need for cash to fund the affairs of the tribes was great. By the middle of the 1960s when Peabody Coal requested the lease, the oil and gas revenues of the Navajo were in the middle of a steep decline. This source of revenue funded most of the expenses of the tribal government: between 1954 and 1971, oil and gas revenue made up no less than 50 percent of tribal income in any year. Faced with growing expenses and declining revenue, the Tribal Council found the proposal enticing. The $2 million per annum for thirty-five years that the company offered seemed a phenomenal amount of money, and with coaxing from the Department of the Interior and the Bureau of Indian Affairs, the lease was signed.[50]

The two mines Peabody Coal Company developed in the Shonto vicinity had a significant impact on the lives of local Navajo people. The coal mining operation was one of the few on-reservation industries that hired many people, and the jobs there were available throughout the year, providing choices for Navajo people that had not previously existed. Employment there paid well, particularly by the standards of the area. By the early 1990s, some of the jobs at the mine paid in the $20 per hour range, and the entire spectrum of Navajo and Hopi people found employment there. Hubert Laughter, well over sixty years of age, found himself working as a heavy equipment operator for $17.79 per hour.[51]

The mine offered many economic advantages. It enabled a wide range of local people to achieve a standard of living previously unavailable in the region. Year-round employment allowed Navajos to remain among their people, work their lands, and bring home sizeable incomes. The economic impact of the mine meant new levels of prosperity, allowing Shonto Navajo greater participation in the market economy.

In material terms, evidence of comprehensive transformation of Navajo culture in the Shonto area showed rapidly. The coming of paved roads and paychecks with which to purchase vehicles made mechanized transportation a viable alternative, replacing the classic orange and green Studebaker horse-drawn wagon. William Binnewies recalled that during his tenure as superintendent of Navajo National Monument during the late 1960s, the pick-up truck era began in the Shonto vicinity. About the same time, Navajo families began to travel to other places, a practice uncommon prior to that time. These symbols of greater exposure to the outside world were the harbinger of a revolution in lifestyle for the people of the western reservation, and the jobs at the mine played an important role in bringing them on.[52]

The mine exacted a toll from the region and its people. Employment at the mine was like working for the railroad. Schedules and practices had to be followed, the work was hard, dirty, and sometimes dangerous, and it acculturated people rapidly. The difference between a Navajo who worked at Black Mesa Mine and anyone who worked at any of Peabody's mines off the reservation was smaller than the difference between the Navajo miner and other Navajos who did not work at the mine. There were few opportunities to follow the Navajo way at Black Mesa Mine.

In contrast, employment at Navajo National Monument offered a compromise position between the Navajo world and the acculturation of hourly wage labor. People with greater experience in Anglo culture, like Hubert Laughter—with military and Park Service background, a stint as a Navajo police officer, and a term in the Tribal Council—were comfortable at the mine. Delbert Smallcanyon and others like him, with limited exposure to and understanding of the Anglo world and little desire for deeper involvement, found themselves more comfortable at a place such as the monument that made concessions to the character of Navajo life. A number of the employees at the monument were singers; some used personal days of leave to perform or participate in Navajo rituals.

This classic trade-off—between material success and cultural sustenance—lies at the core of the colonial experience, but rarely with the many economic options available to the Shonto area Navajo after the coming of the mine and MISSION 66. Although more limited than that of the Anglo middle class, the Navajo situation offered more choices than were available to most nonwhite unskilled workers in the United States. Protected by the preferential treatment in hiring guaranteed by the contract with Peabody Coal and the lack of amenities to attract Anglo workers to the area, and offered the opportunity to choose between assimilation in the extractive industry workplace and a lower-paying transformative option at the monument that accommodated Navajo desires, the people of the Shonto area had weathered the latest replacement of an economy in their region.

But the economic solution offered no guarantee of permanence. The coal mining operation had socioeconomic and environmental consequences. The 1966 agreement allowed the company to establish a slurry pipeline to convey pulverized coal and water to the Mojave Power Plant on the banks of the Colorado River in Nevada. This became the first instance in which the Navajo and Hopi tribes were paid for the use of their water. The Navajo Nation agreed to provide more than 3,000 acre-feet of water each year. For this constant supply, Peabody Coal paid five dollars per acre-foot. The initial agreement created a source of cheap water for the company, but later renegotiations raised the cost significantly in an effort to limit use by the coal company.[53]

The sale of 3,000 acre-feet of groundwater each year and the fact that no water from the Colorado River was used in the slurry meant that there was an impact on the water table in the vicinity of Black Mesa. The water traveled one way—from Black Mesa to the Colorado River—providing jobs and income for Navajo and Hopi people in the area but creating a long-term threat to their survival. The mine was slated to cease operation in 2023, and the possibility that its closure would leave the Shonto area without either jobs or water seemed very real. An economic backbone for the region had been developed, but its long-term cost could be prohibitive.

It was this predicament that characterized the future of the western reservation at the beginning of the 1990s. Economic opportunities existed that had the ability to sustain the loose-knit community in the Shonto region. Yet this economic lifeline had a growing social and environmental cost, offset by the material prosperity that employment offered. Benign forms of dependence such as employment at the monument offered a midpoint between mere wage labor and historic patterns of Navajo life, but there was no doubt that with or without the power of institutions, wage labor had become the dominant form of sustenance in the Shonto vicinity. What the American military could not accomplish—the subjugation and transformation of the western Navajo reservation—was achieved smoothly by the accouterments of technology and material expectations of the modern age.

Pokey Medicine Wing was right. Indian people could make money by raising earthworms; what he failed to take into account was the impact on them of that, or any other, choice. The paradox that the people of the Shonto area faced has become typical of the peripheries— Anglo, Hispano, and Indian—of the American West. The vast material benefits of industrialized society offer an economic option, but they lack a cultural dimension that would help mitigate the change in ways of living that accompanies new economies. Even options that allow for the desire to preserve culture and participate in its rituals are in their very essence transformative; they require behavior that conforms to the modern world even as they make every attempt to allow for the maintenance of cultural heritage. Efforts at economic exploitation have become commonplace, while genuine efforts at accommodation and acculturation have been sporadic at best and nonexistent at worst. As a result, individuals and culture groups have uninformed choices thrust upon them, seeing only part of the equation. Without a comprehensive institutional structure and deprived of the efficacy of historic practices and customs, areas like Shonto face a denouement: they can exchange historical identity derived from place for material gain and thrive economically but suffer culturally. If they reject the manifestations of modernity offered them, they risk the continuation of the pattern of economic marginalization and the destruction of culture from abject poverty. This is truly a devil's bargain.

Notes

1. Christopher Moore, *Coyote Blue* (New York: Simon and Schuster, 1994), pp. 95–96.

2. Dean MacCannell, *The Tourist: A New Theory of the Leisure Class* (New York: Shocken Books, 1976); Dean MacCannell, *Empty Meeting Grounds: The Tourist Papers* (London: Routledge, 1992); John Dorst, *The Written Suburb: An American Site, an Ethnographic Dilemma* (Philadelphia: University of Pennsylvania Press, 1989). For an example of the declensionist mode, see Scott Norris, ed., *Discovered Country: Tourism and Survival in the American West* (Albuquerque: University of New Mexico Press, 1994).

3. Histories of tourism have tended to focus on the experiences of visitors rather than the impact of the "industry" on places visited. The best-known example of this kind of narrative is Mark Twain, *The Innocents Abroad* (Hartford, Conn.: American Publishing Company, 1869). Most scholars have followed this tactic in an effort to open dialogue; see, for example, Earl S. Pomeroy, *In Search of the Golden West: The Tourist in Western America* (New York: Alfred A. Knopf, 1957). See also John Jakle, *The Tourist: Travel in Twentieth-Century America* (Lincoln: University of Nebraska Press, 1985); John F. Sears, *Sacred Places: American Tourist Attractions in the Nineteenth Century* (New York: Oxford University Press, 1988).

4. Donald Worster, *Under Western Skies: Nature and History in the American West* (New York: Oxford University Press, 1992), pp. 106–153; Hal Rothman, *On Rims and Ridges: The Los Alamos Area since 1880* (Lincoln: University of Nebraska Press, 1992); David M. Brugge and Raymond Wilson, *Administrative History: Canyon de Chelly* (Santa Fe: National Park Service, 1976); Michael Welsh, *U.S. Army Corps of Engineers in the Middle Rio Grande Conservancy District* (Albuquerque: University of New Mexico Press, 1983); Sam Stanley, ed., *American Indian Economic Development* (The Hague and Paris: Mouton Publishers, 1973).

5. Bill P. Acrey, *Navajo History: The Land and the People* (Shiprock, N.Mex.: Department of Curriculum Materials Development, Central Consolidated School District no. 22, 1988), pp. 35–44, 73–81; Raymond Friday Locke, *The Book of the Navajo*, 4th ed. (Los Angeles: Mankind Publishing Company, 1989), pp. 35–61; Frank McNitt, *The Indian Traders* (Norman: University of Oklahoma Press, 1962), pp. 270–276; Richard White, *Roots of Dependency: Subsistence, Environment, and Social Change among the Choctaws, Pawnees, and Navajos* (Lincoln: University of Nebraska Press, 1983), pp. 236–249.

6. Neil M. Judd, *Men Met along the Trail: Adventures in Archaeology* (Norman: University of Oklahoma Press, 1968), pp. 29–30.

7. Judd, *Men Met along the Trail*, p. 30; Elizabeth Compton Hegemann, *Navajo Trading Days* (Albuquerque: University of New Mexico Press, 1963), p. 227.

8. C. W. Ceram, *The First Americans: A Story of North American Archaeology* (New York: Harcourt, Brace, Jovanovich, 1971), pp. 64–67; Judd, *Men Met along the Trail*, pp. 4–45.

9. Alfred Runte, *National Parks: The American Experience*, 2nd ed. (Lincoln: University of Nebraska Press, 1987), pp. 82–105; Hal Rothman, *Preserving Differ-*

ent *Pasts: The American National Monuments* (Urbana: University of Illinois Press, 1989), pp. 6–33; Curtis M. Hinsley, Jr., *Savages and Scientists: The Smithsonian Institution and the Development of American Anthropology, 1846–1910* (Washington, D.C.: Smithsonian Institution Press, 1981), pp. 81–230.

10. Rothman, *Preserving Different Pasts,* pp. 70–84.

11. Judd, *Men Met along the Trail,* p. 45; Hal Rothman, *Navajo National Monument: A Place and Its People* (Santa Fe: National Park Service, 1991), pp. 12–21; McNitt, *Indian Traders,* pp. 270–273; Jesse Walter Fewkes, *Preliminary Report on a Visit to the Navaho National Monument, Arizona* (Washington, D.C.: Government Printing Office, 1911).

12. Fred S. Garing, "A Trip to Navajo National Monument, 1910," manuscript, Navajo National Monument Library; McNitt, *Indian Traders,* p. 271; Hegemann, *Navaho Trading Days,* p. 224.

13. Judd, *Men Met along the Trail,* pp. 42–43; Rothman, *Preserving Different Pasts,* pp. 76–82; Byron L. Cummings, *Indians I Have Known* (Tucson: Arizona Silhouette, 1952), pp. 24–33; Robert S. McPherson, *The Northern Navajo Frontier, 1860–1900* (Albuquerque: University of New Mexico Press, 1988), pp. 51–99; William Y. Adams, *Shonto: The Study of the Role of a Trader in a Modern Navaho Community,* Bureau of American Ethnology Bulletin no. 188 (Washington, D.C.: Government Printing Office, 1963), p. 39.

14. McNitt, *Indian Traders,* p. 273; Gladwell Richardson, *Navajo Trader* (Tucson: University of Arizona Press, 1986), pp. 75–82; Hegemann, *Navaho Trading Days,* pp. 264–267; Adams, *Shonto,* pp. 42–43.

15. Richardson, *Navajo Trader,* p. 75; Hegemann, *Navaho Trading Days,* pp. 292–293.

16. Hegemann, *Navaho Trading Days,* pp. 227, 274–275, 293; Adams, *Shonto,* pp. 43–44.

17. Hegemann, *Navaho Trading Days,* p. 312.

18. Donald L. Parman, *The Navajos and the New Deal* (New Haven, Conn.: Yale University Press, 1976), pp. 36–43, 81–94; Lawrence C. Kelly, "Anthropology in the Soil Conservation Service," *Agricultural History* 59 (April 1985):136–147; Sandra S. Batie, "Soil Conservation in the 1980s: A Historical Perspective," *Agricultural History* 59 (April 1985):107–123; George A. Boyce, *When the Navajo Had Too Many Sheep: The 1940s* (San Francisco: Indian Historian Press, 1974), pp. 62–92; Hegemann, *Navaho Trading Days,* pp. 376–384; Adams, *Shonto,* p. 158.

19. White, *Roots of Dependency,* pp. 250–270; Adams, *Shonto,* pp. 4–5, 11.

20. Denis Foster Johnston, *An Analysis of Sources of Information on the Population of the Navaho,* Bureau of American Ethnology Report no. 197 (Washington, D.C.: Government Printing Office, 1966), pp. 124–125; Hegemann, *Navaho Trading Days,* p. 317; Adams, *Shonto,* pp. 158–160.

21. White, *Roots of Dependency,* pp. 230–312; Johnston, *Analysis of Sources,* pp. 125–128.

22. Bob Black interview with Hal Rothman, translated by Clarence N. Gorman and Marylou Smith, Navajo National Monument, January 5, 1991.

23. Black interview; Hegemann, *Navaho Trading Days,* pp. 292–293.

24. Adams, *Shonto*, pp. 68–69.

25. Robert Netting, *Balancing on an Alp: Ecological Change and Continuity in a Swiss Mountain Community* (Cambridge, U.K.: Cambridge University Press, 1981), pp. 1–9, 90–168.

26. Hubert Laughter interview with Hal Rothman, portions translated by Clarence N. Gorman, Navajo National Monument, January 5, 1991.

27. Laughter interview; Hegemann, *Navaho Trading Days*, pp. 297–298; Adams, *Shonto*, pp. 49–50.

28. *Inside Interior*, April 1948, pp. 5–6; Seth Bigman interview by Clarence N. Gorman, Monument Valley, Arizona, March 1991.

29. Adams, *Shonto*, p. 88. For the plight of nonwhite peoples in the nineteenth and twentieth centuries, see Pete Daniel, *Breaking the Land* (Urbana: University of Illinois Press, 1985); Nicholas Lemann, *The Promised Land* (New York: Alfred A. Knopf, 1991); David J. Weber, *Foreigners in Their Native Land* (Albuquerque: University of New Mexico Press, 1974); Robert Rosenbaum, *Mexicano Resistance in the American Southwest: The Sacred Right of Self-Preservation* (Austin: University of Texas Press, 1979).

30. Johnston, *Analysis of Sources*, pp. 127–135; Delbert Smallcanyon interview with Hal Rothman, translated by Clarence N. Gorman, Navajo National Monument, January 4, 1991.

31. Adams, *Shonto*, pp. 1–2, 51.

32. Peter Iverson, *The Navajo Nation* (Westport, Conn.: Greenwood Press, 1981), pp. 56–57; Peter Iverson, "The Emerging Navajo Nation," in Alfonso Ortiz, ed., *Southwest*, vol. 10 of *Handbook of North American Indians* (Washington, D.C.: Smithsonian Institution, 1983), pp. 636–658; Arthur R. Gómez, "The Fabulous Four Corners: Neocolonialism and Subregional Development in the Hinterland West, 1945–1970," Ph.D. diss., University of New Mexico, 1989, pp. 147–153; Raye C. Ringholz, *Uranium Frenzy: Boom and Bust on the Colorado Plateau* (Albuquerque: University of New Mexico Press, 1991), pp. 52–122.

33. Superintendent's Monthly Narrative, March 1958, Navajo National Monument Library.

34. Sanford Hill to Hugh Miller, July 5, 1957, Navajo, D30: Roads and Trails; Edward B. Danson to Hugh Miller, November 25, 1958, Navajo, D3415: Buildings; "MISSION 66 Prospectus: Navajo National Monument, April 20, 1956," A9815: MISSION 66 Programs. Denver Federal Records Center.

35. Rothman, *Navajo National Monument*, pp. 76–112.

36. Calendar Year, A3015: Reports, Travel, Monthly, September 30, 1965; Jack R. Williams to Frank H. Carson, January 27, 1966, Navajo, A3815: Public Relations with Federal, State, and Local Agencies. Denver Federal Records Center.

37. Bob Black interview; Superintendent's Monthly Narrative, 1956–1962, A2823, Navajo National Monument Library.

38. Mary Lou Smith comments as she translated Bob Black's interview, January 5, 1991; Concessionaires, Horse, NPS History file, Navajo National Monument Library.

39. Robert Shankland, *Steve Mather of the National Parks* (New York: Alfred A. Knopf, 1953), pp. 7, 92–99, 120–127; Ronald A. Foresta, *America's National*

Parks and Their Keepers (Washington, D.C.: Resources for the Future, 1984), pp. 52–55; P. J. Ryan telephone conversation, May 25, 1990.

40. P. J. Ryan telephone conversation; William G. Binnewies telephone conversation, May 30, 1990.

41. P. J. Ryan telephone conversation; William G. Binnewies telephone conversation. Carl M. Hinckley to Stewart L. Udall, June 17, 1966; Jack R. Williams to Regional Director, September 2, 1966; Mildred Heflin to Jack Williams, August 28, 1966; Thomas M. Newell to Kevin McKibben, July 26, 1967; Barbara Horton to Frank F. Kowski, April 15, 1968. Letters in file H36, Navajo National Monument Library.

42. Harold Timmons to Clarence Gorman, April 13, 1973, A36, Navajo National Monument Library.

43. P. J. Ryan telephone conversation.

44. Hubert Laughter interview; Robert Holden, "Administrative History," p. 24, unpublished typescript dated 1963, Navajo National Monument Library; Black interview; no author, "Seth Bigman Completes First Season as Interpretive Ranger," *Inside Interior,* November 1948, p. 6.

45. Delbert Smallcanyon interview with Hal Rothman, translated by Clarence N. Gorman, Navajo National Monument, January 5, 1991.

46. John Laughter interview with Hal Rothman, Navajo National Monument, January 5, 1991.

47. John Laughter interview; Hubert Laughter interview; Black interview; Smallcanyon interview.

48. Ronald R. Switzer and John Carlin, "Management Evaluation: Navajo National Monument," August 24–26, 1982, A5427, Southwest Regional Office Interpretation Library; Gorman interview; John Laughter interview.

49. Acrey, *Navajo History,* pp. 287–289.

50. Marjane Ambler, *Breaking the Iron Bonds: Indian Control of Energy Development* (Lawrence: University of Kansas Press, 1990), pp. 58–60.

51. Hubert Laughter interview.

52. William G. Binnewies telephone conversation; Adams, *Shonto,* p. 79.

53. Ambler, *Breaking the Iron Bonds,* pp. 222–224.

Marguerite S. Shaffer

Negotiating National Identity
Western Tourism and "See America First"

In a burst of patriotic fervor that characterized his 1866 travel narrative, *Across the Continent: A Summer's Journey to the Rocky Mountains, the Mormons and the Pacific States,* Samuel Bowles proudly exclaimed, "The Continent is spanned. The national breath is measured. How this Republic, saved, reunited, bound together as never before, expands under such personal passage and footstep tread; how magnificent its domain." Extolling the virtues of the expanding railroad system and expressing a shift in national focus, he concluded, "There is no such knowledge of the nation as comes of traveling it, of seeing eye to eye its vast extent, its various and teeming wealth, and, above all, its purpose-filled people."[1] Bowles's narrative reflected a turn away from the South and the trauma of the Civil War and toward the West and the expanding nation. The structural changes that took hold after the Civil War and came to fruition around the turn of the century reinforced this shift in focus. Between 1865 and the turn of the century, the United States dramatically changed from a society of "island communities" to a modern, urban-industrial nation-state.[2] The construction of a national transportation network, the emergence of a national market, and the development of a national print media mark the central technological, economic, and cultural changes that helped to initiate and define this transformation. These developments represent the broad structural changes that transformed America into a modern nation, but developments in American popular culture also reinforced this nationalizing process. Like brand-name goods, mail-order catalogs, department stores, and mass-circulation magazines, western tourism, as Bowles suggested, imbued the emerging nation with form and substance.

Tourism developed as an elite pastime in the United States during the early nineteenth century with the growth of a leisure ethic, the emergence of adequate modes of transportation, and the establishment of unique attractions. After the Civil War, the completion of the transcontinental rail system, the communications revolution, and the evolution of corporate capitalism instituted touring as an established leisure activity for American elites. The select number of eastern attractions and resorts gave way to a vast array of dramatic natural wonders, ancient ruins, and scenic landscapes scattered throughout the western United States. As a result, a truly national tourism developed, distinct from the earlier practice of vacationing, which was centered predominantly in the East.[3] As a popular cultural practice that rested on the inscription of national identity in the built and the natural environment, tourism drew on the broad changes that were helping to forge a national community. In this way tourism reshaped the built environment of the United States and transformed the symbolic value of American landscape and, in the process, influenced the way in which people defined and identified themselves as "Americans."

The etymology of the tourist slogan "See America First" reflects the role of western tourism in this broad societal transformation. Appropriated and embraced by a variety of constituencies, "See America First" did not represent a unified movement; rather, it reflected a series of evolving ideas about tourism and commerce, scenery and history, the West and the nation. Originally conceived in 1905 as the slogan for a western booster scheme, "See America First" signified a commercially oriented campaign to promote settlement, investment, and tourism in the intermountain West. Inadequate financial backing, however, doomed this original version to obscurity. In 1910 the Great Northern Railway adopted the slogan as its corporate logo and motto. No longer just a regional booster slogan, "See America First" took on the status of a corporate trademark that associated the experience of travel and leisure made possible by the Great Northern with the domesticated western wilderness of Glacier National Park. The Great Northern popularized the slogan, and as World War I closed Europe to American tourists, "See America First" was adopted by a variety of organizations including the Panama-Pacific International Exposition, the Lincoln Highway Association, and the National Park Service to advocate domestic tourism—more specifically, western tourism. Each organization extended the slogan's meaning, defining a new ideal of the West and America through the context of touring. Tracing the evolution of "See America First" from its origins as a western booster idea to its culmination as a popular touring emblem reveals that the messages and meaning generated by the slogan were part of a larger dialogue concerning national identity and national unity that centered on the role and image of the West.[4]

Commemorating the opening of the See America First Conference on the morning of January 25, 1906, Governor John C. Cutler of Utah praised 125 delegates representing boosters, businessmen, and politicians from across the West for the unselfish task they were about to undertake:[5] "You will carry forward a work that has at its very base the inculcation of patriotism, the love of native land." This represented a historic moment in the forging of a united nation, according to Cutler. "The movement that you strive for in this conference will make better citizens of the tens of thousands of Americans who are now living in ignorance of their own land, will through the agencies of school, pulpit and press bring to the young men and maidens of the land a vision of the regions they know nothing of which are yet under the dominion of the flag we all revere." They were there, Governor Cutler proclaimed, "to preach the gospel of a better-known America." During their three days in Salt Lake City these men were showered with words of welcome and praise, they were toasted and cheered, and they were inundated with the charge to "go forth and . . . preach the doctrine of 'See America First.'"[6]

The See America First Conference marked the public introduction of a western booster campaign initiated in Salt Lake City by Fisher

Sanford Harris, secretary of the Salt Lake City Commercial Club. "See Europe if you will, but See America First" became the rallying cry for Harris's scheme, the central argument being that Americans had spent more than $150 million touring Europe during the 1904–1905 touring season and that not only could this money be well spent in America, but also tourism would help to educate ignorant easterners about the wonders and possibilities available throughout the West.[7] Harris imagined the formation of a "tourist trust" organized to promote tourism throughout the intermountain West. The general idea was that this voluntary group comprising western businessmen, civic leaders, representatives from railroad publicity departments, and city and state politicians "would pool their resources" in an effort to advertise the tourist attractions and develop the tourist infrastructure throughout the West, thus stimulating settlement, investment, and "the discovery of America by Americans."[8] Building on the idea that "scenery was a valuable asset," conference delegates laid the groundwork for the formation of the See America First League, whose central role would be to promote the West by articulating "a grand, comprehensive scheme of publicity, involving in its beneficent results the welfare and development of a great industrial empire and calling into its service the best artistic and literary skill of the world, for the accomplishment of its far reaching purpose."[9]

"See America First," as articulated by these western interests, expressed a sense of western identity grounded in the intersection between the West as region and the West as myth, which had taken shape around the turn of the century.[10] Western boosters and businessmen who conceived of the movement embraced a double consciousness. As westerners, they hoped that "See America First" would give the West equal status with the Northeast. As Americans, they believed that the ideal West with its sublime scenery, abundant resources, and virtuous citizens embodied the "true" America. In defining and developing their scheme to promote tourism in the United States, they revealed not only their commercial interests, but also their ambivalence toward the political and economic control exercised by the northeastern industrial core.[11] "See America First" expressed both a fascination with and an anxiety toward the forces of industrialization, incorporation, and urbanization that were transforming the United States into a complex, modern nation-state.

On the one hand, "See America First" as defined by the league expressed the desires of western boosters interested in promoting scenery for the sake of increasing investment and settlement in the West. In this commercial guise, "See America First" rhetoric criticized easterners for their fascination with Europe and argued that the West had just as much to offer as the Old World, if not more. In this context, the slogan manifested a western regionalism in which businessmen and civic leaders sought to reframe the colonial relationship between the West and the northeastern industrial core by representing the West, with its potential for commercial development, as an equal partner to the East in the framework of the nation. In his speeches and writings Harris scolded easterners for their "careless ignorance of the marvelous beauty and wealth" of the West. He argued that many easterners "simply do not know—they are not educated about our throbbing West. They do not realize that some day out of this great West will come a Shakespeare, a Byron and the nation's greatest statesmen."[12] He concluded that "the people of the East seem to be growing effete," as manifested by their obsession with everything European.[13] In this context, the East and Europe were conflated to symbolize elitism, wealth, culture, big business, and Old World provincialism. The West represented democracy, freedom, nature, and economic opportunity. In attracting eastern attention, western businessmen and boosters hoped to unite East and West in a commercial partnership that would strengthen the nation. Thus, the gospel of "See America First" was meant to dispel established myths and fallacies about the West and in the process rectify the unequal economic relationship between the two regions.

On the other hand, "See America First," as promoted by these western boosters, went beyond commercial and regional concerns to deeper anxieties about the transformations taking place in American culture. Over and over Harris returned to the eternal value of western scenery. Mines and farms become "worn out and factories are no longer profitable," Harris explained, "but the river running to the sea, the waterfall turning the old mill wheel, the cool, inviting canyon, the awe inspiring mountain, the laughing lake, the gorgeous sunset, remain forever."[14] Western scenery embodied the promise and potential of the nation, according to "See America First" advocates. "The golden West," Harris explained, "offers a treasure house filled to overflowing with the rarest gems of towering snow-capped mountains; noble rivers, bearing in their broad bosoms the commerce of a nation; blue lakes smiling in the face of unclouded skies; gorgeous sunsets, whose ravishing beauty fills the soul with reverential awe, while over all and around all there is an atmosphere so pure that simply breathing it brings life to the lifeless, hope to the hopeless, and happiness to the miserable." He celebrated "the health renewing, soul-uplifting qualities of outdoor life" available in the West, arguing that the region offered a place where overworked Americans (read easterners) could reinvigorate themselves and revive their sense of patriotism. By encouraging easterners to know the West, Harris implicitly associated the East with corruption and the West with virtue. In his mind, western nature represented the antithesis of the industrial and overly civilized East, providing a therapeutic retreat from the demands of modern living. "The number of jaded, overworked men and women of the crowded cities who feel in their hearts the irresistible 'call of the wild,' is greatly increasing," Harris wrote. "To such as these the fields and streams, the mountains, lakes and canyons of the West lie fallow for the working out of their physical and mental salvation."[15] Essentially Harris argued that even though the frontier seemed to be dwindling and commerce seemed to be transforming the character of American society, the promise of nature as both sanctuary and free land as represented in the West remained in those scattered sublime landscapes.[16] Tourism promised to preserve those landscapes while opening up to development all land not designated as "scenic." In touring the West, Americans could see that promise, in effect consume that promise, and yet simultaneously the West could reap the benefits of progress without suffering the ill effects that had corrupted the East. Thus, tourism became an act of virtuous consumption. In Harris's mind, the program of the See America First League allowed the West and America to have the best of both worlds: the virtues of nature combined with the benefits of commerce.

Despite Fisher Harris's grand ideals, the See America First League had little success. Although Harris embarked on an extensive mission-ary journey throughout the country to preach the gospel of "See America First" and promote the league in 1906, he was unable to gain the nec-essary financial and cooperative support to solidify the organization and actually initiate the publicity program imagined at the conference. He did succeed in adopting the *Western Monthly* magazine, a booster magazine published out of Salt Lake City, to be the official organ of the See America First League. And between 1908 and 1909, he published a few articles promoting the "See America First" idea.[17] But lack of funds, the financial panic of 1907, and the onslaught of what appears to have been tuberculosis sapped his energy and enthusiasm, and by the fall of 1909 Harris was dead, and the See America First League had faded from the public record. The slogan, however, remained.

On May 25, 1910, the Great Northern Railway completed the con-struction of a twenty–by–fifteen–foot billboard in front of its general offices in St. Paul, Minnesota. The large oil-colored painting portrayed a scene of Lake McDonald and the surrounding Rocky Mountains in the newly created Glacier National Park. The slogan "See America First" was inscribed across the top. The St. Paul *Pioneer Press Dispatch* noted that two hundred of these billboards, depicting twenty different scenes in the park, were being erected "along the trunk lines near Chicago, Detroit, Cleveland, Philadelphia, New York, Boston and Buffalo" to boost Glacier National Park and the "See America First" movement.[18] These billboards represented just one component of what *Printer's Ink* described as an "extensive campaign of newspaper, magazine and out-door advertising." Herbert J. Smith reported that the Great Northern was launching a multimedia advertising campaign "to attract tourists to the new Glacier National Park in northern Montana." All new Great Northern advertisements displayed the "See America First" emblem illustrated by photographic images of scenes throughout the park. The campaign was "an effort to take full advantage of the opportunities" presented by the "natural attraction" of the park.[19] As Louis W. Hill, president of the Great Northern Railway, explained, "There is a vari-ety of beauty in Glacier National Park . . . which is not surpassed any-where in the world. Americans spend millions of dollars in Europe each year to see sights which are already equaled in this country. They need to be educated to realize this, and Glacier National Park should go far to help the 'See America First' movement."[20]

As the Great Northern Railway began to develop and promote Glacier National Park as a romanticized western retreat, it initiated an extensive advertising campaign, adopting "See America First" as its new motto and logo to associate the Great Northern with the newly formed park. Through the use of its corporate resources the Great Northern Railway appropriated what had been a motto for local western boosters and publicized it on a national scale. The company literally and figuratively reimagined the landscape of northwestern Montana, reconstructing and packaging the park to create a myth of the West that signified an idealized America. In the process, it not only popularized the "See America First" slogan, but also gave it new meaning.

By 1915 Glacier had two rustic luxury hotels, nine chalet complexes, three teepee camps, and a series of roads and trails that stretched throughout the park.[21] Not only did the physical arrangement of the hotels, chalets, and teepee camps compel tourists to walk or ride through the area—experiencing the scenic vistas, the glaciers, the dense forests, and the mountain streams firsthand—but also the atmosphere of these accommodations provided a context for understanding this wilderness experience in terms of America's past, present, and future.

The Glacier Park Hotel served as the gateway to the park. "Here the east and the west meet, the American and the European, finding pleasure in the associations with bronzed and hardy mountaineers," explained one promotional brochure.[22] Modeled on the Forestry Building at the 1905 Lewis and Clark Exposition, the hotel was celebrated for its "Forest Lobby," a three-story enclosed courtyard supported by "splendid fir-tree pillars four feet in thickness"[23] which brought "the outdoors indoors."[24] The lobby was decorated with Blackfeet Indian rugs and blankets, oak furniture, and tree-trunk lamp stands and was lighted by Japanese lanterns. It also contained an open campfire set up on a bed of stones. Telephone booths, a drugstore, a cigar stand, a railroad ticket office, and a haberdasher were situated in the midst of this rustic decor.[25] Blackfeet Indians in full war dress and rough-clad western guides brushed shoulders with newly arrived guests outfitted in the latest styles from Chicago and New York. By design and by chance, the hotel straddled boundaries of past and present, primitive and modern, East and West.

The ideal of western wilderness represented in the rustic atmosphere of the hotel rested on symbols of conquest: harvested forest, friendly Indians and their crafts, and the heads and skins of slain animals. These images suggested a timeless and harmonious past—an American frontier just civilized by Anglo-Americans, a simple but strenuous life on the edge of western wilderness. They marked an imagined past that worked to provide security, authority, and legitimacy to those living in the present.[26] In effect, the rustic decor, which represented an ideal of the American frontier tamed by vigorous men, encouraged white upper-class tourists to identify with that triumph, to find power in recognizing themselves as the legitimate heirs of the Anglo-Americans who had conquered the frontier.

The Blackfeet Indians were central to this imagery of wilderness and the American frontier. Not only were the cultural artifacts of the tribe appropriated to decorate the hotels and chalets, but the Indians and their culture were employed as a decorative presence throughout the park. In an attempt to smooth over any conflict concerning Blackfeet claims to park lands, the Great Northern symbolically adopted the Blackfeet as the official mascots of the park.[27] During the Glacier Park season a number of Indians from the reservation were paid to camp in a large teepee set up adjacent to the Glacier Park Hotel and to perform a weekly powwow. Other Indians were employed to escort tourists from the Great Northern trains that stopped at the East Glacier Station up to the Glacier Park Hotel.[28] The Great Northern also set up a series of "teepee village camps" to encourage walking tours of the park.[29] Promotional literature encouraged visitors who chose to eschew the hotels and chalets and tour the park on foot to follow "the dim and little-traveled trails of the Indian and ranger, into the wilderness, but always through a region of indescribable beauty, with new scenic surprises at every turn."[30]

This Indian imagery presented a double-sided message. The Blackfeet with their animal-skin teepees, their colorful blankets, their

feather-and-bead headdresses, and their primitive ceremonies represented an era and a lifestyle unscathed by the ravages of civilization. As
one promotional pamphlet explained, the Blackfeet "were one of the
last tribes to come in contact with the white man and still retain most
of their primitive customs and manner of living. Tourists are afforded
an excellent opportunity to observe their rites and ceremonies. Their
history and legends are perpetuated in the names of many of the mountains, lakes and glaciers of the Park."[31] Although the presence of the
Blackfeet and their artifacts conveyed an ideal of western wilderness
and the primitive to elite white travelers searching for an alternative to
modern society, their presence also reinforced a racial hierarchy. As
objects on display, they implicitly became objects of conquest that had
been subdued by a more advanced race; in consuming this Indian imagery, tourists were implicitly encouraged to become vicarious con-
querors.

Glacier's image was further embellished by references to Europe,
suggesting that the park offered not only western wilderness, but also
sublime scenery. Even before the Great Northern began its building
program, Glacier had been referred to as the Switzerland of America.
The chalet complexes spaced along the mountain passes on lake edges
and among the glacial valleys were based on authentic Swiss designs
and modeled on the hut system in the Swiss Alps.[32] The Great Northern encouraged tourists to walk or ride from one chalet camp to the
next to fully enjoy the variety of wonders in the park, which they described as the "Alps of America." Waitresses outfitted in Swiss cos-
tumes served the clientele at both the hotels and the chalets. At one
point, Louis Hill had even envisioned an advertising campaign in which
a map of the Swiss Alps would be superimposed over a map of the
park. The idea was abandoned when he saw how small the park was in
comparison to Switzerland.[33]

The Great Northern was not simply trying to re-create Switzerland
in America by using the Swiss motif in the park. Instead, the Swiss
references served to locate the park in the context of Europe. Great
Northern publicists knew that it would be difficult to compete with the
popularity of European tourism: the museums, the scenery, the rem-
nants of antiquity, and its association with refinement and culture. The

company counted on the Swiss motif to assure potential tourists that Glacier offered not only suitable tourist accommodations, but also magnificent natural landscapes guaranteed to inspire the intellect. In combination with western wilderness imagery, the Swiss references suggested that American scenery was superior to that of Europe because it remained untainted by the effects of excessive civilization.

In many respects, the company's use of the slogan as defined by Hill revolved around issues of class and who could control the meaning of America, as well as around issues of race and the construction of whiteness.[34] Hill not only built a vacation chalet in Glacier for himself and his family, he also fashioned himself as the ultimate host for the park. His careful attention to the design of the park, his close monitoring of guests and services, and his active involvement in publicizing the park to friends and business associates suggest that Hill imagined the park as an exclusive wilderness resort. According to Hill's vision, Glacier offered upper- and upper-middle-class white Americans a chance to escape the ills of the modern city and reimagine themselves as the heirs of Anglo frontiersmen and pioneers who had succeeded in civilizing the West.[35] In this way, the manifestation of "See America First" constructed by the Great Northern revealed some of the larger anxieties about the changes taking place in American society, specifically concerning the increasing presence and visibility of ethnic and racial diversity in American society, as well as the seeming increase in power of the "lower" classes.[36]

On another level, Great Northern's "See America First" publicity campaign also worked to mask the commercial aims of the company. Tourism, specifically travel to Glacier, was framed as an act of patriotism rather than an act of consumption. Through their journeys, Great Northern tourists became good citizens. As one grateful Glacier Park visitor wrote to Hill, "This is just a little note of warm congratulation of the vision you have had for the West; every stand taken against super civilized modern life, is a right stand for the American people, if they are going to continue their energetic leadership of straight forward accomplishment in this present day world." "See America First," she concluded, "is a great slogan and it is splendid that you have opened up such a country for us to glory in. It is so uniquely America. Our spoiled East would gain immeasurably by getting some big free spirit of the West, that can only be acquired on the trails and tracks in places like Glacier."[37] The Great Northern's use of the slogan manifested a certain ambivalence about the relationship between the corporation, the citizen-consumer, and the emerging consumer society during this period. Specifically, the Great Northern, by representing itself as an altruistic nation builder, masked the more problematic image of railroad corporations as greedy monopolies preying on yeoman farmers and free laborers.[38]

According to the Great Northern Railway, to "See America First" was to experience Teddy Roosevelt's robust western frontier: the home of the Blackfeet Indians conquered and befriended by brave westerners and the sight of unequaled sublime scenery.[39] It was to be refashioned as a modern-day explorer or an aristocratic sportsman and test one's strength and will against the western wilderness. Simultaneously, the fast transcontinental train, the luxury hotels, the European-style accouterments reminded tourists that they were never far from modern conveniences and civilized taste and style. This assortment of images brought together to define the Glacier Park experience revealed the components of a myth of America that was meant to reconcile the conflicts of a nation struggling to define itself. In this manner, the Great Northern popularized the "See America First" idea.

The period between 1914 and 1917 marked a pivotal moment for the establishment of "See America First" as a generic tourist slogan. In July of 1914 the outbreak of war stranded 150,000 Americans in Europe.[40] The war effectively closed Europe to American tourists. Simultaneously, it intensified the discourse of patriotism and loyalty in the United States.[41] In the context of this rising fervor of patriotism, "See America First" transcended its ties to the Great Northern Railway and Glacier National Park and emerged as a popular touring slogan celebrating the possibilities of touring throughout the American West. Seeing America first, in essence, not only became an expression of economic nationalism, as in "Buy American," it also served to juxtapose an idealized and untainted America with a destitute Europe. The West was central to this image. An editorial in *Collier's* magazine promoting the "See America First" idea explained that it was the patriotic duty of American citizens to see the wonders of their own country.[42] Similarly, the secretary of the interior, Franklin K. Lane, likened the "See America First" idea to a kind of "preparedness" for American scenery.[43] In this atmosphere, "See America First" took on some of the tenor of reactionary patriotism.

Promoters for the Panama-Pacific International Exposition in 1915 were quick to seize the "See America First" idea to promote the exposition.[44] Opening in the wake of the closing of European borders, the exposition provided American tourist industries and organizations with a podium from which to proclaim the possibilities of touring in America. After Congress recognized San Francisco as the official site for the 1915 fair, Charles C. Moore, president of the Panama-Pacific International Exposition, extolled the significance of San Francisco as a site in relation to the rest of the nation. In the tradition of the "See America First" idea, he wrote, "I know men who have never been west of Buffalo, New York, yet who go frequently to Europe, perhaps once a year. Such men would become better citizens of this country were they to see the West." He went on to explain, "In the choice of a western city as the exposition site the educational advantage of a trip across the continent was one of the impellingly favorable factors, and it is undeniable that the lure of the West will be the magnet that will draw tens of thousands to whom the Exposition will be merely incidental, an exciting cause for greater experience." According to Moore, Yellowstone, the Grand Canyon, Yosemite, Alaska, and even a voyage through the newly opened Panama Canal would "be some of the great educational features by which those who visit the Exposition will have the opportunity to learn of their own country under the most enjoyable conditions and at a minimum of cost."[45] If one had to pick a moment at which touring the United States (rather than Europe) became fashionable, this was the moment.

The use of "See America First" by exposition promoters and exhibitors suggested that the "true" America could be seen in western scenery, where the promise of nature, representing both divine sanction of an American empire and the wealth of natural resources supporting that empire, offered an inspiring alternative to the decaying civilization of the Old World. The major transcontinental railroads all contributed elaborate displays to the exposition, glorifying the scenic wonders along their lines. In addition, a number of railroads including the Union Pacific and the Santa Fe set up concessions in the commercial section of the fair, marketing a re-created touring experience for fair-goers. The Union Pacific went so far as to reconstruct "the most noted objects in [Yellowstone] park," including Eagle Nest Rock, the Hot Spring Terraces, the Great Falls of the Yellowstone, the Old Faithful Geyser, and finally, the "crowning feature," a reproduction of the Old Faithful Inn.[46] Similarly, the Santa Fe constructed a model of the Grand Canyon for fair-goers to explore. The model reproduced to scale "a trip of 200 hundred miles in length through a gorge thirteen miles across from rim to rim, 8000 feet deep . . . omitting no essential feature from the panorama." In addition to the replica of the El Tovar Hotel situated at the entrance to the concession, there was also a model village of Pueblo Indians, depicting "The Life of a Vanishing Race."[47]

In popularizing "See America First," the Panama-Pacific Exposition helped to establish not only the American attractions that were to be seen, but also the context in which they were to be understood. Guidebooks, in combination with the scenic reproductions such as those of the Grand Canyon and Yellowstone, as well as displays of lantern slides, moving pictures, photographs, and paintings, touted emerging tourist sites across the West. To "See America First" as directed by Panama-Pacific officials and exhibitors was to see those natural landscapes of the West that had been deemed sublime, scenic, or extraordinary. These dramatic western landscapes reinforced the central ideology of the exposition, which celebrated the United States as an increasingly powerful, imperial nation. In commemorating the completion of the Panama Canal, the exposition sought to position the United States in a larger narrative of progress that essentially built on the "westward the course of empire" ideal. As Robert Rydell has explained, the fair "sought to preserve people's faith in the idea of progress—with all its interlaced connotations of technological advance, material growth, racism, and imperialism—and to reshape that faith with a particular reference to the challenges posed by domestic and international turmoil."[48] The western tourist attractions celebrated at the fair were meant to provide physical proof of this emerging American empire.

While the Panama-Pacific Exposition was using "See America First" to promote tourism in the West as a patriotic ideal, the Lincoln Highway Association had also adopted the slogan to encourage the novel idea of automobile touring along its proposed transcontinental road, which ran from New York City to Chicago, along the Platte River to Salt Lake City, and on to Cheyenne, Wyoming, and Reno, Nevada, finally traversing California via Sacramento and reaching its final destination in San Francisco.[49] In a pamphlet entitled *Following the Path of Progress*, A. R. Pardington, vice president of the Lincoln Highway Association, detailed the progress made on the highway in its first year and encouraged automobile tourists to use the new highway to "See America First."[50] Pardington argued that the experience of automobile touring along the Lincoln Highway offered scenery, roads, and places of historic interest that equaled or surpassed the possibilities of touring in Europe. "From New York to San Francisco," he explained, "the tourist over the Lincoln Highway is treated to a moving, ever-changing panorama of beauty and interest; he traces the footsteps of the pioneer and follows the path of the frontier as it moved ever westward." In this way tourists came in contact with "a cross section of America; her people, her thousand interests, her tradition, her history, her beauty, her resources, her magnitude, her power." West of Chicago, tourists could experience the "memories of early days" such as the tragic adventure of the Donner party who perished trying to reach California, the fortitude of the forty-niners, the bravery of stage drivers and Indian fighters, and "the thrilling adventures of these hardy men who formed the vanguard of civilization in laying the Union Pacific."[51] Traveling by automobile along the Lincoln Highway, according to Pardington, brought tourists face to face with American history.

In the spring of 1915 Newton A. Fuessle reiterated these themes in a series of three articles he wrote for *Travel* magazine detailing the possibilities for touring on the Lincoln Highway.[52] Using the chaos of the European war as a backdrop, Fuessle noted that Americans were finally beginning to discover the wonders of their own country. "The tremendous significance which the whirl of sinister developments in Europe's theater of war has given to the 'See America First' movement, has clothed the project of the Lincoln Highway Association with singular importance," he explained. The highway brought tourists to the heart of America—"its life and manners, history and traditions, hopes and dreams and ambitions, its multitude of interests, its tangle of industries, its wealth of resource, power, color and endless beauties." The highway not only revealed America's rich past, but also displayed its promising future. It objectified America as a nation: "Teaching patriotism, sewing up the remaining ragged edges of sectionalism, revealing and interpreting America to its people, giving swifter feet to commerce, gathering up the country's loose ends of desultory and disjointed good roads [with] ardor and binding them into one highly organized, proficient unit of dynamic, result-getting force, electric with zeal, it is quickening American neighborliness, democracy, progress and civilization." In his survey of the highway, Fuessle described in detail the route of the Lincoln Highway and the unique sights and experiences the tourist could anticipate, arguing that only through this firsthand experience of automobile touring made possible by the Lincoln Highway could the tourist come to truly understand America. He wrote, "One may whirl across the continent a score of times as a railway passenger and never sense the slightest fraction of the feeling of nearness to the States and cities traversed"; in contrast, he explained, "The Highway affords an incomparable inspirational course in Americanism."[53]

Fuessle perhaps most clearly defined the significance of "See America First" as it was used by the Lincoln Highway Association. Transcontinental automobile touring allowed tourists to move beyond the simple act of viewing, to actually experience both history and nature. Not only did the automobile allow the individual to exercise complete control over the touring experience, thus gaining a more intimate interaction with the people and places across America, but also the emerging road network vastly increased the number of potential tourist attractions. In effect the automobile completely transformed the tourist experience. In contrast to viewing the landscape cinematically as it flashed by the train window, the automobile brought the tourist into the landscape. From the perspective of the automobile, tourists could not only admire the scenic views and vistas as they had from the train window, they could also stop and explore. They could vicariously experience the people and places of America. Thus, as automobile touring became increasingly popular after World War I, prescriptive literature publicizing the landscapes of tourism began to promote historic sites, places associated with historic events, and the local color of particular places, in addition to the scenic attractions typically associated with railroad tourism. Touring came to be understood as a much more intimate, personal, and authentic experience. Prescriptive material promoting automobile touring underscored this notion of authenticity, focusing on firsthand experience. Using the rhetoric of "See America First," organizations such as the Lincoln Highway Association argued that an extensive network of good roads not only served to physically bind America into a united nation, but also worked to promote a shared national identity by manifesting a cross section of the "real" America for the tourist to experience firsthand. That "real" America, according to the Lincoln Highway Association, was to be found in touring the West—retracing the westward course of history.[54]

Building on this wave of popularity for "See America First," the National Park Service also embraced the slogan, giving it the official sanction of the national government and thus completing the transformation from western booster slogan to popular tourist emblem. As the Park Service's official motto, "See America First" came to embody an established relationship between tourism and national identity that moved beyond the concerns of private organizations or corporations interested in defining a national clientele. In this manifestation "See America First" defined a ritual of citizenship.

In the fall of 1914, as plans for the Panama-Pacific Exposition began to solidify, Secretary Lane initiated a campaign to develop and publicize the national parks, especially Yosemite so that it might be ready for the crowds that would arrive in San Francisco for the exposition.[55] Lane turned to a former University of California classmate, millionaire Stephen Tyng Mather, to launch this new publicity and development campaign.[56] In January of 1915 Mather was sworn in as assistant secretary of the interior. Lane charged him with the task of establishing "a business administration" to manage the fourteen existing national parks and the eighteen existing national monuments.[57] Mather began by organizing an extensive publicity campaign for the parks, building on the "See America First" idea.

The Third Annual National Parks Conference held at the University of California in Berkeley during the Panama-Pacific Exposition initiated this national parks publicity campaign. In his introductory speech, Mather articulated his ideas about the necessity for park publicity. "The parks," he said, "must be, of course, much better known that [sic] they are to-day if they are going to be the true playgrounds of the people that we want them to be. There is much that can be done in making them better known. There are many ways in which they can be brought home to the great mass of eastern people." Those at the conference agreed that "the policy of the present Administration to exploit the move to 'see America first' is a step in the right direction, and should be commended by the American public to the extent that they will make it their duty as well as their pleasure to assist in this patriotic movement."[58]

Mather hired Robert Sterling Yard "to work up a nationwide publicity campaign" to "get the people behind the parks."[59] Yard, who had worked with Mather on the *New York Sun* and later edited *Century* magazine and the Sunday edition of the *New York Herald*, was hired as the national parks publicity chief.[60] Although Yard was a self-admitted "tenderfoot" when it came to western wilderness, he proceeded to organize a park publicity bureau.[61] He began gathering information about travel to foreign countries and the promotion of tourist sights and then set out to tour the parks, gathering "information about our own scenic resources." On his return he established a national parks news service and began writing articles for magazines, issuing press bulletins, and "encourag[ing] the preparation of publicity material by everybody in and out of government who had talents to be exploited."[62]

Yard's research and travels culminated in two important publications published in 1916 that promoted the parks under the rubric of "See America First": the *National Parks Portfolio*, an expensive picture book, and a less expensive pamphlet, *Glimpses of Our National Parks*.[63] The portfolio was composed of a series of pamphlets describing Yellowstone, Yosemite, Sequoia, Mount Rainier, Crater Lake, Mesa Verde, Glacier, and Rocky Mountain, the most prominent national parks, in addition to one on Grand Canyon National Monument. Each park description was illustrated by a number of dramatic photographs, interspersed with brief tables providing an overview of all the parks, and bound together in an expensive cloth folder. The book came out in the midst of the congressional debate over the National Park Service Bill, and every member of Congress received a copy. In total, 275,000 copies were distributed by the U.S. government free of charge to a select list of recipients considered as potential park supporters. *Glimpses of Our National Parks* was simply a scaled-down version of the *National Parks Portfolio* geared toward the tourist.[64]

Both the *National Parks Portfolio* and *Glimpses of Our National Parks* were meant to educate the American people about the "wonders" of their own country, to instill a scenic patriotism that would unite the touring public in support of the national parks. In his preface to the portfolio Mather drew on the established "See America First" argument. "This Nation is richer in natural scenery of the first order than any other nation," he wrote, "but it does not know it. . . . In its national parks it has neglected, because it has quite overlooked, an economic asset of incalculable value." He went on to explain, "The main object of this portfolio, therefore is to present to the people of this country a panorama of our principal national parks. . . . Each park will be found highly individual. The whole will be a revelation." Mather noted that this was the first "representative presentation of American scenery of grandeur" to be published, and he dedicated it to the American people. "It is my great hope," he concluded, "that it will serve to turn the busy eyes of the Nation upon its national parks long enough to bring some realization of what these pleasure gardens ought to mean, of what so easily they may be made to mean, to this people." Essentially, Mather was encouraging greater recognition of the western landscapes enshrined by the parks, and in this way his publicity campaign represented another version of "See America First" that centered on promoting the West.

The *National Parks Portfolio* functioned as a catalogue of the parks, displaying, codifying, and enumerating the dramatic natural landscapes that the government had set aside as "playgrounds for the people." The colorful descriptions of the eight major western parks and the Grand Canyon—combined with more than two hundred photographs of mountain views, lakes and waterfalls, glaciers, wild animals, and rustic hotels—stated that the national parks embodied a physical experience that promised "thrills . . . never before experienced," "fairyland and the awe of infinity," "romantic Indian legend," along with health and peacefulness. Each section detailed the spectacles of one park, providing information on scenic character, the geological formations, wildlife, the Indians if applicable, and park accommodations.

The purpose of the portfolio was to establish the parks as national assets, making them valuable national property rather than simply land set aside by the national government and thus designated as "unusable." It accomplished this by presenting the parks as ceremonial landscapes, icons of the nation.[65] Written descriptions celebrated the "sublimity" of the park landscapes, suggesting that they had the ability to inspire and uplift. The many photographs captured scenic views from their most alluring perspective, transforming the natural landscape into pristine iconographic images. In a number of the photographs, solitary viewers or groups of sightseers were pictured surveying the landscape, in effect worshipping the natural icons that embodied the nation. In each section the text reasserted that the parks not only promised an "unrivaled" experience, but also were valuable for their natural formations, which allowed for the firsthand study of nature. As Secretary Lane wrote, they were "the public laboratories of nature study for the Nation."

Most important, they belonged to "the people." As landscapes administered by the U.S. government it was necessary that they embody the democratic imperative of the nation. At the end of each descriptive section readers were reminded that the national parks belonged to them. However, it was clear that the imagined tourists, as evidenced by the photographs, were white upper- and middle-class Americans who could afford to travel by train or automobile and spend a week or more vacationing in the parks. In promoting the national parks, the portfolio gave official government sanction to the preservation of western scenery. But the justification for preservation was based not so much on the aesthetic or intrinsic value of nature as on the educational and nationalizing value of scenic western landscapes.[66]

Like the portfolio, *Glimpses of Our National Parks* sought to establish the value of national parks as national assets. "The national parks, unlike the national forests, are not properties in a commercial sense, but natural preserves for the rest, recreation, and education of the people. They remain under nature's own chosen conditions. They alone maintain 'the forest primeval,'" wrote Yard. In separating the parks from the realm of commerce, *Glimpses of Our National Parks* defined their value in other terms, most notably through their potential to educate. Yard encouraged tourists to explore the national parks: to go "hunting . . . with a camera in Yellowstone," to study the formation of glaciers in Mount Rainier, to ponder the development of prehistoric civilizations in Mesa Verde, or to consider Major John Wesley Powell's "perilous passage" in the Grand Canyon. The dramatic land formations, the ancient Indian ruins, the giant trees, and the volcanic and glacial phenomena all revealed nature in its "pristine" form, untouched by man. In stating that the value of the parks rested on their "extraordinary scenic beauty" and "remarkable phenomenon," Yard set up an implicit opposition between nature as represented in the parks, and the ordinary built and natural environment. He also attempted to define the preserved nature of the parks in terms of highbrow culture; his celebration of the educational value of dramatic western landscapes of the parks and his promotion of nature study raised the national parks to a level above the crass concerns of commercialism and the cheap amusements of common tourist attractions. "Every person living in the United States," Yard wrote, "ought to know about these eight national parks and ought to visit them when possible, for, considered together, they contain more features of conspicuous grandeur than are readily accessible in all the rest of the world."[67] Building on a long-established national mythology that identified America as "nature's nation," Yard essentially argued that the natural landscapes embodied in the national parks evinced America's greatness.[68]

Mather supplemented and further spread Yard's publicity work through a series of well-advertised park tours, speaking to chambers of commerce, wilderness groups, automobile associations, and other interested organizations to disseminate his ideas about developing the parks and making them more accessible to the American people.[69] He met with railroad representatives to negotiate reduced rates, suggesting that they issue "park tour tickets which [would] enable tourists to buy tickets at the starting point for a definite tour of national parks, all accommodations paid for and arranged in advance." Moreover, he asked the railroads to include information about the parks in their tourist brochures.[70] He also supported the formation of a national park-to-park highway. In addition, Mather cultivated valuable working relationships with both Gilbert Grosvenor, editor of the *National Geographic* magazine, and George Horace Lorimer, editor of the *Saturday Evening Post*. These connections ensured a constant flow of park publicity.[71]

In 1918 the administrative policy for the newly established National Park Service was outlined in an official letter from the secretary of the interior to Mather. In defining the criteria for the creation of new national parks, the letter stated that the Park Service should seek out "scenery of supreme and distinctive quality or some natural feature so extraordinary or unique as to be of national interest or importance." Not only did these guidelines set the criteria for the establishment of new national parks, but they also defined the value of existing parks. The national park system, according to the 1918 annual report of the secretary of the interior, "constituted one of America's greatest national assets."[72] This celebration of the dramatic natural scenery of the West, the remains of ancient civilizations, and pristine wilderness—the landscapes embraced by the parks—moved beyond the rhetoric of economic nationalism to express an ideal of nationhood. By focusing on wilderness, scenery, and ruins, park publicity glorified not the commercial and industrial developments that were catapulting the United States to world power but the natural landscapes and ancient ruins of the West that were symbolic of America's origins. The essence of American identity, according to the narrative of nationalism constructed by the Park Service, rested primarily in western wilderness, landscapes once inhabited by more primitive civilizations but then left untouched by modern development, still symbolizing the bounty of American nature. These unique landscapes embodied the wilderness of the North American continent that had helped to forge a distinct American nation.[73] Thus, by the early 1920s the National Park Service had established itself as a primary supporter of the "See America First" idea, and the national parks—which at this time were concentrated in the western United States—had become not only the nation's preeminent tourist attractions, but also the nation's quintessential landscapes.

"See America First" as defined by the National Park Service gave official sanction to the slogan and in the process consummated the growing popularity of domestic, or more specifically, western tourism. To "See America First" in the national parks was to witness American wilderness firsthand, to come to know the American land, and thus to become a better citizen. In promoting the national parks, the Park Service was essentially advocating a kind of secular pilgrimage where tourists could actually see and experience the nation's shrines and thereby reaffirm their love of country and their connection to the nation.[74] In this way, the official sanction of the government also served to legitimize the inherent patriotism of "See America First" and define an organic nationalism that linked the nation to an idealized territory or homeland. American scenery, specifically national park wilderness located primarily in the western United States, came to stand for the essence of America.

The story of the "See America First" slogan is the story not only about the development of tourism in the West, but also about the negotiation of national identity as connected with the natural landscapes of the West. From western booster slogan to corporate motto to national emblem, "See America First" articulated a series of shifting concerns connected with the emergence of America as a modern nation-state. On the surface, the development of tourism in the West embodied the process of nation building at the level of popular and commercial culture. Tourism—as a leisure activity tied not only to the emergence of a leisure class and a leisure ethic, but also to the transportation and communications revolutions of the turn of the century—perhaps best manifested the possibilities and desires of this emerging consumer culture.

At a deeper level, the messages and meanings that emerged around "See America First" to define western tourism reflect a broader dia-

logue concerning the relationship of the West as region to this emerging nation-state. In the vocabulary of tourism, this dialogue revolved
around the actual and symbolic values of dramatic western landscapes.
An ambiguous national ideal emerged out of the cultural practice of
tourism as defined by the various invocations of "See America First."

Pristine yet domesticated nature came to symbolize the promise of
America as a nation. On the one hand, nature represented the abundant resources bestowed by God on America—resources capable of
fueling a vast empire—and tourism offered a new means of tapping
into those resources. On the other hand, nature represented a conflicted
ideal of an area of free land that could sustain America as virtuous
republican empire, as well as a place for therapeutic escape where the
self could be reinvigorated and patriotism could be rekindled; in this
sense tourism offered a means of preserving those sacred spaces. This
contradictory celebration of nature as resource (progress and commerce)
and nature as safety valve (preservation) reveals an ambivalence about
the emergence of the United States as a modern, corporate nation-state.

In expressing the regional concerns of an insecure West, in defining the consumption of western scenery as a patriotic act, and in sec-
tioning off and elevating that scenery to the status of sacred national
space, various "See America First" advocates sought to capitalize on
western scenery while simultaneously masking the commercial and
corporate underpinnings of their actions. Western boosters, railroad
executives, tourist advocates, and National Park Service administra-
tors used "See America First" in an effort to reap the benefits of western tourism, and in the process they embraced the broad structural
changes that were transforming American society. In this sense, the
scenery of the West became just one more commodity to be mined,
marketed, and exported. But these constituencies simultaneously used
"See America First" to define and legitimate their own visions of America
as nation. In this guise, western scenery symbolized an ideal of the
nation grounded in a nostalgic republican tradition that linked pristine
nature with an ideal of virtuous citizenship. From this perspective, nature as represented by dramatic western landscapes had to be protected
from the ravages of commercialization.

This tension between commerce and preservation expressed through the evolving invocations of "See America First" reveals the ideological process of nation building. The modern nation-state extended from the technological, the economic, and the social infrastructure that began to solidify in fin de siècle America. But cultural nationalism grew out of a nostalgic ideal of America as nature's nation. The tourist's West offered the potential of containing both.

Notes

1. Samuel Bowles, *Across the Continent: A Summer's Journey to the Rocky Mountains, the Mormons and the Pacific States* (Springfield, Mass.: Samuel Bowles & Co., 1866), pp. 1–2.

2. Robert H. Wiebe, *The Search for Order, 1877–1920* (New York: Hill and Wang, 1967); Alan Trachtenberg, *The Incorporation of America: Culture and Society of the Gilded Age* (New York: Hill and Wang, 1982); Nell Irvin Painter, *Standing at Armageddon: The United States, 1877–1919* (New York: Norton, 1987).

3. Dona Brown, *Inventing New England: Regional Tourism in the Nineteenth Century* (Washington, D.C.: Smithsonian Institution Press, 1995); M. H. Dunlop, *Sixty Miles from Contentment: Traveling the Nineteenth-Century American Interior* (New York: Basic Books, 1995); John F. Sears, *Sacred Places: American Tourist Attractions in the Nineteenth Century* (New York: Oxford University Press, 1989).

4. A number of people, the most notable of whom are Louis W. Hill and Charles Lummis, claimed authorship of the "See America First" slogan. Both men's claims as originators of the slogan were so successful that historians have reinforced these claims. For examples see Anne Farrar Hyde, *An American Vision: Far Western Landscape and National Culture, 1820–1920* (New York: New York University Press, 1990), pp. 284–286; Alfred Runte, "Pragmatic Alliance: Western Railroads and the National Parks," *National Parks and Conservation Magazine* 48 (April 1974):14–21; Alfred Runte, *National Parks: The American Experience,* 2nd ed. (Lincoln: University of Nebraska Press, 1987), pp. 82–105; Dudley C. Gordon, *Charles F. Lummis: Crusader in Corduroy* (Los Angeles: Cultural Assets Press, 1972), pp. 133, 149–156; Michael Kammen, *Mystic Chords of Memory: The Transformation of Tradition in American Culture* (New York: Vintage Books, 1993), p. 276. For a complete overview of the history of the "See America First" slogan see Marguerite S. Shaffer, "See America First: Tourism and National Identity, 1905–1930," Ph.D. diss., Harvard University, 1994.

5. "Real Work Has Only Now Begun," *Salt Lake Tribune,* January 28, 1906.

6. "Governors, Delegates Welcome!" *Salt Lake Tribune,* January 26, 1906.

7. Clipping, *Salt Lake City Telegram,* October 24, 1905, Scrapbook III, and Salt Lake City Commercial Club to Whomever, October 24, 1905, Scrapbook III. Fisher Sanford Harris Manuscripts, Special Collections, Perkins Library, Duke Uni-

versity, Durham, N.C. (hereafter cited as Harris MSS). For a history of Fisher Harris's use of "See America First," see Marguerite S. Shaffer, "See America First: Re-Envisioning Nation and Region through Western Tourism," *Pacific Historical Review* 65 (November 1996):559–581.

8. C. F. Carter to Salt Lake City Commercial Club, October 19, 1905, Scrapbook II, 1905–1906, Harris MSS.

9. *The "See America First" Conference, Salt Lake City, Utah, January 25–26, 1906* (Salt Lake City: Tribune Job Printing Co., 1906), pp. 9 and 12–13.

10. Robert G. Athearn, *The Mythic West in Twentieth-Century America* (Lawrence: University of Kansas Press, 1986); Donald Worster, "New West, True West: Interpreting the Region's History," *Western Historical Quarterly* 18 (April 1987):141–156; Richard Slotkin, *The Fatal Environment: The Myth of Frontier in the Age of Industrialization* (New York: Atheneum, 1985); William H. Truettner, ed., *The West as America: Reinterpreting Images of the Frontier* (Washington, D.C.: Smithsonian Institution Press, 1991).

11. For a discussion of the economic relationship between the West and the nation see William G. Robbins, *Colony and Empire: The Capitalist Transformation of the American West* (Lawrence: University of Kansas Press, 1994). For arguments that the West was not a "colonial economy" of the northeastern industrial core see Gene M. Gressley, "Colonialism: A Western Complaint," *Pacific Northwest Quarterly* 54 (1963):1–8; Leonard J. Arrington and Thomas G. Alexander, *A Dependent Commonwealth: Utah's Economy from Statehood to the Great Depression,* ed. Dean L. May (Provo, Utah: Brigham Young University, 1974). For an alternative interpretation see Timothy W. Luke, "Internal Colonialism in the American Mountain West: A Preliminary Study," *Southwest Economy and Society* 5 (summer 1981):28–50.

12. "Great Move to Promote the West," *Salt Lake Tribune,* April 5, 1906.

13. Fisher Harris, "Are the People of the East Growing Effete?" *Western Monthly,* June 1909, p. 8.

14. Fisher Harris, "Europe vs. America," *Western Monthly,* December 1908, p. 15.

15. Clipping, *Los Angeles Arrowhead,* December 1905, Scrapbook III, Harris MSS.

16. For applications of republican theory and rhetoric in defining America into the twentieth century see Dorothy Ross, "The Liberal Tradition Revisited and the Republican Tradition Addressed," in John Higham and Paul Conkin, eds., *New Directions in American Intellectual History* (Baltimore: Johns Hopkins University Press, 1977), pp. 116–131; T. J. Jackson Lears, *No Place of Grace: Antimodernism and the Transformation of American Culture, 1880–1920* (New York: Pantheon, 1981); T. J. Jackson Lears, "From Salvation to Self-Realization: Advertising and the Therapeutic Roots of the Consumer Culture, 1880-1930," in Richard Wightman Fox and T. J. Jackson Lears, eds., *The Culture of Consumption: Critical Essays in American History, 1880-1980* (New York: Pantheon, 1983), pp. 3–38.

17. Parely P. Jenson, "Current Comments and Announcements," *Western Monthly,* December 1908, p. 87.

18. "To Advertise Glacier National Park," *St. Paul Pioneer Press Dispatch,* May 26, 1910.

19. Clipping, Herbert J. Smith, "Booming a New National Park," *Printer's Ink,* enclosure in H. A. Noble to L. W. Hill, June 17, 1910, President's Office Subject Files: Publicity, File 4325. Great Northern Railway Records, Minnesota Historical Society, St. Paul (hereafter cited as GNRR).

20. "To Advertise Glacier National Park."

21. Michael J. Ober, "Enmity and Alliance: Park Service–Concessioner Relations in Glacier National Park, 1892–1916," master's thesis, University of Montana, 1973; James W. Sheire, *Glacier National Park: Historic Resource Study* (Washington, D.C.: National Park Service, Office of History and Historic Architecture Eastern Service Center, 1970); Alan S. Newell, David Walterm, and James R. McDonald, *Historic Resource Study, Glacier National Park and Historic Structures Survey* (Denver: National Park Service, Denver Service Center, 1980).

22. *Hotels and Tours: Glacier National Park* (Great Northern Railway, 1914), p. 6. Railroads, Warshaw Collection of Business Americana, National Museum of American History Archives Center, Smithsonian Institution, Washington, D.C. (hereafter cited as Warshaw Railroad Papers).

23. *See America First: The Great Northwest Annotated Time Table* (Great Northern Railway, 1916), p. 63, Advertising and Publicity Department: Advertising Literature, File 4551, GNRR.

24. *Glacier National Park* (Great Northern Railway, 1915), n.p., Glacier National Park Company: Histories and Related Records, File 5, GNRR.

25. John Willy, "A Week in Glacier National Park," *Hotel Monthly,* August 1915, pp. 45–48.

26. David Thelen, "Memory and American History," *Journal of American History* 75 (March 1989):1117–1129; Eric Hobsbawm, "Introduction: Inventing Traditions," in Eric Hobsbawm and Terence Ranger, eds., *The Invention of Tradition* (Cambridge, U.K.: Cambridge University Press, 1983); David Lowenthal, "The Place of the Past in the American Landscape," in David Lowenthal and Martyn J. Bow, eds., *Geographies of the Mind* (New York: Oxford University Press, 1976).

27. Mark David Spence, "Crown of the Continent, Backbone of the World: The American Wilderness Ideal and Blackfeet Exclusion from Glacier National Park," *Environmental History* 1 (July 1996):29–49; Brian Reeves and Sandy Peacock, *"Our Mountains Are Our Pillows": An Ethnographic Overview of Glacier National Park* (Denver: National Park Service, Denver Service Center, 1995).

28. "A Report on Glacier National Park for Season 1913," from J. A. Shoemaker to L. W. Hill, C. R. Gray, W. P. Kenney, October 7, 1913, President's Subject Files: Chairman's File Glacier Park Publicity, File 4, GNRR.

29. L. W. Hill to W. P. Kenney, June 3, 1914, President's Subject Files: Publicity, File 4325, GNRR.

30. *Walking Tours: Glacier National Park* (Great Northern Railway, 1914), n.p., Warshaw Railroad Papers.

31. *Hotels and Tours: Glacier National Park,* p. 30.

32. Fred K. Leland to Louis W. Hill, March 27, 1911; Fred K. Leland to Louis Hill, February 16, 1911; Robert C. Auld, "The Alpine House: Distinctive Type in

Spite of Many Mangled Reproductions in This Country," *Arts and Decoration,* enclosure in Walter A. Johnson to James B. Hill, March 21, 1911. Letters in President's Office Subject Files: Advertising 1903–1916, File 3903, GNRR.

33. H. H. Parkhouse to W. R. Mills, May 29, 1914; W. R. Mills to H. H. Parkhouse, June 19, 1914; H. H. Parkhouse to W. R. Mills, June 22, 1914. Letters in President's Subject Files: Publicity, File 4325, GNRR.

34. Carlos Schwantes, *Railroad Signatures across the Pacific Northwest* (Seattle: University of Washington Press, 1993), pp. 157 and 209–213.

35. Shaffer, "See America First," pp. 105–115.

36. Painter, *Standing at Armageddon;* John Higham, *Strangers in the Land: Patterns of American Nativism, 1860–1925* (New York: Atheneum, 1985).

37. Emily Bayne Bosson to Louis Hill, August 21, 1921. L. W. Hill Papers, James J. Hill Reference Library, St. Paul, Minn. (hereafter cited as L. W. Hill Papers).

38. For examples of other railroad corporations that embraced this tactic see Alfred Runte, "Promoting Wonderland: Western Railroads and the Evolution of National Park Advertising," *Journal of the West* 31 (January 1992):43–48; Runte, "Pragmatic Alliance."

39. Richard Slotkin, "Nostalgia and Progress: Theodore Roosevelt's Myth of the Frontier," *American Quarterly* 33 (winter 1981):608–637; G. Edward White, *The Eastern Establishment and the Western Experience: The West of Frederic Remington, Theodore Roosevelt, and Owen Wister* (New Haven, Conn.: Yale University Press, 1968), pp. 185–202.

40. John A. Jakle, *The Tourist: Travel in Twentieth Century North America* (Lincoln: University of Nebraska Press, 1985), p. 102.

41. For discussion of American nationalism during World War I see Higham, *Strangers in the Land,* pp. 194–233; Philip Gleason, "American Identity and Americanization," in *Concepts of Ethnicity* (Cambridge, Mass.: Belknap Press, 1982), pp. 80–109; David M. Kennedy, *Over Here: The First World War and American Society* (New York: Oxford University Press, 1980), pp. 37–38. For a discussion of how advertisers adopted the language of nationalism to sell products see Charles F. McGovern, "Sold American: Inventing the Consumer, 1890–1940," Ph.D. diss., Harvard University, 1993.

42. "See America First," *Collier's,* October 31, 1914, n.p.

43. Robert Sterling Yard, "Director of the Nation's Playgrounds," *Sunset,* September 1916, p. 27.

44. Burton Benedict, *The Anthropology of World's Fairs: San Francisco's Panama Pacific International Exposition of 1915* (Berkeley, Calif.: Scholar Press, 1983); Robert W. Rydell, *All the World's a Fair* (Chicago: University of Chicago Press, 1984).

45. Charles C. Moore, "San Francisco and the Exposition: The Relation of the City to the Nation as Regards the World's Fair," *Sunset,* February 1912, p. 198.

46. *California and the Expositions, 1915* (Union Pacific System, 1915), pp. 16–19, Panama-Pacific International Exposition, Reel 169, no. 6. Worlds Fairs Microfilm Collection, National Museum of American History, Smithsonian Institution, Washington, D.C. (hereafter cited as Worlds Fairs Microfilm Coll.).

47. Robert A. Reid, *The Blue Book: A Comprehensive Official Souvenir View Book of the Panama-Pacific International Exposition at San Francisco*, 2nd ed. (Panama-Pacific Exposition Company, 1915), p. 312, Panama-Pacific International Exposition, Reel 169, no. 4, Worlds Fairs Microfilm Coll.; Guy Richard Kingsley, "Progress of America's Great Panama Canal Celebration," *Overland Monthly*, October 1914, p. 6; Hamilton Wright, "The Panama-Pacific Exposition in Its Glorious Prime," *Overland Monthly*, October 1915, p. 297; Rydell, *All the World's a Fair*, pp. 227–228.

48. Rydell, *All the World's a Fair*, p. 219.

49. Drake Hokanson, *The Lincoln Highway: Main Street across America* (Iowa City: University of Iowa Press, 1988); Lincoln Highway Association, *The Lincoln Highway: The Story of a Crusade That Made Transportation History* (New York: Dodd, Mead & Co., 1935).

50. *Following the Path of Progress* (Detroit: Lincoln Highway Association, 1914). U.S. Department of Transportation Library Manuscripts, Department of Transportation, Washington, D.C. (hereafter cited as DOT MSS). Selections of this essay were reprinted in the *American Motorist* and attributed to A. R. Pardington; see A. R. Pardington, "Following the Path of Progress," *American Motorist*, January 1915, pp. 28–29.

51. *Following the Path of Progress*, p. 2. See also *The Complete Official Road Guide of the Lincoln Highway* (Detroit: Lincoln Highway Association, 1915).

52. Newton A. Fuessle, "The Lincoln Highway—A National Road," *Travel*, February 1915, pp. 26–29; March 1915, pp. 30–33, 57; April 1915, pp. 30–33.

53. Fuessle, "Lincoln Highway," February 1915, p. 26.

54. For discussions of nationalist ideologies based on the notion of possessive individualism see Richard Handler, "Authenticity," *Anthropology Today* 2 (February 1986):2–4; Richard Handler, "On Having a Culture: Nationalism and the Preservation of Quebec's 'Patrimonie,'" in George W. Stocking, Jr., ed., *Objects and Others: Essays on Museums and Material Culture* (Madison: University of Wisconsin Press, 1985), pp. 192–217.

55. Robert Sterling Yard, "Historical Basis of National Parks Standards," *National Parks Bulletin*, November 1929, p. 3. U.S. National Park Service, Stephen Tyng Mather Papers, Bancroft Library, University of California, Berkeley (hereafter cited as Mather MSS).

56. Robert Shankland, *Steve Mather of the National Parks*, 3rd ed. (New York: Knopf, 1970); Donald C. Swain, *Wilderness Defender: Horace M. Albright and Conservation* (Chicago: University of Chicago Press, 1970); Horace M. Albright and Robert Cahn, *The Birth of the National Park Service: The Founding Years, 1913–33* (Chicago: Howe Brothers, 1985); John Ise, *Our National Park Policy: A Critical History* (Baltimore: Johns Hopkins University Press, 1961); Hal Rothman, *Preserving Different Pasts: The American National Monuments* (Chicago: University of Illinois Press, 1989), pp. 89–118.

57. Stephen Tyng Mather, "The National Parks on a Business Basis," *American Review of Reviews*, April 1915, p. 429.

58. *Proceedings of the National Parks Conference, Berkeley, California, March 11, 12 and 13, 1915* (Washington, D.C.: Government Printing Office, 1915), pp.

11, 79. See also "Heads of National Parks Are to Meet," *San Francisco Examiner,* February 15, 1915; "To Make the Parks People's Own," *Los Angeles Times,* March 8, 1915; "National Park Chief Opens Sessions To-Day," unidentified clipping; "Steps Taken to Make U.S. Parks More Accessible," *Christian Science Monitor,* March 18, 1915. Scrapbook, vol. 4, Clippings Re Public Official Career, 1915–1916, Mather MSS.

59. Robert Sterling Yard, "Historical Basis of National Parks Standards," p. 3, U.S. National Park Service, carton 1, Mather MSS.

60. Shankland, *Steve Mather of the National Parks,* p. 59.

61. *Proceedings of the National Park Conference,* p. 151.

62. Horace M. Albright, "Making the Parks Known to the People," *Living Wilderness,* December 1945, p. 6, S. T. Mather Clippings, carton 1; "World Will Be Told of State's Wonder," *Rocky Mountain News,* September 3, 1915, Scrapbook, vol. 9, Personal Clippings, 1915–1929. Mather MSS.

63. U.S. Department of the Interior, *The National Parks Portfolio* (New York: Scribners, 1916) and *Glimpses of Our National Parks* (Washington, D.C.: Government Printing Office, 1916).

64. Albright, "Making the Parks Known to the People"; Ise, *Our National Park Policy,* p. 196; Shankland, *Steve Mather of the National Parks,* pp. 97–98; Swain, *Wilderness Defender,* pp. 57–58.

65. Kenneth A. Erickson, "Ceremonial Landscapes of the American West," *Landscape* 22 (autumn 1977):39–41; John F. Sears, *Sacred Places,* p. 5.

66. Runte, *National Parks,* pp. 82–105.

67. *Glimpses of Our National Parks,* pp. 3, 7–8, 45.

68. Perry Miller, "The Romantic Dilemma in American Nationalism and the Concept of Nature," in *Nature's Nation* (Cambridge, Mass.: Belknap Press, 1967), 196–207; Lowenthal, "The Place of the Past in the American Landscape."

69. See clippings in scrapbooks, vols. 4–7, Mather MSS.

70. "Colorado—A Game Sanctuary," *Rocky Mountain News,* March 26, 1915; "Trying to Turn Travel to Wonderlands of the U.S." Scrapbook, vol. 4, Clippings Re Public Official Career, 1915–1916, Mather MSS.

71. Scrapbooks, vols. 4–7, esp. vol. 5, Clippings Re Public Official Career, 1916–1919, Mather MSS. See also Shankland, *Steve Mather of the National Parks,* pp. 85–92.

72. U.S. Department of the Interior, *Annual Report of the Secretary of the Interior, 1918,* pp. 119, 122.

73. Hyde, *An American Vision.*

74. Benedict Anderson, *Imagined Communities: Reflections of the Origin and Spread of Nationalism* (London: Verso, 1983); Sears, *Sacred Places;* Wilbur Zelinsky, *Nation into State: The Shifting Symbolic Foundations of American Nationalism* (Chapel Hill: University of North Carolina Press, 1988).

Part 3

Understanding

Helen Ingram

Place Humanists
at the Headgates

We are familiar with the power of images. More than merely conveying reality, images actually construct reality. The image of starving children in Somalia, for example, constructs and defines a problem that
leads to the intervention of American military forces in an African nation, an intervention justified by reasons of humanity. Only months
later, a different image of a frightened and wounded American helicop-
ter pilot surrounded by jeering, dancing Somalians so changes the construction of the problem that Congress presses for hasty abandonment
of the project. It is not that Americans are witless and passive receptors
of manipulated mass communication. Rather, different images give cred-
ibility to alternative and competing models of how the world works
and where power and moral responsibility lie. Public policy action,
whether foreign or domestic, is driven by underlying perspectives, ex-
planations, and rationales that impart order and meaning to events.

The way in which nature is treated in public policy in the American West is determined by the dominant models and associated images
that organize our thinking. For instance, a utilitarian perspective sub-
jugates nature to providing goods and services for humans and favors
"natural resources" as a more appropriate label for what I and many
others would prefer to call "habitat" or "environment." From the resources perspective, the birds, rocks, and trees have little value in and
of themselves; their importance is measured solely according to the
benefits to people that they provide. The utilitarian mode of thinking

about nature is being strongly questioned today. However, the irreparable damage done to the natural world in places where human needs and desires have prevailed over all else suggests that we should learn to be more skeptical about conventional modes of thinking about our surroundings.

Acting upon inappropriate constructions of public issues can leave a bitter legacy. In regard to water, more than any other so-called natural resource, our inheritance from past public management is continuing and thereby aggravating already serious problems. Water is particularly appropriate as a theme for this chapter because it is a fundamental resource, especially in the arid West, where it is essential to all life. Water is a common tie that binds many aspects of nature together. Yet, not only have the ways we think about water alienated us from our natural setting, the models and ideas we have held have divided human communities. The struggle to secure ample high-quality water has fostered mistrust and misunderstanding and has created disharmony. Water conflicts have driven wedges between neighbors, and the lines of division are both historic and modern. Examples include

> Divisions among nations. Here in the Southwest water has been the most divisive issue between the United States and Mexico, and a sense of injustice lingers about the ways we have divided the Colorado River and the Rio Grande. Even after having defined an international agreement over trade, there is no agreement over groundwater even though transboundary aquifers are being seriously depleted at numerous locations along the border. As a result, riparian habitats and drinking-water supplies dependent upon transboundary water are being gravely threatened.

> Divisions among states. The eleven states that share the most important river in the West, the Colorado, have been continually at odds over water quantity and quality. The longest Supreme Court case in history involved Arizona's struggle with California over ownership of water in the river. This struggle continues today as Arizona strains to put to use all of its allotment so that the water allocated to Arizona is not somehow captured by Nevada and California.

Divisions between rural and urban areas. Growing urban demands threaten rural areas that are the sources of new supplies for urban areas that have outgrown their natural watersheds. The historic battle between Owens Valley and the city of Los Angeles that William Kahrl wrote about is being repeated all over the West.[1] The city of El Paso, for example, spent more than $11 million and seven years trying to import water from rural Doña Ana County in New Mexico.[2] Despite the fact that rural residents of that county were economically dependent upon the El Paso Metropolitan Area, they refused to share even one drop and fought and won using the courts and administrative systems.

Cultural and ethnic conflict. European and American settlers of the West claimed the best lands and most of the water, while Native Americans were confined to reservations with poor farming lands and little water. What water they had was inadequately protected by the government through a legal concept of "reserved water rights," or paper promises that their water would be available in the future when communities had advanced sufficiently to be able to make use of it. Now that Indians are laying claims to their reserved rights and are demanding "wet" instead of "paper" water, all available water is already in use by farmers, miners, energy developers, and urban areas. The values and cultures slighted in past water development—including natural areas, endangered species, rural Hispanics, and Native Americans—contend with one another for a marginal, residual share. The unsatisfactorily resolved struggle between the Spanish-ancestry farmers and Pueblo villages in the upper Rio Grande region is a tragic illustration of such a contemporary cultural conflict.[3] The battle between the Ute Mountain Utes and the environmentalists protecting the habitat of the squawfish in the Animas–La Plata area is another example of past decisions that have left the present with no good choices.[4]

At the same time that nations, states, regions, and cultures have battled over water, another kind of warfare has been going on. Different professions, disciplines, and perspectives have vied with one another to become the dominant model for framing water issues and their solutions. The power among various contestants has shifted over time. It is my contention that the inadequacy of these modes of thinking is responsible for the serious water problems we now must solve in an atmosphere of suspicion and hostility. The engineers, the lawmakers, lawyers, and political power-wielders, and the economists have spoken with conflicting voices, different images, and very different prescriptions about what we should do concerning water problems. In the meantime, the voice of the humanists speaking through literature has been all but ignored.

The engineering profession more than any other has interpreted water problems for society and framed the solutions to those problems. Its dominance is not surprising. After all, since Roman times engineers have made life for humans safer and better by constructing dams and aqueducts that move water from where it naturally occurs to where humans want to use it. Without the Bureau of Reclamation engineers, the great empires of the West never could have been constructed. Lights would not burn in Los Angeles and Las Vegas, and the groundwater pumps that are the heartbeat of desert cities would cease to throb.

Engineering is a wonderful tool, but we have let the tool take charge. Throughout the 1950s and 1960s we dammed, ditched, and diverted almost every stretch of running water in the West. Several of my students have referred to this period in reclamation history as the Golden Age of Concrete. Engineers have been able to perform great feats such as the construction of Hoover and Glen Canyon Dams because they see access to water as a problem they are able to solve through the slide rule and computer, accurate measurements, correct equations, and construction according to blueprints. By the nature of their disciplinary training, engineers are positive and oriented toward action rather than reflection. They approach floods, droughts, and contamination as plumbing issues requiring a plug here and a pump there, and a pipe over yonder. They are applied scientists and yearn to span chasms with bridges, scrape the sky with great buildings, and harness water resources to serve human needs.

While many engineers I have known are wise enough to know better, nothing in their tool kit prepares them to address whether the something they propose is really preferable to leaving things alone. They envision the problems created by their solutions as simply needs for more engineering expertise. As a result of past overreliance on engineering solutions, we face a host of environmental, economic, and social problems. The consequences of engineering works have been addressed by still other engineering works in an escalating spiral of more bizarre difficulties and expensive solutions. Note California's Kesterson Reservoir, where return flows from constructed irrigation projects contain such high levels of selenium that ducks hatched there are genetically flawed.[5] Similarly, Tucson residents shake their heads as engineers tell them it will take many years and millions of dollars to deal with eroding and leaking municipal and household pipes dissolved by Central Arizona Project water, imported from the Colorado River, which has a chemical composition very different from their previous groundwater supply to which their pipes were accustomed.

More than anyone else, historians and creative writers have understood and publicized the costs of resolving water problems through large-scale water works and interbasin transfers. Historian Donald Worster has made us aware of the relationship between large-scale irrigation and water-supply projects and the concentration of wealth and power in the hands of the few. He has argued that the vision of early reclamationists such as William Smythe to unlock the stored riches of the centuries through the blessing of irrigation was terribly flawed.[6] Instead of the egalitarian democratic society envisioned by Nevada's congressman Francis Newlands, who framed the Reclamation Act of 1902, the unequal distribution of the fruits of water development has created classes and regions that now feel bitter and disinherited.

Many creative writers have told us of the profound environmental damage done by engineering works. No one has written more memorably about dams than Edward Abbey, whose classic *The Monkey Wrench Gang* begins with eco-raiders blowing up the Glen Canyon Dam. Abbey writes of the dam and the channelized, subsidized, salinized river,

> Great River—greater dam. Seen from the bridge the dam presents the gray sheer concave face of concrete aggregate, implacable and mute. A gravity dam, eight hundred thousand tons of solidarity, countersunk in the sandstone of the Navajo formation, fifty mil-

lion years emplaced, of the bedrock and canyon walls. A plug, a block, a fat wedge, the dam diverts through penstocks and turbines the force of the puzzled river.

What was once a mighty river. Now a ghost. Spirits of sea gulls and pelicans wing above the desiccated delta a thousand miles to seaward. Spirits of beaver nose upstream through silt-gold surface. Great blue herons once descended, light as mosquitoes, long legs dangling, to the sandbars. Wood ibis croaked in the cottonwood. Deer walked the canyon shores. Snowy egrets in the tamarisk, plumes waving in the river breeze.[7]

The perspective of lawmakers, lawyers, and political entrepreneurs on water is very different. While engineering is grounded in physical reality, water law reflects political power and judicial precedent. Legislation and the law—as made and interpreted by legislators, lawyers, and judges—have exerted as much influence over water flows as the physical rule of gravity. What is generally called (on the Colorado) the Law of the River has been more important than the dams and diversions because the law has determined whether and where such structures can be erected. Cases over water rights crowd the judicial system. There are probably more water lawyers, for instance, in the state of Colorado than in any nation on the globe.

Whether or not members of Congress have effectively protected their state's water interests has spelled electoral success or defeat. Even the environmentalist statesman Morris K. Udall once told me that water issues, particularly the Central Arizona Project, took up more of his time than any other legislative matter in his career. Water rights—including the doctrine of prior appropriation and the concept of beneficial use—have determined who can use water, how, and when. Water law has encouraged holders of water rights to believe that they have absolute hegemony over the blessings of nature. Senior rights holders have been led to believe that they have no obligation to the larger community welfare and that they could protect their rights only by subjugating and utilizing every drop of their legal allocation. The rules of "first in time, first in right" and "use it or lose it" are solemnly spoken in the West as if they had the moral force of the Golden Rule even though their effect is quite the opposite.

Legal instruments such as the Colorado River Basin Compact of 1922 divided the flow of the Colorado as if the whole could be broken down into parts like making change for the dollar. This set a precedent for resolving other interstate water fights such as have occurred on the Rio Grande, the Pecos, and the Arkansas. Once states had a firm legal ownership, the challenge was to put the water to work in economically beneficial ways or lose it downstream to some other state. State delegations to Congress battled one another for federally subsidized water projects. I have spent much of my scholarly career tracing the Byzantine and intricate processes of vote-trading and logrolling involved in building political support for omnibus water legislation. Water projects have been planned by putting together features that favor a variety of local stakeholders including farmers, miners, energy developers, and cities. Individual projects have been strung together like beads on a string. The results reflect neither hydrologic nor engineering rationality but rather political feasibility, that is, securing enough congressional votes to get a bill through Congress. As a number of humanities scholars have pointed out, water politics and law have fed false expectations and have led to bitter disappointments.

Despite the heavily political nature of the process, the arenas in which water policies are forged are not democratic. Those with direct economic interests in exploitation have had the largest voice, and access to information has been restricted and the content of analysis biased so that the true costs of development are seldom revealed. In consequence, conflict has magnified rather than abated as advantaged and disadvantaged clash. As historian James Earl Sherow notes in *Watering the Valley,*

> When their aspirations fell short and their water systems failed, as was wont to happen during drought, the road to conflict opened. Occasionally people fought one another with guns, as had the angry people of Victor who took back "their" water from the citizens of Colorado Springs. Far more often, people responded with hired

assailants or protectors (depending on their relative position in litigation) called water lawyers. The attorneys took to court the questions concerning the equitable distribution of water flow. As users claimed more rights to the river flow than the stream could ever normally supply, and as urban, industrial, and agricultural demands continued apace, water lawyers multiplied with the inevitable conflict.[8]

The false democracy, inequity, and bitterness that arise from power politics in water resources are the central theme in Frank Waters's novel *People of the Valley*. He tells the story of Irish merchants, the Murphys (called the Mophries by their Hispanic neighbors), who settled and prospered in northern New Mexico. Even though they were long-time residents, inwardly they remained gringos and Irish. As gringos they held to a certain cold objectivity that enabled them to set themselves apart from the land and the people. As Irishmen, they had a natural gravitation toward politics. Through politics they established a separate water district and convinced people to vote for bonds to construct a dam to control floods and measure water allotments. But the respected community elder known only as Maria was instinctively distrustful of the dam. That this dam could be built only for the benefit of the people of the valley and yet the Mophries would be eager to support it did not coincide in Maria's mind: a reservoir was planned, and to make room for it, some people would lose their land. Waters writes, "There was this about it, it was more than a dam, it was a step in progress. And progress men define as that step toward giving the greatest good to the greatest number of people. Now Maria believed neither in the majority nor in the minority. She believed in all men. Good for the strong at the expense of the weak she saw as a natural inevitability. But also she saw that intentionally wrong dealt the few can never be paid for by the right derived from it by the many. Maria believed in fulfillment instead of progress. Fulfillment is individual evolution. It requires time and patience. Progress, in haste to move mass, admits neither."[9] In a parable that speaks to the fate of many rural minorities including Mormons and Native Americans, as well as Hispanics, the community was torn apart as some members lost their land and squandered their small compensations. The Mophries continued to profit through each transaction, for they were involved in construction and resettlement. Only when Maria restored the sense of community in spite of the conflicts aroused by the dam was the future of the people secured.

Water law and politics in the West have served well the aim of providing water resources for economic development in the West. At the same time, fairness and the welfare of indigenous minorities have often been disregarded. The loss of control over water as much as the loss of land has damaged rural cultures and diminished the rich diversity so important to western society. As Waters's Maria observed, it is very difficult to build a strong social edifice on the foundations of inequity.

Economists view water as a commodity that should be priced at its "real" value and allocated toward the highest economic use. This economic perspective has come to replace engineering and water law in terms of intellectual respectability, if not in application and practice. The perspective is attractive because it provides powerful arguments against the large-scale construction works that have been damaging to the environment. The expectation is that higher water prices would promote conservation. Economists are right in thinking that too much water is now being used at least partly because it is too cheap. Further, turning many decisions on water allocation over to the markets would seem to remove the lawyers and politicians from their privileged positions. Consequently, economists have become the major architects of reform policies that will allow buyers and sellers to determine water allocation in the future.

The economic perspective exhibits some serious flaws, however, and markets by themselves are unlikely to reverse the errors of the past or avoid making new ones. Broader community values at stake in water allocation are not likely to be protected in unfettered market transactions. In rural-to-urban water sales, for instance, the selling price of the farmer may well reflect the present worth of water in agriculture, but it will not reflect the value the rural area places upon keeping water rights in the community to provide a viable resource base for the future. Without secure water rights, rural areas may be unable to retain sufficient population and economic vitality to plan or to attract new opportunities.

Humanists have pointed out that water has long had a community value that transcends the individual property interest. Spanish colonial water law, according to historian Michael Meyer, set an important example. Meyer notes, "The water retained by the Spanish American town was held in trust for the benefit of the entire community. It was not the property of the inhabitants of that town, either individually or collectively, but rather was the property of the corporate body itself."[10]

A historic and powerful tradition of American public interest is applied as a guiding force in many important policy areas. A dollar value is not put on such things as the Bill of Rights, or protecting health and welfare, or protecting wilderness. Ethicist Mark Sagoff has argued that Americans see themselves not only as private consumers but also as members of a larger community that supports environmental protection and public welfare for reasons other than benefit-to-cost ratios.[11] Water may run uphill toward money, but it also should flow steadily and strongly toward the public welfare.[12]

Decisions involving water are simply too closely tied to collective well-being for the community to separate itself from water decision making. Writer Stanley Crawford reinforces the notion of water as the lifeblood of the community in his lovely and sensitive book *Mayordomo: Chronicle of an Acequia in Northern New Mexico*, a superb example of humanist scholarship. In *Mayordomo*, Crawford chronicles a year spent as a ditch master on an *acequia*, or irrigation canal. He writes,

> Next to blood relationships, which rule the valley, come water relationships. The arteries of ditches and bloodlines cut across each other in patterns of astounding complexity. . . . As *mayordomo* you become the pump, the heart that moves the vital fluid down the artery to the little plots of land of each of the cells, the *parciantes*. Water relationships would be simple and linear were they not complicated by all those other ways that human beings are connected with and divided from each other: blood, race, religion, education, politics, money. Against human constrictions and diversions, the *mayordomo* must pump water seven months of the year. . . . A

mayordomo has to deal with people whole, often angry, in their own backyards, on their own property, regarding a commonplace substance that can inspire passion like no other, with all connections everywhere firmly in place, including who beat up on who twenty years before in the village schoolyard.[13]

That water has the power to unite and connect as well as divide communities is also the message of perhaps the most widely read contemporary water novel, John Nichols's *Milagro Beanfield War*.[14] Although Joe Mondragon, the central character whose ancestors had farmed the land for centuries, had lost his water right to those able to pay for it, he was reasserting something quite different from lawlessness when he opened the headgate to his field and began to water his beans. He was affirming the generations-old connection of his people to land and place and to the values of independence and self-reliance. Through this simple act related to water, Joe was able to bring together previously fragmented and quarreling neighbors. Irrigating a crop central to their culture re-created community loyalties and fostered optimism about the community's ability to confront problems.

The economic value of irrigating pinto beans was certainly no measure of cultural value, and that is exactly the point that economists frequently misunderstand. The excessively narrow, overly exclusive perspective economists bring to water returns me to the title of this essay, "Place Humanists at the Headgates." The opening and closing of gates in water delivery systems determine which interests and values are served, by directing the flow of water to one area or another. Nichols's *Milagro Beanfield War* used the symbolic image of opening the headgate to Joe Mondragon's field to suggest that water policy needs to be directed differently. Values of fairness and equity need to take a more central position in water-allocation decisions.

Choices on water use must reflect respect for the diverse cultures that contribute to the distinctiveness of the western region. Ranchers, Native Americans, Hispanics, Mormons, miners, environmentalists, as well as city-dwellers and others, should have the right to employ water as long as their use does not degrade the resource or harm others.

The history of water in the West includes numerous past injustices and is highly relevant to what we must decide today. We have an obligation to obey promises that were made in good faith in the course of past negotiation and compromise, such as federal reserved water rights for national parks and Indian peoples. The present use of water resources should take account of future generations. It is important that use of a basic resource and social good such as water not be a part of a "Faustian bargain" that sacrifices future well-being to the present generations' uncontrolled material appetites.

When engineers, politicians, or economists have taken control of water-resources decision making, a singular, exclusivist perspective has dominated. Humanists, it seems to me, would be better gatekeepers because they are respectful of value pluralism. They would be able to recognize the importance of the engineers' concern that waterworks actually work, that is, be rationally designed to function. They would understand the political actors' preoccupation with political feasibility. The importance of efficiency and prevention of waste of societies' economic resources would thus be placed in a more balanced perspective. Most important, humanists would emphasize the rights of ordinary people to participate in the public deliberations that should govern water choices.

On the occasion of the sixtieth anniversary of the Colorado River Compact, signed at Bishop's Lodge in Santa Fe, a group of scholars and public officials gathered to discuss new directions for thinking about the Colorado. A political philosopher, Lawrence Scaff, and I suggested a list of five distributive principles—reciprocity, value pluralism, participation, promises, and responsibility—as tests for equity in water policy. We intended our ideas to contribute to a process of deliberation, a broad discussion that would create a new water ethic and a new image of fairness in western water policy. In Prescott, ten years later, I called upon humanists to take their rightful role as leaders of the discussion, and I urge immediate action toward this end. We must place humanists at the headgates.

Notes

1. William L. Kahrl, *Water and Power* (Berkeley: University of California Press, 1982).

2. John Falk-Williams, *Water and the Cities of the Southwest,* Western Water Policy Project Discussion Series Paper no. 3 (Denver: Natural Resources Law Center, University of Colorado School of Law, 1990).

3. F. Lee Brown and Helen Ingram, *Water and Poverty in the Southwest* (Tucson: University of Arizona Press, 1987).

4. Helen Ingram, *Water Politics: Continuity and Change* (Albuquerque: University of New Mexico Press, 1990).

5. Marc Reisner, *Cadillac Desert: The American West and Its Disappearing Water* (New York: Viking Penguin, 1986), p. 486.

6. Donald Worster, *Rivers of Empire: Water, Aridity, and the Growth of the American West* (New York: Pantheon, 1985).

7. Edward Abbey, *The Monkey Wrench Gang* (Salt Lake City: Dream Garden Press, 1975), p. 12.

8. James Earl Sherow, *Watering the Valley: Development along the High Plains Arkansas River, 1870–1950* (Lawrence: University of Kansas Press, 1990), pp. 167–168.

9. Frank Waters, *People of the Valley* (Chicago: Swallow Press, 1969; orig. pub. 1941), p. 134.

10. Michael Meyer, *Water in the Hispanic Southwest: A Social and Legal History* (Tucson: University of Arizona Press, 1984), p. 157.

11. Mark Sagoff, *The Economy of the Earth* (Cambridge, U.K.: Cambridge University Press, 1988).

12. John Opie, *Ogallala: Water for a Dry Land* (Lincoln: University of Nebraska Press, 1993), p. 242.

13. Stanley Crawford, *Mayordomo: Chronicle of an Acequia in Northern New Mexico* (Albuquerque: University of New Mexico Press, 1988), pp. 23–25.

14. John Nichols, *The Milagro Beanfield War* (New York: Henry Holt & Co., 1974).

Char Miller

Tapping the Rockies
Resource Exploitation and
Conservation in the Intermountain West

The Rocky Mountains have loomed large in the American imagination, though the meaning attributed to this stunning landscape has
changed over time. In the narrative of nineteenth-century western migration, for instance, the mountains were impediments, an elevated
topography that had to be conquered before the pioneers could reach
the promised lands of the Pacific slope. That image is what Emmanuel
Leutze sought to capture in his *Westward the Course of Empire* (1847),
a massive painting depicting the successful struggle of a wagon train to
top an imposing and rugged ridge: in the foreground a buckskinned
guide standing astride the continental divide huzzahs and points west
toward the beckoning, golden sun; in the soft glow of its new light, a
mother cradles a babe. Only in that West out beyond this fierce high
country would America be reborn.

Leutze's iconography of triumph and regeneration struck a chord,
so much so that his work has been on permanent display in the ro-
tunda of the U.S. Capitol, a political celebration of a cultural ideal;
breaching the Rockies was a means to an end. No more. In the late
twentieth century, the Rockies are an end unto themselves: a source of
any number of vital natural resources, the range is also a playground
upon which another set of cultural ambitions and desires are worked
out. High country is now good. We all want to get high, whether our
mountainous regions of choice are the Rockies, Wasatch, or Cascades,
the Sierra Nevada or the Sangre de Cristos. But the most massive of

these—the Rockies—seem to fill a special space in the contemporary fascination with tall places. They do so in any event for David Robinson, star center for the San Antonio Spurs, who was in 1995 declared Most Valuable Player in the National Basketball Association, a man who, at 7'2", knows something about *being* a tall place. One of his favorite scriptures is Jeremiah 50:6, in which faithlessness is likened to sheep who are driven away from the mountaintops and herded down to the hills, where they forget "their own resting place," the place where they are most who they are. This is an intriguing passage for one who, like Robinson, has a second home in Aspen; there, amidst its thin atmosphere, he finds himself and comes close to his God.[1]

The Rockies also serve those for whom faith in the almighty dollar is the touchstone of conscience. Radio listeners in the Lone Star State are repeatedly warned, for example, that they can slake their "Texas-sized thirst" (I think that means extra-large) only if they "reach for the Rockies," that is, grab and drain a chilled Coors Lite. During the spring of 1995, cable television offered up a different hard pitch, a seemingly interminable commercial featuring a boyish John Denver, his soft mane intact, first lounging before a blazing fire, later resting in an alpine meadow, all the while lip-synching lyrics to a retrospective album of his golden oldies, including, of course, "Rocky Mountain High!" This land is for sale.

Or this land is gone. That is one possible message conveyed by the seductive architecture of the new Denver International Airport, with its provocative superstructure—Teflon-coated, white-tented peaks sailing above the terminals—and its stunning interior, particularly the faux forest primeval that rises up into a glass-enclosed, bright blue sky. As *New York Times* architectural critic Herbert Muscamp has mused, perhaps "the airport's stylized version of nature is to be read as a kind of paradise lost: the rendering of God's own country into a man-made artifact."[2] We have cut the mountains down to our size.

There is a cost, then, that comes from hawking this extraordinary landscape, from selling a set of values that these very high places are said to embody: of divinity, leisure, and recreation, of soft-lit romantic fantasies and rugged confrontations between self and nature. One can hardly sing of this eden, this acadia, and then wonder why narrow mountain highways are jammed, housing developments are springing up like mushrooms, and ski lifts are clogged. Sorting out the dilemmas posed by the contradictory image of "rush hour in the Rockies" is no easy task, for they depend upon a cultural conundrum: the simultaneous and conflicting desires to preserve and utilize this threatened scenic resource.

The past offers no simple set of guidelines for how to balance these impulses of preservation and use. When westerners at the turn of the nineteenth century, for instance, grappled with this same conundrum, when they too were forced to determine the best way to live within and work on the land, they were as perplexed as are their descendants at the end of the twentieth century. But out of that earlier confusion and struggle emerged a set of critical legal and political resolutions that generated the language through which these decisions ever since have been debated. Digging into that past helps uncover some of the developmental strains endemic to the modern West.

One of the central issues confronting the intermountain West in the post–Civil War era was not the impact the region's tiny human population had upon the landscape but the impress of its domesticated animals, specifically the massive herds of sheep and cattle that then grazed on public lands. The size of these herds is astounding. In 1890 in Colorado, for example, a state with a human population totaling a bit more than 400,000, there were approximately 1.7 million head of sheep and more than 1 million head of cattle.[3] The competition for land that such numbers induced, Joseph Nimmo (then chief statistician for the Treasury Department's Bureau of Statistics) observed dryly, was "subject to frictional resistances and embarrassments,"[4] a bureaucratically coy way of saying that the pitched battles fought over this terrain were vicious and violent, a fierce set of range wars between cattle drovers and sheep herders that dominated land-use patterns. The boundaries they finally agreed upon, the "dead lines," were quite literal in their determination of where each form of grazing could occur: a cow or sheep that strayed across the line was at risk of being gunned down, an act of vigilante justice.

Vigilantism, by its very definition, suggests that there was then little federal authority imposed on publicly owned land. Seemingly the only restraints on the movement of herds throughout this vast intermountain landscape were those imposed by the limits of forage and water. Indeed, by the late 1800s, the concept of "free use" or "free grass" had become a crucial element in the presumed stability of the regional economy and was vigorously touted and protected through a political culture that bound together cattle- and woolgrower associations, newspapers, and officeholders at all levels and of all partisan persuasions. Together these forged a potent consensus that shaped a national commitment to the maintenance and expansion of this form of agricultural production. Nimmo, for instance, acknowledged in his seminal report that "the range and ranch cattle business . . . is one of the most attractive and important commercial and industrial enterprises of the present day." It was so, he argued, because the "occupancy of the public lands throughout the central and northern portions of the great dry area for range cattle purposes" had "subdued and utilized such lands for the production of a cheap and nutritious article of food." Although there were aspects of the industry that he critiqued—particularly its desire to secure long-term leases that would effectively limit human settlement and establish land monopolies—he accepted intense grazing on public lands as a given, sanctioned as a matter of social utility. He had no beef with an industry of this magnitude and consequence, for which "preservation" of the land was an utterly foreign concept; "use" was all.[5]

The consequences of unrestrained development, however, and the vicious cycle of economic greed and environmental despoliation it set in motion, were escalating toward the close of the nineteenth century. With improved rail transport to the burgeoning eastern urban markets, rails that also brought a surge of migrants into western states, the pressure on this region's lands intensified. Seeking quick profits that grazing on the public lands would underwrite, ranchers drove ever larger numbers of cattle and sheep onto the ranges, an overstocking that unleashed intense speculation, a boost in production that dropped prices and consequently led to the release of still more herds into mountainous pastures. The carrying capacity of the land was thus overwhelmed. Noted Albert Potter, who had been a rancher before he became the first head of the Forest Service's Grazing Section, "vegetation was cropped by hungry animals before it had a chance to reproduce; valuable forage plants gave way to worthless weeds."[6] This observation could apply equally to Colorado or California, Washington or New Mexico; in each, Potter continued, "the highest and most inaccessible slopes and alpine meadows" were under siege. Stripping these lands only forced an increased demand for newer, more distant and greener range to maintain herd size, sustain income, and protect market share. If this sounds like the feeding frenzy that surrounds, say, late-twentieth-century condominium development, it should: in theory at least there is little difference between the drum of thundering hooves and the pneumatic *thwack-thwack-thwack* of staple guns.[7]

Reining in this form of uncontrolled growth in the nineteenth century was unthinkable, largely because a vocabulary of restraint did not yet exist; a new rhetoric had to be created that would, through a set of scientific, economic, and political principles, establish a different relationship between humans and the land on which they lived. By the late nineteenth century the broad outlines of this new perspective had begun to emerge, the central thrust of which was that the nation's natural resources and agricultural production were interwoven parts of a whole. Those who developed this nascent ecological vision believed, for example, that the massive herds of free-ranging sheep in the valleys, foothills, and slopes posed a series of dangers: they not only decimated grasses and plants, but also disrupted the health of forests, polluted streams and rivers, and increased the threat of forest fires. "Free grass" was anything but free.

The same conclusions could be drawn about other forms of unrestrained resource exploitation in the Rockies—lumbering, mining, and cattle ranching, in particular. Their combined devastation of the landscape in fact is what forced a growing demand for some federal controls, and those local and national figures who demanded such regulation came to call themselves conservationists. It was an old term, but an apt one: it was necessary to conserve, they argued, to slow national consumption of resources, managing or regulating demand so that

Americans might have a continuous supply of natural resources well into the future. Perhaps the most articulate and controversial spokesman for this concept was Gifford Pinchot, a European-trained American forester who founded the U.S. Forest Service in 1905, who was one of the chief architects of the late-nineteenth-century conservationist movement, and who claimed even to have invented the term "conservation" (he didn't). But he offered a snappy sound bite that captured the essence of the movement's ethos: its goal, he wrote, was to produce "the greatest good, for the greatest number, for the longest time."[8] There are problems with this definition (for example, who defines what the greatest good is, and is it possible to produce such a lofty, if perhaps contradictory outcome?), but he was convinced that only a rigorous pursuit of conservation would enable this democratic society to provide a steady stream of goods and services to bolster the citizenry's standard of living. Opposed to social inequality, respectful of the land, and determined to account for the needs of subsequent generations, conservation seemed to solve some of the most pressing problems confronting an industrializing America.

Yet there was no mechanism by which to implement the principles of conservation on the public lands. This was partly a result of a bureaucratic jumble, in which the nation's publicly owned forests, then called forest reserves, were placed under the jurisdiction of the Interior Department, while the Bureau of Forestry, which Pinchot had headed since 1898, was situated in the Department of Agriculture; the nation's foresters had no forests on which to practice their ideas of conservation. Yet even if either department had wanted to implement conservationist policies on these lands—and in the late nineteenth century that was not their commitment—neither had the authority to police activities on them. The sheep and cattle could roam at will; lumber companies could harvest wood with little restraint.

That situation changed markedly during the first decade of the twentieth century. When Theodore Roosevelt replaced the assassinated William McKinley, Pinchot found in the new president an ally who would work closely with him to transfer the nation's forests to the Agriculture Department, a transfer that brought with it the legal power for forest rangers to arrest trespassers without first securing a warrant.

Livestock associations and other western resource special-interest groups quickly challenged this unprecedented authority in the courts, but in the end they failed to establish their case. By 1911, through a series of landmark judicial decisions, the U.S. Supreme Court had upheld the congressional act that gave the Secretary of Agriculture (and thus Pinchot's Forest Service) the ability "to regulate the occupancy and use of and to preserve the forests from destruction."[9] The federal government could then control access to and activities upon public lands.

This was no small victory. Its policy implications, for example, were immense; henceforth, the Forest Service could, in the words of one historian, "administer the national forests under scientific management in the public interest," management practices that could include issuing restrictions on grazing to "improve soil and watershed stability," implementing badly needed scientific studies to determine how to preserve and utilize western lands, and developing reforestation and revegetation programs designed to repair stripped-over terrain. Through human stewardship, the West could be repaired and renewed.[10]

The same notion of stewardship might also regenerate human life out beyond the 100th meridian, or so novelist Hamlin Garland asserted. Indeed, he believed that the newly empowered forest rangers, and the federal agency they represented, would become symbols of a long-overdue cultural revolution in the intermountain region, constituting in his opinion "the most significant movement in the West at this moment." Speaking through Forest Supervisor Redfield, one of the protagonists of his novel *Cavanagh: Forest Ranger* (1910), Garland lashed out at the frontier rough and tumble: "From the very first the public lands of this state have been a refuge for the criminal—a lawless no man's land; but now, thanks to Roosevelt and the chief Forester, we at least have a force of men on the spot to see that some semblance of law and order is maintained." Establishing peace was only one part of the Forest Service's charge. As they enforced "ultimate peace and order over all the public lands," Garland was confident that the "picturesque West," the land of "the free-range stockman and his cowboy cohorts," who may have been "admirable subjects for fiction" (including his own), would give way to the "civilized West." It was "the forest ranger, riding his solitary trail," who was "the vidette of the real civilization which is to bring in 'the real West,'" the ranger who "represents the future and not the present, the Federal not the local spirit." Gifford Pinchot could not have said it any better.[11]

He did not even try. Instead, in his preface to Garland's novel, the chief forester could only applaud the writer's "sympathetic understanding of the problems which confronted the Forest Service before the Western people understood it"; that someone outside the agency recognized and appreciated its struggles was heartening. Perhaps *Cavanagh* would facilitate the forest rangers' introduction of federal sovereignty, the "new order," to the West.[12] By itself, Garland's fictional account of the crying need for a powerful federal government did not carry the day, but the "new world" it described and helped usher in has since come of age. Surely a measure of its successful implementation can be found in the current animosity that Newt Gingrich and the Neo–Sagebrush Rebellion have directed toward the cultural assumptions embedded in the Progressive-era federal land policies that Theodore Roosevelt's administration initiated at the beginning of this century. Past political commitments have become the source of contemporary conflict; the new has become old.

Likewise, present-day complaints implicitly draw upon earlier resistance to the conservation principles Roosevelt and Pinchot had articulated. Those who opposed the implementation of the conservation ethos of the early twentieth century, for example, did so in ways both subtle and blunt; in particular, they mounted a series of raucous public meetings to which Pinchot was regularly invited, and which he usually attended. During these boisterous assemblies, westerners shored up their political support, championed states' rights as the only means to blunt an aggressive executive branch, and sought alternately to browbeat or sweet-talk the nation's forester into changing his allegiances. He never yielded, of course, which only heightened the dramatic, if ritual-like tension of these encounters, which were often (and aptly) held in the opera houses or theaters of Denver, Salt Lake City, Boise, Wallace, or Cheyenne. That they became ritualistic is important: these meetings served as middle grounds, zones in which each side of the debate could stake its claims, establish the legitimacy of its position, and seek to moderate, even as it came to a grudging appreciation of the opposition's perspectives. Civic peace was (largely) maintained through civil dialogue.

But civility did not mean a dearth of disagreement. Each of these confabs had its share of verbal fireworks and tense confrontations— none more so than the Denver Public Lands Convention, held in mid– June 1907, which attracted several thousand delegates from the western states. Called by the Colorado legislature "for the purpose of discussing the relation of the states to public lands, and, if possible, [to] agree upon some policy in regards these lands to be urged upon the general government,"[13] the conference's timing reflected an upsurge in western frustration with Rooseveltian conservation policies. During the preceding six months, for instance, congressional representatives from the West had beat back attempts to institute grazing regulations on the public domain and had vigorously attacked but failed to derail increases in the Forest Service's budgetary appropriations as well as in Pinchot's salary. They seemed to hit paydirt when, through the Fulton amendment, named for Charles Fulton of Oregon, the anticonservationists were able to amend annual appropriations legislation to include language prohibiting the president from creating or expanding forest reserves within Oregon, Washington, Montana, Colorado, and Wyoming; against what many in Congress had once felt was an unstoppable federal conservation juggernaut, the legislative branch had finally flexed its muscles.[14]

Only to be flattened in turn: Roosevelt, who knew he had to sign the appropriations bill by March 4, 1907, schemed with Pinchot and the Forest Service staff to withdraw more than 16 million acres of public land, some to augment old national forests, the bulk establishing twenty-one new forests in six western states. When the president announced the creation of the so-called midnight reserves, his opponents were livid and, in Roosevelt's felicitous phrase, "turned handsprings in their wrath." However dire their threats, the chief executive believed they "could not be carried out, and were really only a tribute to the efficiency of our action." When he and Pinchot then met with a delegation of aggrieved western representatives, he let them see, Pinchot later reported, that the "joke was on them. It was their kind of joke, and the meeting ended in a highly temporary era of good feelings."[15]

Highly temporary indeed, as in two weeks—for that is how rapidly state legislators in Colorado met and agreed to issue a call for the Denver meetings, which were billed as a showdown with the federal government. The initial announcement, later toned down, rebuked Washington for having usurped "the rights of the states and its citizens to develop and acquire title to these public lands and to utilize [the] resources."[16] At Denver, then, the question of whose lands these were would be thoroughly ventilated, a question that was of considerable constitutional concern: at stake was whether the states or the federal government had ultimate sovereignty over public lands. It was all a matter of boundaries.

That the Roosevelt administration expected to lay down any lines at all provoked an intense hostility that led some to charge that the government was waging war on its citizens, pursuing what one Colorado newspaper lambasted as a "Russian policy" of arbitrary and authoritarian rule on the range. "Very few of the autocratic monarchs of the world," the *Steamboat Pilot* trumpeted, "would so dare to set aside the will of the people this way."[17] Another, more playfully, mocked the administrative pose of omnipotence:

> Wise old guy this Baron Pinchot
>   Seeks to fence in all the earth,
> While we sit here and watch his doings
>   In a manner full of mirth. . . .
>
> But while you're building fences
>   Of barbed wire and the like,
> Remember that the cowboys
>   May decide to go out on strike.
> Maybe when they're through with you
>   And you their wrath have felt,
> Your pet scheme will be blasted,
>   And your scalp hang from their belt.[18]

Lurking beneath this bold rebuke, however, evident in the poet's use of the conditional tense—"*maybe* when they're through with you" (emphasis added)—was the fear that the insurgency would falter before an unbending federal government. That fearful reality was most vividly captured in a cartoon that appeared in the *Rocky Mountain News.* Sitting upon a regal throne, wearing a bejeweled crown, a severe-looking Gifford Pinchot holds in his right hand a mace, symbol of monarchical power. Arrayed behind him, mounted on powerful steeds, are six forest rangers, their right arms raised, brandishing whips, markers of unchecked authority. In the foreground are abject westerners, cowering, hats in hand, deferentially posed on bended knees; the stockman, the irrigationist and miner, the new settler and pioneer are no longer masters of their own fate. Over all rules the chief forester with an iron hand.[19]

Defusing that charged atmosphere was Pinchot's goal at the Denver Public Lands Convention. Yet in this regard, the first two days of that conference only made his work more complicated: his opponents fed off one another's animosity, and in speech after speech they excoriated the Roosevelt administration in general and Pinchot in particular. Senator Henry Teller of Colorado was among those who blasted the chief forester's claim of federal sovereignty: "We cannot remain barbarians to save timber. I do not contend that the government has the right to seize land, but I do contend that we have the right to put it to the use that Almighty God intended."[20] Such blunt and contentious rhetoric emboldened the audience, so that when on the afternoon of the convention's third day Pinchot finally strode across the stage of the Brown Theater, he was meet with a storm of catcalls and jeers. He was on the spot.

There was no place he would rather have been. "If you fellows can stand me," he said wryly when he finally gained the crowd's attention, "I can stand you"—a deft retort that quieted the hecklers. Pinchot then launched into his standard declaration about the critical relationship between national forests, conservation practices, economic growth, and political equity. Creating the vast national forests had had a series of beneficial effects, he declared: "government-regulated timber auctions prevented monopoly and the consequent excessive price of lumber";

they consequently stabilized markets and ensured that there was "no question of favoritism or graft." As the federal presence helped regularize life in the intermountain region, so did it serve the public in other, no less complicated ways. For those living in an often arid region, Pinchot was also at pains to emphasize what he considered to be a critical connection between woods and water, noting that forested lands protected "watersheds of streams used for irrigation, for domestic water and manufacturing supply, and for transportation." For these reasons alone, he asserted, "the protection of irrigation throughout the west would justify the president's forest policy." Rather than resist federal conservation policies, western insurgents should embrace them.[21]

Some of his listeners must have absorbed his message, for when Pinchot concluded his address to the hitherto heckling crowd, he was reportedly cheered "lustfully." Not all were convinced, of course, and in follow-up speeches they continued to tear into the federal government's assumptions to and flaunting of its regulatory powers. Yet these more intransigent delegates and speakers were apparently shocked when, following Pinchot's speech, the Public Lands Convention's resolutions were announced. Although the platform called for an end to federal intervention in western affairs and asked for a reevaluation of national forest legislation and regulatory activism, these resolutions were couched in temperate language quite unlike the incendiary rhetoric and blustery sloganeering that had characterized the public speeches and back-room discussions. As one newspaper editorial put it, the resolutions sent the delegates packing, "roaring as mildly as a suckling dove."[22]

Credit for the apparently pro-conservation victory lay in part with behind-the-scenes maneuvering on the resolutions committee, which inexplicably had been stacked with a goodly number of Pinchot supporters. Pinchot's presence itself was influential—that he confronted his detractors face to face, and stated his position forcefully, helped his cause. That cause was helped too by his assertion of the definitive role conservation played in the government's decision-making process. The web of mutuality governing the relationship between the people and the land on which they lived—all set within the interconnectedness of trees, water, and soil, of high country and lowlands—not only defined the paramount problem facing the West, but was also its inspired solution. Each human context and need was important, Pinchot observed, each legitimate interest must be acknowledged and fulfilled where possible, but no interest, individual or combined, could be expected to supplant the carrying capacity of the land itself. "The protection of the forest and the protection of the range by wise use," he had reminded his Denver audience, "are two divisions of a problem vastly larger and more important than either. This is the problem of the conservation of all our natural resources," a matter for careful consideration. "If we destroy them, no amount of success in any other direction will keep us prosperous." His generation was confronted with a question, in short, that spanned "both the present and the future." Private, short-term interests must give way to public, long-term needs.[23]

Pinchot's strategy of conflict resolution helped transform the often vociferous early-twentieth-century debate over conservation. His goal, after all, was to decenter the narrow, specific concerns of particular resource groups, thereby forcing each to acknowledge the legitimate needs of the complex collective, an approach that thrust the public good, which he equated with the principles of conservation, to center stage. Conservation, then, became the basis for discussion, muscling aside the demands for "free grass" or "free range." In this way he was able to rein in and thus moderate the once-dominant voice with which grazing interests spoke in the then-contemporary political discourse. No wonder his opponents sneeringly referred to him as "Czar Pinchot"; no wonder his supporters embraced him as a savior.

His approach to conflict resolution still seems pertinent, as does his deep commitment to building a broad-based coalition fully in support of the conservation ethos. In this sense there may not be a world of difference between his time and our own, between the dilemmas once posed by sheep and those now by skiers.

That correspondence, naturally enough, can be extended only so far: we do not live in the Progressive era, and despite our occasional ovine-like behavior, people are not sheep. This is especially evident when measuring our relative impact on land, water, and sky: the human imprint is far more indelible than that of a herd of woolly quadrupeds.

Managed properly, their hoofprints leave but ephemeral marks upon the ground. Our footprints, by contrast, whether in the form of housing or resort villages, roads or tunnels, reservoirs or water treatment plants, are set in concrete. Our presence is considerably more permanent.[24]

It is that quest for permanence that has generated so much political controversy and economic stress in the contemporary West. At times unrecognized and unrestrained, it has already led to the obliteration of some of the magnificent and rocky vistas Americans flock to behold (and that, once beheld, want to live within); the sight of terraced, suburban tract housing rising high into the foothills is a sign of the degree to which we are capable of loving these elevated landscapes to death. Once that deadly embrace is complete, all that will be left of the Rockies, for example, will be the coarse and disquieting representations now pitched in beer commercials, evoked in popular song, and ironized in airport architecture. That in turn will mark the end of the trail, a cultural trail, that is, America's century-long faith in the restorative power of high country, what Hamlin Garland once claimed was "the clean sanity of the hills."[25]

Notes

A version of this chapter was presented to the "Boom in Mountain Living Conference," Keystone, Colorado, June 1995. I am grateful to Bill Rowley for his bibliographical guidance.

1. *San Antonio Express News,* May 27, 1995, p. 3S.

2. Herbert Muscamp, "A Wonder World in the Mile High City," *New York Times,* May 7, 1995, p. B4.

3. Joseph Nimmo, *Report in Regard to the Range and Ranch Cattle Business of the United States* (New York: Arno Press, 1972), p. 55; William D. Rowley, *U.S. Forest Service Grazing and Rangelands: A History* (College Station: Texas A & M University Press, 1985), pp. 4–10.

4. Nimmo, *Report,* p. 50.

5. Nimmo, *Report,* pp. 46–55.

6. Albert F. Potter, "The National Forests and the Livestock Industry," quoted in Rowley, *U.S. Forest Service Grazing and Rangelands,* p. 16.

7. Rowley, *U.S. Forest Service Grazing and Rangelands,* pp. 3–21; National

Academy of Sciences 1896 report quoted in Henry Clepper, *Professional Forestry in the United States* (Baltimore: Johns Hopkins University Press, 1971), p. 74.

8. Gifford Pinchot, *The Fight for Conservation* (New York: Doubleday, Page & Co., 1910), p. 48.

9. Clepper, *Professional Forestry in the United States*, pp. 70–71, 80–81.

10. Clepper, *Professional Forestry in the United States*, p. 81.

11. Hamlin Garland, *Cavanagh: Forest Ranger* (New York: Harper & Brothers Publishers, 1910), p. 201; Hamlin Garland, "My Aim in *Cavanagh*," *World's Work*, October 1910, p. 13569.

12. Gifford Pinchot, "Introduction," in Garland, *Cavanagh*, pp. vii–viii.

13. G. Michael McCarthy, *Hour of Trial: The Conservation Conflict in Colorado and the West, 1891–1907* (Norman: University of Oklahoma Press, 1977), p. 211.

14. McCarthy, *Hour of Trial*, pp. 200–209; Elmo Richardson, *The Politics of Conservation: Crusades and Controversies, 1897–1913* (Berkeley: University of California Press, 1962), pp. 33–35.

15. Gifford Pinchot, *Breaking New Ground* (New York: Henry Holt, 1947), pp. 299–300; McCarthy, *Hour of Trial*, pp. 200–210.

16. Quoted in McCarthy, *Hour of Trial*, p. 210.

17. *Steamboat Pilot*, June 5, 1907.

17. Glenwood *Avalanche-Echo*, June 12, 1907.

19. "Czar Pinchot" cartoon, *Rocky Mountain News*, September 20, 1908.

20. McCarthy, *Hour of Trial*, pp. 221–226.

21. Pinchot's speech in Denver was reprinted in the *Idaho Daily Statesman*, June 21, 1907.

22. Quoted in Richardson, *Politics of Conservation*, p. 39.

23. *Idaho Daily Statesman*, June 21, 1907. For Pinchot's policy of cooperation see Gifford Pinchot, "Grazing in the Forest Reserves," *Forester* (November 1901):276–280. See also Rowley, *U.S. Forest Service Grazing and Rangelands*, pp. 44–47.

24. See "Grappling with Growth," a special issue of *High Country News*, September 5, 1994, pp. 6–23.

25. Garland, *Cavanagh*, p. 267. Some of these issues were manifest in the "Boom in Mountain Living Conference," held in June 1995 and reported in *Snow Country*, September 1995, pp. 58–62. William B. Cronon, "The Trouble with Wilderness," in Char Miller and Hal K. Rothman, eds., *Out of the Woods: Essays in Environmental History* (Pittsburgh: University of Pittsburgh Press, 1997), brilliantly captures some of the cultural tensions embodied in the American conception of wilderness.

Robert Gottlieb

The Meaning of Place
Reimagining Community
in a Changing West

To enter the Pico Farmers' Market in Santa Monica, similar to the experience available at any of the nearly three dozen farmers' markets spread throughout urban southern California, is one way to step into the complex, diverse world and shifting landscapes of one part of the American West.[1] Guatemalan instruments greet the buyer with the soft, sensual music of Chiapas, while the explosion of colors—from sunflowers to azaleas to flowering cacti grown in the semidesert of eastern San Diego County by immigrants from the Mexican state of Nuevo León—provides a visual entry into what has become both a cultural and a literal feast of opportunities and product. Oden melons from the Mojave Desert, hot habanera peppers that can burn your lips if you touch them, green and red bell peppers from Vista, peaches and plums and four-inch organically grown grapes from Dinuba, honey sticks for the kids in a panoply of flavors and colors, fish caught that morning in the Channel Islands, bagels from grains grown without preservatives, *nopales* grown in the Imperial Valley that are found in numerous bodegas, Persian limes that are popular with the large Iranian population of westside Los Angeles, sweet corn pecked by birds and grown on farms without imported labor, tomatoes from Oxnard that taste like tomatoes, baby bok choy and Japanese eggplant and Chinese cabbage and the array of Asian vegetables that are also a southern California staple: for all these experiences and more, the Pico market is an articulation of contemporary urban southern California.[2]

These markets define a new urban landscape. They can be seen as cultural as well as economic meeting grounds, providing a distinctive sense of place. Such meeting grounds also contrast with the atomized concept of place associated with the increasing privatization of landscape and cityspace that prevails in areas such as urban southern California. It is here, in a global city such as Los Angeles, where one also finds food megastores built with ten-foot fences and police substations and where cultural diversity is represented as ethnic gangs, and guns, and danger, and separation.[3]

I've introduced the experience of the Pico market as one way to rethink how the West and its many communities and sights and sounds are characterized and analyzed. But describing this region as in transition or in evolution becomes itself problematic, given that "the West" is an elusive term to begin with and that the field of western history, as Patricia Limerick reminds us, is in "a constant crisis of definition."[4]

As historians have argued, the West can be defined as a region or as a set of regions, or as a shifting frontier (at least the residual idea of frontier that survives as part of the popular imagination in theme parks or other cultural representations).[5] For some, the West consists of borderlands that are also permeable to the flow of capital and of labor and, increasingly, of pollution as well as cultural identities.[6] Yet this notion of an open border or a recirculating border has also resulted in a peculiar western nativism. This nativism is reflected in California's mean-spirited and convulsive Proposition 187, which seeks to purify our public schools by nativist cleansing, and in those self-defined Aryan movements of the Pacific Northwest for whom westernness is an invented Americanism, purified by Anglo hardiness as well as by race, religion, and creed.[7]

For those who focus on resources and landscape, the West is "rural," a set of discrete communities whose livelihood today is being threatened by the restructuring of the resource economies.[8] It is in relation to this conception of a rural West where the counteroffensive by the Wise Use movement seeks (often successfully) to pit a notion of community (represented by the survival of the resource-based industries and their jobs) against the concept of protected nature (represented, according to the Wise Use ideologues, by the big-city, backpacking, envirorecreationists).[9] But is the West predominantly rural (as measured by jobs, population, or industry activities), or is it urban (as defined by those same variables)? Isn't it more accurate to see the West as a collection of powerful and expanding metropolitan areas; areas that not only demonstrate the expanding reach of the urban spaces of the West, but also influence, if not dominate, extraurban life and therefore the region as a whole, as many western historians are now prepared to argue?[10]

Similarly, there are arguments about how to define "environment," as it is so often associated with the West. Some historians see the West as the birthplace of the environmental movement. In this setting, the West becomes distinctive Nature, a wilderness without people, or at least a place where people encounter a natural environment of large, open spaces.[11] For those advocates of wilderness, the western environment becomes a place to preserve, to set apart from human contact and daily life. Others (myself included) have argued, however, that the concept of environment needs to be bounded by daily life experiences, western or otherwise, and that human environments and natural environments (or Nature and Second Nature, to borrow from William Cronon) are not divisible.[12]

And, finally, for the purposes of this discussion, there is the compelling concept of the West transformed from resource colony to empire, with its ever-expanding physical as well as economic, political, and cultural boundaries. The West as empire has multiple reference points, whether situated as the resource economy of the trans-Mississippi West, specifically constructed beyond the 98th or 100th meridian;[13] the empire of the Pacific Basin, recognized for its central role within the global economy; the major urban centers that have dominated a series of intersecting regions;[14] or the military economy that exploded in size and reach during World War II and subsequently during the cold war.[15]

Each of these themes—resource economy, Pacific Basin, major urban centers, and military presence—was developed by Peter Wiley and myself more than fifteen years ago in *Empires in the Sun,* our book about the contemporary West in the post–World War II years, and in our weekly "Points West" newspaper column that we sent out to about thirty-five papers during the early 1980s. The theme of the West shifting from colony to empire (or into evolving, intersecting empires) served as our point of departure in characterizing and situating western regions in the twentieth century. We elaborated on this theme by analyzing the massive infrastructure of water development projects, power plants, metal mining, fossil fuel and timber operations, and an industrializing agriculture. These developments, in turn, constituted the West's expanding resource economy, consisting of projects whose backers were seeking in part to establish a western autonomy, to achieve more independence from Wall Street and other nonwestern financial centers in breaking free of the colony-type relationships and interdependencies of earlier periods. And while western resource development remained dependent on Washington for funding and a wealth of subsidies (reinforcing that well-known, well-worn western expectation of federal largesse that would simultaneously breed political resentment), the resource economy also became locally constructed. Indeed, the federal bureaucracies, whether through the regional offices of the Bureau of Reclamation or the Forest Service or the cooperative management agreements of the Bureau of Land Management or the field offices of the Agriculture Department, came to be viewed during much of the twentieth century as an extension of locally derived power.[16]

Western water policy perhaps best exemplifies the intricate patterns of local and federal power and, in particular, the crucial role of local interests (both irrigated agriculture and urban development) in establishing a continuing cycle of water development and expansion characteristic of those relationships and the policies for which they became responsible. By the turn of the century, the federal role—centered on a newly formed Reclamation Service (later named the Bureau of Reclamation)—was deemed essential for building and financing and subsequently subsidizing the massive infrastructure of projects and facilities that dotted the seventeen western states served by the Bureau of Reclamation. But relations between the bureau and local constituencies, modeled to a certain extent on the Army Corps of Engineers' pervasive "iron triangle" set of relationships between executive branch agencies, Congress, and local interests, were predicated not on management or planning or even equity considerations (a mission that had fully eroded during the heyday of the Bureau of Reclamation in the post–World War II period) but on considerations of local agricultural or urban development. Lobbying and trade organizations, such as the National Water Resources Association, became both the occasion for and the manifestation of such federal/local relationships, the meeting ground for what came to be called the water industry. Organized around the integration of public agencies and private interests, of local and federal players, and of agriculture and urban representation, the western water industry established its own domain of water policy decision making outside public scrutiny. At the same time, the water industry successfully captured the capital and resources necessary to put in place the Bureau of Reclamation's elaborate infrastructure for development.[17]

Many of these developments in the post–World War II era, it turned out, involved the kinds of massive projects and massive plans worthy of the assumptions of empire. And what plans they were! They included, among others, the myriad of deals for the Upper Basin authorized through the Colorado River Storage Project,[18] the distributive politics associated with the Central Arizona Project,[19] and the monumental and much-hyped Pacific Southwest Water plan and the North American Water and Power Alliance's monstrous extravaganza of five-hundred-mile trenches and water flowing from the outer reaches of British Columbia to the Mexican border to the south and the Great Lakes to the east ("And it will take forty years to do an EIR!" quipped Colorado's water czar).[20] Aside from the activities of the western water industry, the plans also involved other public/private, federal/local relationships and megadeals, such as the "Grand Plan" of the Southwest-California-Northwest power grid based on coal-fired plants, nuclear plants, and big hydropower projects;[21] the massive land grabs and market dominance of California's agro-industrial entities and chemical manufacturers;[22] and, perhaps most extravagant of all, Exxon's plans (instantly designed and as rapidly abandoned) to build six huge oil shale pits in western Colorado, each measuring a half-mile deep, 3.5 miles long, and 1.75 miles wide, with enough rock excavated each day for an entire Panama Canal.[23] This, indeed, was the stuff of empire!

The rapid emergence of these contemporary resource developments, it should be noted, was not wholly unanticipated, given earlier cycles of boom and bust in resource extraction and in the resource dependencies of the West. But it was the breadth and scale of such projects, spanning the relatively short period of the 1930s through the 1970s, that distinguished for us this era of western empire building. At the same time, this nexus of resource developments coincided with the era of the cold war and its enormous and far-reaching impact on both resource activities and the economy, the environment, and the politics and culture of the West. It has become, in fact, increasingly commonplace for contemporary historians to say that the politics and economy of the West in the postwar, expansionary years were embedded in a cold war praxis. In the building and testing and storage of bombs and missiles, the mining and milling of uranium and yellowcake, the production of plutonium, the construction of arsenals and bases, the establishment of research labs and experimental facilities, the funding of massive aerospace companies and their thousands of subcontractors, and, perhaps most pervasive, the overall development of the culture of this cold war, much of the West—from Mormon Utah to suburban southern California—was clearly and deeply affected.[24]

The western economies likewise had long been influenced by, and frequently depended upon, the federal government's military activities. Yet the post–World War II period, as with the Grand Plans of regional resource development, was different because of the scale of the projects and, perhaps most pernicious, the expectations of permanent boom in California, the Northwest, and parts of the Southwest and intermountain West.[25] The militarization of the western economy was integral to its expansion. Among other noteworthy influences, it involved the creation of new communities and urban growth, the transformation of rural areas, the influx of new population through inmigration in a search for jobs, cheap immigrant labor used at the interstices of military production, and the evolution of small companies and start-up firms into massive companies constructed out of federal contracts to build missiles or planes or bombs or other nuclear-era devices. Writing in 1967, James Clayton calculated that fully one-fourth of all Department of Defense military and civilian personnel, one-third of all military prime contract awards (including one-half of all research and development contracts), and two-thirds of all missile awards were let to companies and organizations located in thirteen western states, creating a new type of dependency-expansionary cycle.[26]

These huge expenditures in federal funds dwarfed even the resource megaprojects and were, at times, responsible for those same resource developments. Take, for example, the influence of the navy's huge base of operations in the San Diego area. It was the navy, primarily, that induced the Metropolitan Water District of Southern California to expand into the San Diego region by guaranteeing a continual, imported water supply in exchange for annexation and a monopoly over those same sources of imported water.[27] San Diego, in fact, was one of those instant cities that have dotted contemporary western history, though in this case it should be viewed primarily as a military creation, its naval base the key actor in stimulating an infrastructure for future growth and development. Indeed, already by 1960, San Diego had become what one observer characterized as a "metropolitan-military complex."[28]

The cold war's influence in the West was framed in part by the significant shift westward, toward the Pacific, of the country's military, economic, and political interests, a process that was significantly heightened during World War II. In *Empires in the Sun,* we documented how the Six Companies (the consortium of California and intermountain West companies that captured the federal contract to build Hoover Dam and subsequently helped lay the groundwork for an emergent western region–based capitalism) became powerful players in the new, post–World War II cold war economy.[29] The consortium achieved this position in part by winning an additional set of contracts to build some of the major military or military-related industrial facilities aimed at the Pacific during World War II. This became a mobile, expansive capitalism in its most militarized form. An executive of the Six Companies put it this way: "A [military] contractor has to set up a tremendous organization where nothing exists, house and feed thousands of workers, establish his own communications. That is what an army does. In both instances you have to move into the 'enemy's' territory, destroy him, then clear out and set yourself up somewhere else."[30]

These new western region capitalists—engineering and construction firms including the participating members of the Six Companies such as Kaiser, Bechtel (out of which the Fluor and Ralph M. Parsons companies evolved), Utah International, and Morrison-Knudsen, as well as the big aerospace giants such as Lockheed, Boeing, and General Dynamics—collectively presided over the great military-induced expansions of the regional economies of the West in the 1940s, 1950s, and 1960s. At the same time, these companies grew rapidly by developing their Pacific Basin ties. In the process, western companies emerged in the cold war era as major multinational players, achieving a kind of a quasi-military or "national security" status in international, and primarily Pacific Basin, arenas.[31]

This was also the era of Pacific Basin megadeals, the modern Pacific version of the old Atlantic-triangle trade policies. It was in this setting that new trade and material flows were established and multiplied, as, for example, when iron ore mined in Peru would be shipped on a fleet of convertible ore carriers built in San Diego to carry the ore to Japan and then sail on to Indonesia where crude oil would be picked up for shipment to refineries on the West Coast.[32] Fossil fuel development could also flow both ways. The much-hyped Japanese market for low-sulfur coal in the 1970s and early 1980s, for example, induced all kinds of convulsive activities in the West associated with the coal trade: new pressures for mining in Utah, plans to build slurry lines through the interior West, proposals for West Coast dredging and port expansion in places such as Seattle and Long Beach. All of these were based on the premise that the geopolitical and resource economy ties in the Pacific Basin were worth the environmental costs, the push for low-paying jobs, and the heavy subsidies required.[33] These in turn became indicative of how the West was becoming newly dependent on, as well as exploitative of, its Pacific Basin ties.

The "empire" message was partly a matter of scale: companies (and regions) that think big are capable of undertaking the megaprojects unprecedented in their restructuring impact, whether in terms of resource use, industrial expansion, population growth, or extending the boundaries of what the *Los Angeles Times* liked to call the "Pacific Littoral."[34] "Thinking big," the motto of the *Los Angeles Times,* as well as the philosophy of some of the other promoters of western regional expansion such as the *Denver Post* or the *Arizona Republic,* was also the motif of the big western engineering and construction firms. These companies, tied into both the military economy and the Pacific Basin nexus of trade and resource flows, were instrumental in designing and promoting some of the huge resource projects characteristic of the post–World War II era. It was Bechtel, for example, that pushed the concept, during the 1960s, of a coastal, nuclear-powered desalting plant that would enable the Metropolitan Water District to envision endless water supplies fueling endless urban expansion and population growth in its six-county megaregion that stretched from the desert to the sea.[35] The southern California–based Ralph M. Parsons Company outdid even its northern California rival with its $200 billion (original cost estimates that continued to ratchet up another $100 billion each decade!) North American Water and Power Alliance (NAWAPA) scheme. For some, such as the state of Washington's Scoop Jackson, NAWAPA was a serious threat, and analysts such as Marc Reisner have elevated the plan as a major controversy in the western resource policy debates. But NAWAPA never really had a significant chance for approval. Indeed, for Parsons, NAWAPA was a device, a way to demonstrate that the company could "think big." "If you don't think big," Army Corps of Engineers colonel Robert W. Reiner said in support of NAWAPA, "you don't accomplish big things." And the Parsons Company's strategy in touting its proposal was aimed as much at its Pacific Basin clients as at the water agencies, Bureau of Reclamation officials, and politicians such as Los Angeles County supervisor Kenneth Hahn, who would trot out NAWAPA every chance he could get and thereby create all kinds of regional fears that once again an insatiable urban southern California was coveting those distant imported water sources.[36]

Much of the "thinking big" philosophy associated with western empire building was urban based, with Los Angeles (the "supercity," as its business leaders liked to proclaim) both symbol and substance of this expansionary model of development. Water availability in arid environments such as Phoenix, Las Vegas, San Diego, and, of course, Los Angeles was one part of that model. These cities extended Lewis Mumford's concept of urban ecological imbalance in ever more pronounced ways.[37] In the urban West, regional centers of power became increasingly dependent on distant sources for their water, energy, food, and, in reversing the flow, for disposing of wastes and spreading pollutant emissions into faraway, nonurban spaces. The Grand Canyon and the Kaiparowits Plateau not only came to be located within the urban orbits of Los Angeles and Phoenix because of their coveted resources and energy-generating potential, but also served as a depository for the unwanted by-products of urban expansion. All too often, dirty air became synonymous with "place" in the West.

Western cities were also expressions of directed military spending and launching pads for the new Pacific Basin forms of global economy and exchange. The global cities concept was the visible, prominent side of the flow of capital and labor.[38] Yet communities of multiple languages, ethnic underclasses, toxic hot spots, food insecurity and homelessness, and creative immigrant energies establishing new cultural, linguistic, and urban landscape hybrids were the darker, often more complex side of the environments of those same cities. "Place" in the urban West was becoming multiethnic and multidimensional. These were locations constituting a more idiosyncratic melting pot than the imagined unidimensional, frontierlike West settled by sturdy Anglo stock who were presumed to have shaped the region's character of democratic individualism.[39]

Today, it has become clear that the "West as empire" image—whether of the global city facing the Pacific, the resource megaproject, the huge military expenditures, or the continuing cycle of expansion in urban growth or resource use—is dated at best, perhaps misleading when exploring these historical shifts in regions and places. The 1960s and 1970s, which for many signified an era of continuing expansion, gave way to the 1980s, the New Morning in America epoch launched by our most western and empire-conscious of contemporary presidents, Ronald Reagan.

Empires in the Sun concluded with a snapshot of the transition to the Reagan presidency, with the interest groups of the West and other regions lined up at the White House door. This was to be a period marked by the anticipation of a signal expansion of that characteristic western mix of government largesse and free-market deregulation. It was also a moment of great expectations about renewed empire build-

ing. These expectations had been heightened, given that ∈
plans in the West had been challenged, sometimes suspen/
derailed during the 1970s. Big water projects were no
built. Pacific Basin ties were no longer being singularly u.......
our shores. Even the military economy seemed vulnerable in the wake
of that extraordinary Pacific Basin debacle, the Vietnam War. Ronald
Reagan, the empire-oriented interest groups assumed, would turn it
around. The new president would open the West for land grabs ("I am
a part of the Sagebrush Rebellion," his newly appointed secretary of
the interior, James Watt, had proclaimed in his confirmation hearings).[40]
Reagan would, it was also assumed, push ahead aggressively with vast
new sums for the military and its contractors, talk tough with the Japanese, initiate all kinds of new water projects, build new nuclear plants,
and renew mineral leasing and energy exploration.[41]

But what happened? Where were Ronald Reagan and his emissaries when the empire builders needed them most? The results, interest-
ingly, turned out to be problematic. I recall a meeting I attended in Salt
Lake City in 1982 of the National Water Resources Association. The
keynote speaker was none other than James Watt, formerly of the Den-
ver-based Mountain States Legal Foundation, a self-proclaimed "public interest" law firm for the empire builders that had also worked
closely with western water industry interests.[42] With his appointment
as secretary of the interior, Watt, the resource developers assumed, would
have the power to make western water and energy development projects
a reality once again. Just weeks after his confirmation, Watt had already declared that "no area [of federal lands in the West] should be
excluded" from energy exploration.[43] A new Cabinet Council on Natural
Resources, headed by Watt and including several Cabinet heads (but
with no representation for the Environmental Protection Agency), was
in fact given the task of setting resource and environmental policy for
the administration.[44]

It seemed clear, given his background and his public statements,
that Watt saw the task of reorienting western resource policy as his
cause célèbre. Indeed, with his lay-minister style and hothouse rhetoric, James Watt was the western antienvironmental, antigovernment
preacher at his most fulsome.[45] "You know the Enemy," he exhorted

his water industry hosts at the National Water Resources Association conference, speaking darkly of the Democratic-environmentalist alliance. "You have built the West, made it what it is today, but they want to tear it down," Watt declared, alluding to environmentalist dreams of decommissioned dams and power plants. "Join the crusade," he implored the water delegates. "Be ready for the call!"[46]

But the call to what? the delegates asked themselves. In the past, friendly secretaries of the interior would announce, at association gatherings, new water-project starts, new appropriations for the megaprojects, new ways to protect agriculture or mining or urban water interests. But Watt was not able to announce any new water projects. The budget crunch was also putting a squeeze on Bureau of Reclamation spending.[47] And the new buzzword out of Washington was cost sharing on projects. This term invariably sent shivers through the subsidy-oriented resource developers. This was no longer the highly contested 10 percent cost-sharing figure of the Carter years. Instead, the Reaganites were declaring the need for 35 percent cost sharing, according to another erstwhile western water industry hero, the Army Corps of Engineers' William Gianelli.[48]

The failure to deliver new projects for the water industry raised a corresponding set of questions about the direction of the Reagan revolution itself. Deregulatory efforts were prominent, though only partially successful, as the environmental movement, for one, effectively used legal action to overturn policies while tapping into widespread pro-environment sentiment—including western sentiment—that helped to place constraints on resource development and continued to elevate environmental concern.[49] Military spending had increased exponentially, maintaining some level of confidence among the empire builders that the expansionary impulse had yet to crest. Yet even military spending was unpredictable and uneven in its growth impacts.[50] It compounded, along with the uncertainty in resource development, widening gaps within the global cities, as well as huge trade imbalances, exposing the uneven and, ultimately, ephemeral nature of the 1980s boom. Ronald Reagan, the sagebrush rebel and western cowboy personified, also turned out to be the harbinger of a new identity for the West: the empire under stress.

In the Reagan, Bush, and now the Clinton years, "most favored region" status has not prevented the West from experiencing sharp declines in its economy and a continuing crisis in resource management and in landscape and environment, while contending with massive upheavals in its urban, rural, and regional identities. With the end of the cold war, military spending crashed, and with it crashed assumptions about continuing western expansion. An article from 1962 by James Clayton about defense spending in California and the West is revealing in this respect. Clayton argued that the danger of a cyclical turn in military spending was always possible, given previous downswings. What was most feared, however, among military-dependent westerners, was the specter of collapse, caused by significantly diminished military spending. But that, Clayton and others argued, was an implausible outcome, advocated predominantly by "disarmament nuts" who were not to be taken seriously.[51]

But Reagan's military–spending gambit—applauded for its role in hastening the disintegration of the Soviet Union and its Eastern European counterparts—created the unintended consequence of western regional economic decline. The aerospace industry was not only downsizing, it was departing and shutting down. Military bases were closing. Weapons production was at a standstill. The Department of Defense and Department of Energy became increasingly known for the number of Superfund sites their facilities had created. The military economy had given way to a mitigation and remediation economy. And although these changes were national in scope, their impact on the West was substantial, if not exceptional, particularly for the ways in which the region found itself vulnerable.

The 1980s and 1990s had brought crucial changes to western cities as well. Homelessness had arrived in the West, while remaining entrenched in the East. The erosion of safety nets, the declining status of the working poor, swings in employment, industry relocation and abandonment—all these had become notable in this region as well. Western cities, with their own patterns of immigration, were becoming a particular variation of a First World/Third World metropolis, where not only did the rich get richer and the poor get poorer, but the colors of the residents changed as well.[52]

The rural West was also in turmoil. When Reagan and Bush helped secure increased timber production for a restructuring timber and pulp and paper industry (and the Clinton administration temporized on some of those same issues, much to the embarrassment of its presumably empowered mainstream environmental supporters), the flow of timber did not stabilize communities; it went elsewhere, as exports to the Pacific, while jobs went south and east to the Carolinas.[53] The big fights around grazing—the battleground of "Cattle Free by '93"—masked the fact that the western cattle industry, including ranchers and meatpackers, had become increasingly whipsawed by the global food economy.[54] The executives of the ConAgras and the Cargills were much more akin to the multinational managers, financiers, and corporate attorneys of the global city than to those much celebrated—and maligned—grizzled westerners who ranched or farmed and who were also finding it increasingly hard to survive.[55]

The evolution of the cattle and meatpacking industry, including changes taking place in the western United States, has highlighted the differences between regional development and regional identities in contrast with trends toward globalization. Grazing in the West has become essentially a subset of an intricate system of beef production, marketing, and distribution characterized, for example, by the emergence of what Sanderson has called the "world steer."[56] In this system, the western region's part in the making of the world steer was perhaps more directly associated with the use of immigrant labor in huge packing plants, such as Montfort's facility in Greeley, Colorado, than with the image of the steak-eating, free and independent cowboy on the range, bringing the cattle home after roaming the open spaces of the West.[57] The restructuring of the meat industry, not environmental claims on grazing lands, was influencing the ranching industry in ways that created stresses on what had been presumed to be a way of life.

This West under stress (or at least a West whose land, institutions, and urban and rural spaces have been and are still being restructured) is not best understood, I would argue, as a "New West" or a "New New West." Instead, the West remains a continuing and more elaborated battleground over what is meant by "place" in this region, my starting point in this essay. To identify Los Angeles as a "place" in the

West, it is no longer adequate to situate it exclusively through the metaphor of the global city or even the expanding metropolis. Los Angeles is not City Walk, Universal Studio's recreation of urban space without edges, a community without conflict or divisions, or, perhaps most significantly, a place without colors or languages or the smells and sounds of a complex urban terrain. To see Los Angeles is to see the incredible murals in Estrada Courts in East Los Angeles where the mural movement was born. It's the view of the food court in Koreatown Plaza where seventy varieties of *kimchi* can be found. It is the jazz corridor along Central Avenue where jams at the Dunbar Hotel played to another wave of inmigration at another time. And it is back to the Pico Farmers' Market in Santa Monica, where the sounds and tastes and smells of that other Los Angeles can be found, another kind of place in this semiarid environment where different roots have taken hold.[58]

These different places are urban as well as rural. They are regional in location, or by watershed, or foodshed, or air basin, or land patterns of development. They can signify other, alternative ways of defining what constitutes a place. The practice of exploiting the land, so western in so many ways, for example, can give way and has given way to a different, more interactive relationship to the land, which is also so western and embedded in the history of the region. This "ethic of place," as Charles Wilkinson has argued, involves different ways to think about a region.[59] It involves, as the Western States Center has sought to implement in its organizing strategies (in part to counter the Wise Use–resource development ideologues), a concept of place where community is reconstituted and secured.[60] It is a concept of place where a food system can be defined by "locality and seasonality" within the construct of a regional foodshed rather than by the "distance and durability" factors that characterize the global food system.[61]

Finally, these alternative concepts of place evoke a notion of the West, not as empire but as home. It is here, in this West, where the idea of home or of place offers a connection to the land, to the people, and to the myriad of experiences that survive, stubbornly, outside the orbit of a globalizing, restructuring, reductionist, and, ultimately, disconnected empire.

Notes

A version of this chapter appears in James Ronda, ed., *Thomas Jefferson and the Changing West: From Conquest to Conservation* (Albuquerque: University of New Mexico Press, in cooperation with the Missouri Historical Society, 1997). Reprinted by permission of the University of New Mexico Press.

1. United States Department of Agriculture, *1994 National Farmers Market Directory* (Washington, D.C.: USDA Agricultural Marketing Service and Transportation and Marketing Division, March 1994).

2. Walter Goldschmidt, *As You Sow* (New York: Harcourt Brace, 1947).

3. Andrew Fisher and Robert Gottlieb, *Community Food Security: Policies for a More Sustainable Food System in the Context of the 1995 Farm Bill and Beyond* (Los Angeles: University of California—Los Angeles, Lewis Center for Regional Policy Studies, 1995).

4. Patricia N. Limerick, "Making the Most of Words: Verbal Activity and Western America," in William Cronon, George Miles, and Jay Gitlin, eds., *Under an Open Sky: Rethinking America's Western Past* (New York: W. W. Norton & Co., 1992).

5. Richard White and Patricia N. Limerick, *The Frontier in American Culture,* ed. James R. Grossman (Berkeley: University of California Press, 1994).

6. Mario Barrera, *Race and Class in the Southwest: A Theory of Racial Inequality* (Notre Dame, Ind.: University of Notre Dame Press, 1979); Alan Weisman and Jay Dusard, *La Frontera: The United States Border with Mexico* (San Diego: Harcourt Brace Jovanovich, 1986); Helen Ingram, *Water Politics: Continuity and Change* (Albuquerque: University of New Mexico Press, 1990).

7. Bill Tamayo, "Proposition 187: Racism Leads to Deaths and More Poverty," *Poverty & Race* 4 (January–February 1995); Philip Weiss, "Off the Grid," *New York Times Sunday Magazine,* January 8, 1995; Louis Sahagun, "A Wave of Distrust in the West," *Los Angeles Times,* February 3, 1995.

8. Charles F. Wilkinson, *Crossing the Next Meridian: Land, Water, and the Future of the West* (Washington, D.C.: Island Press, 1992).

9. Harvey Jacobs, "'Wise Use' versus 'The New Feudalism': Social Conflict over Property Rights." Paper presented to the 35th Annual Meeting of the Association of Collegiate Schools of Planning, Philadelphia, Pennsylvania, October 29–31, 1993; Ron Arnold and Alan Gottlieb, *Trashing the Environment: How Runaway Environmentalism Is Wrecking America* (Bellevue, Wash.: Merrill Press, 1993); Richard M. Stapleton, "Greed vs. Green," *National Parks* 66 (November–December 1992):32–37; Michael O'Keefe and Kevin Daley, "Checking the Right: Conservative Backlash against the Environmental Movement," *Buzzworm* 5 (May–June 1993):38–44.

10. Carl Abbott, *The Metropolitan Frontier: Cities in the Modern American West* (Tucson: University of Arizona Press, 1993); Gerald D. Nash, *The American West in the 20th Century: A Short History of an Urban Oasis* (Englewood Cliffs, N.J.: Prentice Hall, 1973).

11. Stephen Fox, *John Muir and His Legacy: The American Conservation Movement* (Boston: Little Brown & Company, 1981); Richard White, "American Environmental History: The Development of a New Historical Field," *Pacific Historical Review* 3 (August 1985):297–335.

12. William Cronon, *Nature's Metropolis: Chicago and the Great West* (New York: W. W. Norton, 1991); Robert Gottlieb, *Forcing the Spring: The Transformation of the American Environmental Movement* (Washington, D.C.: Island Press, 1993).

13. Donald Worster, *Rivers of Empire: Water, Aridity, and the Growth of the American West* (New York: Pantheon Books, 1985); Peter Wiley and Robert Gottlieb, *Empires in the Sun: The Rise of the New American West* (Tucson: University of Arizona Press, 1982).

14. Carl Abbott, "The Metropolitan Region: Western Cities in the New Urban Era," in Gerald D. Nash and Richard W. Etulain, eds., *The Twentieth Century West: Historical Interpretations* (Albuquerque: University of New Mexico Press, 1989).

15. Gerald D. Nash, *The American West Transformed: The Impact of the Second World War* (Bloomington: Indiana University Press, 1985); Ann Markusen, Peter Hall, Scott Campbell, and Sabina Dietrick, *The Rise of the Gunbelt: The Military Remapping of Industrial America* (New York: Oxford University Press, 1991).

16. Wilkinson, *Crossing the Next Meridian;* Jeanne Nienaber Clarke and Daniel McCool, *Staking Out the Terrain: Power Differentials among Natural Resource Management Agencies* (Albany: State University of New York Press, 1985); Paul J. Culhane, *Public Lands Politics: Interest Group Influence on the Forest Service and the Bureau of Land Management* (Baltimore: Johns Hopkins University Press, 1981); Robert Gottlieb and Margaret FitzSimmons, *Thirst for Growth: Water Agencies as Hidden Government in California* (Tucson: University of Arizona Press, 1991).

17. Ingram, *Water Politics;* Gottlieb and FitzSimmons, *Thirst for Growth.*

18. U.S. Congress, *Colorado River Storage Project.* Hearings before the Subcommittee on Irrigation and Reclamation of the Committee on Interior and Insular Affairs, House of Representatives, 83rd Cong., 2nd sess., on H.R. 4449, H.R. 4443, and H.R. 4463 (Washington, D.C.: GPO, 1954); Elmo Richardson, *Resource Development and Preservation in the Truman-Eisenhower Era* (Lexington: University Press of Kentucky, 1973).

19. Frank Welsh, *How to Create a Water Crisis* (Boulder, Colo.: Johnson Books, 1985); Rich Johnson, *The Central Arizona Project, 1918–1968* (Tucson: University of Arizona Press, 1977).

20. Nathan W. Snyder, "Water from Alaska." Paper presented at the 1977 Irrigation Symposium, November 16, 1977, Fresno, California, in *1977 Proceedings of the Irrigation Symposium* (Fresno: Fresno State University and the International Irrigation Association, 1977); Robert Gottlieb, *A Life of Its Own* (San Diego: Harcourt Brace Jovanovich, 1989).

21. Wiley and Gottlieb, *Empires in the Sun.*

22. Donald Pisani, *From the Family Farm to Agribusiness: The Irrigation Cru-*

sade in California and the West, 1850–1931 (Berkeley: University of California Press, 1984); Don Villarejo, *New Lands for Agriculture* (Davis: California Institute for Rural Studies, 1981).

23. Eleanor J. Tracy, "Exxon Gets Serious about Shale," *Fortune,* May 18, 1981, pp. 62–64; Bob Anderson, "Oil Shale Future: Jewel or Synfuel?" *High Country News,* April 3, 1981; Karen Tumulty, "Exxon and Tosco Corp. Scrap Oil Shale Project," *Los Angeles Times,* May 3, 1981, p. 1.

24. Ann Markusen and Joel Yudken, *Dismantling the Cold War Economy* (New York: Basic Books, 1992).

25. Roger W. Lotchin, *Fortress California, 1910–1961* (New York: Oxford University Press, 1992); Markusen, Hall, Campbell, and Dietrick, *Rise of the Gunbelt.*

26. James Clayton, "The Impact of the Cold War on the Economies of California and Utah, 1946–1965," *Pacific Historical Review* 36 (November 1967):449–473.

27. Joel Schwarz, *A Water Odyssey: The Story of the Metropolitan Water District of Southern California* (Los Angeles: Metropolitan Water District, 1991); Gottlieb and FitzSimmons, *Thirst for Growth.*

28. Lotchin, *Fortress California,* p. 302.

29. Charles J. Murphy, "The Earth Movers I: Winning the Epic of the Six Companies of the West," *Fortune,* August 1943, pp. 99–107.

30. Charles J. Murphy, "The Earth Movers II: They Turn to Shipbuilding and Change the Face of the West," *Fortune,* September 1943; Wiley and Gottlieb, *Empires in the Sun.*

31. Dan Cordtz, "Bechtel Thrives on Billion-Dollar Jobs," *Fortune,* January 1975, pp. 91–93; Markusen, Hall, Campbell, and Dietrick, *Rise of the Gunbelt.*

32. Wiley and Gottlieb, *Empires in the Sun.*

33. Western Coal Export Task Force, *Western U.S. Steam Coal Exports to the Pacific Basin, Summary Report of the Joint Study of the Western Coal Export Task Force and the Working Groups of Japan, the Republic of China, and the Republic of Korea* (Denver: Western Governors' Policy Office, 1981); Robert Gottlieb, "The Coal Rush Countdown," *PSA* (June 1982):79–82.

34. Robert Gottlieb and Irene Wolt, *Thinking Big: The Story of the Los Angeles Times, Its Publishers, and Their Influence on Southern California* (New York: Putnam, 1977).

35. "Contracts for Study of Sea Water Conversion," *Twenty-eighth Annual Report* (Los Angeles: Metropolitan Water District of Southern California, 1966), pp. 151–152.

36. Marc Reisner, *Cadillac Desert: The American West and Its Disappearing Water* (New York: Penguin Books, 1987); Snyder, "Water from Alaska"; Reed McClure, "Hahn Urges Columbia River to Be Tapped to Supply Water," *Los Angeles Daily News,* September 12, 1981.

37. Lewis Mumford, "The Theory and Practice of Regionalism," *Sociological Review* 20 (January 1928):18–33; Carl Sussman, ed., *Planning the Fourth Migration: The Neglected Vision of the Regional Planning Association of America* (Cambridge, Mass.: MIT Press, 1976).

38. Saskia Sassen, *The Global City* (Princeton, N.J.: Princeton University Press, 1991); John Friedmann and Goetz Wolff, "The World City Hypothesis: An Agenda for Research and Action," *International Journal of Urban and Regional Research* 63 (1982).

39. Abbott, *Metropolitan Frontier.*

40. Elizabeth Drew, "A Reporter at Large," *New Yorker,* April 4, 1981, p. 104.

41. Norman Vig and Michael E. Kraft, eds., *Environmental Policy in the 1980s: Reagan's New Agenda* (Washington, D.C.: CQ Press, 1984).

42. Robert Gottlieb and Peter Wiley, "The Watt Report," *Nation,* January 17, 1981.

43. Rich Jaroslovsky, "Reagan's Drive to Open More Public Land to Energy Firms May Spark Major Battle," *Wall Street Journal,* April 1, 1981.

44. Marc K. Landy, Marc J. Roberts, and Stephen R. Thomas, *The Environmental Protection Agency: Asking the Wrong Questions* (New York: Oxford University Press, 1990).

45. "Interior Department: Religious Fervor," *National Journal,* April 25, 1981, pp. 720–722.

46. Gottlieb, *Life of Its Own;* Andy Pasztor, "James Watt Tackles Interior Agency Job with Religious Zeal," *Wall Street Journal,* May 5, 1981.

47. Water Information News Service, "Administration Requests Reduced Water Budget," February 2, 1983.

48. "Cost Sharing," *Western Resources Wrap-up,* vol. 20, December 2, 1982; William R. Gianelli, *Water Resources: People and Issues* (Washington, D.C.: U.S. Army Corps of Engineers, EP 870-1-24, August 1985).

49. Andy Pasztor, "Reagan Goal of Easing Environmental Laws Is Largely Unattained," *Wall Street Journal,* February 18, 1983; Jonathan Lash, *A Season of Spoils: The Reagan Administration's Attack on the Environment* (New York: Random House, 1984).

50. Markusen and Yudken, *Dismantling the Cold War Economy.*

51. James Clayton, "Defense Spending: Key to California's Economic Growth," *Western Political Quarterly* 15 (June 1962):280–293.

52. Mike Davis, *City of Quartz: Excavating the Future in Los Angeles* (New York: Vintage Books, 1992).

53. Maureen Smith, *The Paper Industry and Barriers to Recycling: An Environmental Argument for Industrial Restructuring* (Los Angeles: University of California, Department of Urban Planning, 1992).

54. Lourdes Gouveia, "Global Strategies and Local Linkages: The Case of the U.S. Meatpacking Industry," in Alessandro Bonanno, Lawrence Bush, William Friedland, Lourdes Gouveia, and Enzo Mingione, eds., *From Columbus to ConAgra: The Globalization of Agriculture and Food* (Lawrence: University of Kansas Press, 1994).

55. Mustafa Koc, "Globalization as a Discourse," in Bonanno et al., *From Columbus to ConAgra;* Harriet Friedmann, "Distance and Durability: Shaky Foundations of the World Food Economy," in Philip McMichael, ed., *The Globalization of Agro-Food Systems* (Ithaca, N.Y.: Cornell University Press, 1994).

56. Steven E. Sanderson, "The Emergence of the 'World Steer': International and Foreign Domination in Latin American Cattle Production," in F. Lamond Tullis and W. Ladd Hollist, eds., *Food, the State, and International Political Economy* (Lincoln: University of Nebraska Press, 1986).

57. Carol Andreas, *Meatpackers and Beef Barons: Company Town in a Global Economy* (Niwot: University of Colorado Press, 1994).

58. Madeline Janis-Aparicio, Gilda Haas, and Robin Cannon, "Sell L.A. in All Its Tastes and Colors," *Los Angeles Times*, March 18, 1994.

59. Charles F. Wilkinson, *The Eagle Bird: Mapping a New West* (New York: Pantheon Books, 1992).

60. Jeff Malachowski, Western States Center, personal communication, 1993.

61. Harriet Friedmann, "After Midas's Feast: Alternative Food Regimes for the Future," in Patricia Allen, ed., *Food for the Future: Conditions and Contradictions of Sustainability* (New York: John Wiley and Sons, 1993).

Contributors

Mike Davis is a widely known and respected journalist and the author of *City of Quartz: Excavating the Future in Los Angeles*. Among his many projects is a coedited volume with Hal Rothman entitled *The Grit beneath the Glitter: Tales from the Real Las Vegas*. He teaches urban theory at the Southern California Institute of Architecture in Los Angeles.

William deBuys is an author and professional conservationist who resides in Santa Fe, New Mexico. He is the author of two highly acclaimed books—*Enchantment and Exploitation: The Life and Hard Times of a New Mexico Mountain Range* and, with photographer Alex Harris, *River of Traps*.

Dan L. Flores is Hammond Professor of History and Environmental Studies at the University of Montana in Missoula. He is the author of a series of influential and provocative articles about environmental history and *Caprock Canyonlands: Journeys into the Heart of the Southern Plains*.

Robert Gottlieb is one of the leading scholars and writers about the American West. He is the author of numerous books about water, including *A Life of Its Own: The Politics and Power of Water*, as well as *Forcing the Spring: The Transformation of the American Environmental Movement*. He teaches at the University of California—Los Angeles.

Helen Ingram is the Warmington Endowed Chair and Professor at the University of California—Irvine, where she holds joint appointments with the School of Social Ecology and the Department of Politics and Society. Among her specialties is the relationship of water resources to political power and equity in the American West. Her first book, a study of the 1967 Colorado River Basin Projects Act, was updated in a new edition: *Water Politics, Continuity and Change*. Her most recent coauthored book, *Divided Waters*, deals with U.S.–Mexico transboundary water resources.

Char Miller is a professor of history at Trinity University in San Antonio, Texas. His articles on the history of American forestry and the Forest Service frequently appear in scholarly and popular journals. Forthcoming works include *American Forestry: Nature, Politics, and Culture, Out of the Woods: Essays in Environmental History*, and a volume redefining the life of Gifford Pinchot.

Stephen J. Pyne is a professor of history at Arizona State University, Tempe, and the author of numerous volumes on fire history throughout the world, including *Fire in America, World Fire, Vestal Fire*, and *Burning Bush: A History of Fire in Australia*.

Hal K. Rothman is a professor of history at the University of Nevada—Las Vegas, where he edits the journal *Environmental History*. His most recent books are *The Greening of Nation? Environmentalism in the United States since 1945* and *"I'll Never Fight Fire with My Bare Hands Again."* His next book is *Devil's Bargains: Tourism and Transformation in the Twentieth-Century American West*.

Marguerite S. Shaffer is an assistant professor of history at the University of North Carolina—Wilmington. She has published in *Pacific Historical Review* and other journals and has received grants from the Smithsonian Institution, Dumbarton Oaks, and the Huntington Library. Her article is derived from her first book, *See America First: Tourism and National Identity, 1905–1930*, which is forthcoming.

Donald Worster is the Hall Distinguished Professor of American History at the University of Kansas and one of the founders of modern environmental history. His works, including *Dust Bowl: The Southern Plains in the 1930s* and *Rivers of Empire: Water, Aridity, and the Growth of the American West*, have garnered countless awards as he defined and redefined various subfields. His most recent work is *An Unsettled Country: Changing Landscapes of the American West*. He is a popular speaker and lecturer and one of the clearest voices of environmental history that reaches the public.

Index